The Life of Prayer

OTHER CROSSWAY BOOKS BY EDITH SCHAEFFER

The Art of Life
Lifelines
L'Abri

The Life of Prayer

EDITH SCHAEFFER

CROSSWAY BOOKS • WHEATON, ILLINOIS
A DIVISION OF GOOD NEWS PUBLISHERS

The Life of Prayer.

Copyright © 1992 by Edith Schaeffer.

Published by Crossway Books, a division of
Good News Publishers, 1300 Crescent St., Wheaton, Illinois 60187.

First printing, 1992

Printed in the United States of America

ISBN 0-89107-649-2

"The Gallant Trees" was taken from *Windows* by Amy Carmichael with
the permission of the Dohnavur Fellowship in England.

Material by Mortimer J. Adler is reprinted with the permission of
Macmillan Publishing Company from *INTELLECT: Mind Over Matter.*
Copyright © 1990 by Mortimer J. Adler.

Bible quotations taken from *Holy Bible: New International Version,*
are identified by NIV. Copyright © 1978 by the New York International
Bible Society. Used by permission of Zondervan Bible Publishers.

Quotations from the *King James Version* of the Bible are identified by KJV.

00	99	98	97	96	95	94	93	92
15	14	13	12	11	10	9 8	7 6	5 4	3 2	1

Contents

ONE
Who Is There?

"HELP . . . H E L P . . . help . . . meeee" . . . "help . . . h e l p . . . help . . . meeee . . ." The cry comes from a throat strangled with fear, calling out where she fell, sliding down the shale-like stones of a quarry. The echo of her own voice comes back, the same voice, a bit muted but with the same tone of fear casting more fear into the heart of the one calling. Again, again, again, and again, always the reply is an echo . . . bouncing back from an impersonal wall, hollow, meaningless. Nobody is within hearing. The call for help trails out into emptiness.

"I'm lost . . . HELP ME, help . . . HELP . . . H E L P . . . ." The man's hopeless cry is swallowed up in sounds of slithering snakes and alligator barks, among swishing apes swinging from tangled trees, and myriad bird calls as his feet try to move on among roots that merge into unrecognized tropical plants and sudden liquid mud that seems like glue. Lost. Lost in a jungle of roots and trees, of bushes and animals, of sounds overlapping sounds. Lost—with no landmark to give guidance, with no answering voice to the cry, with no compass; nobody with an intellect is there within earshot. The silence is the silence of impersonal sounds unable to respond with any kind of help, adding vulnerability to fear of loneliness . . . in an empty universe.

Human beings can find themselves alone in an ocean while a ship is sinking, alone in a desert in a sandstorm, alone in a blizzard having lost all landmarks, alone in a prison, alone with an enemy approaching. There are *many* fearful situations where help is needed and one is out of earshot of any person with ears to hear the call, with ideas as to how to help, and with the power to carry out that help. Human beings recognize their need of outside help in a diversity of physical situations.

However, aloneness is not restricted to physical aloneness. One can feel the sharp keenness of being alone in the midst of beauty and safety. Aloneness in a tea room by Lac Leman, looking at swans gliding on the lake and spring flowers bordering the quay with a riot of color. Aloneness in the midst of a filled concert hall, listening to the most gorgeous symphony one's ears could possibly hear. Aloneness in an art museum looking at paintings by kindred spirits that reach out with understanding across the gulf of time. Aloneness on a tractor plowing a field for planting for yet another springtime, wondering, "Who will gather the harvest?" Aloneness in the midst of a crowded city or village market, with no one to relate to. The cry of the human heart, whether in danger or needing someone to talk to, knows no boundary of space or time. Throughout the centuries human beings at various points in life have come to excruciating times of knowing they need help, even while declaring that they are totally self-sufficient. People have discovered that they need help physically, emotionally, spiritually and have called "help," in one way or another, to one person or another, or to vast emptiness where there is no answer . . . except an echo.

> . . . and call upon me in the day of trouble; I will deliver thee, and thou shalt glorify me. (Psalm 50:15 KJV)

Who is speaking? To whom are we to call?

> He shall call upon me, and I will answer him; I will be with him in trouble; I will deliver him, and honor him. (Psalm 91:15 KJV)

Who is declaring He can answer the person calling? *Who* declares that He can be with the one calling in the midst of his or her trouble? Who has power to deliver the one caught in fearsome difficulties?

"God," you say, but you haven't said anything clear yet. The letters *G o d* do not clear away the smog of mistaken ideas that not only fill the atmosphere of our world today, but which are taught, written about, spoken, chanted, and accepted as full explanation as to what is meant by the word *prayer.*

But, you may say, "Calling on God *is* prayer."

It depends upon what god you are calling on, as to whether anyone is listening, or has power to help, or is able to be with you.

God speaks to Israel through Jeremiah to make clear the difference between false gods and the one true God.

Hear what the Lord says to you, O house of Israel. This is what the Lord says:

"Do not learn the way of the nations
 or be terrified by signs in the sky,
   though the nations are terrified by them.
For the customs of the peoples are worthless;
   they cut a tree out of the forest,
   and a craftsman shapes it with his chisel.
They adorn it with silver and gold;
   they fasten it with hammer and nails
   so it will not totter.
Like a scarecrow in a melon patch,
   their idols cannot speak;
they must be carried
   because they cannot walk.
Do not fear them;
   they can do no harm
   nor can they do any good."
No one is like you, O Lord;
   you are great, and your name is mighty in power . . .

"Tell them this: 'These gods who did not make the heavens and the earth, will perish from the earth and from under the heavens.'"

But God made the earth by his power;
   he founded the world by his wisdom
   and stretched out the heavens by his understanding.
                              (Jeremiah 10:1-6, 11, 12 NIV)

When God gave the second commandment, He made it very clear that it was, and always would be, sin to worship false gods. The word *god* is used to refer to false gods, the gods made in the form of idols, or the gods made by people's imaginations. False gods are continually referred to and the contrast is made clear. Worship is only to be given to the one true God, and He is the Creator of the universe. "In the beginning God created the heavens and the earth." God is defined as the Creator in the very beginning of the Bible, and that distinction is always there.

> Thus saith God the Lord, he who created the heavens, and stretched them out; he who spread forth the earth, and that which cometh out of it; he who giveth breath unto the people upon it, and spirit to them that walk in it: I, the Lord, have called thee in righteousness, and will hold thine hand, and will keep thee, and give thee for a covenant of the people, for a light of the Gentiles. To open the blind eyes, to bring out the prisoners from the prison, and those who sit in darkness out of the prison house. I am the Lord: that is my name; and my glory will I not give to another, neither my praise to graven images. Behold, the former things are come to pass, and new things do I declare; before they spring forth I tell you of them. (Isaiah 42:5-9 KJV)

The glorious passages of Isaiah should all be read, but in this context of God's commandment to "have no other gods before me" it is imperative to see something of the clarity of contrast, as if seen in the brilliant light of lightning during a storm. There is no mistake, no shadow of doubt that there is only one God, and we are meant to know that we are to be very careful to not come to worship a false god, to not pray to a false god.

Why?

First, because it is like calling "help" into an empty quarry, or crying out for someone to respond in the tangle of a jungle where there is no one to hear, or foundering for a lifeboat in an empty sea! The first reason for not praying to a false god is that there is no other god who *can* hear and answer. The only answer possible would be from an impostor.

Second, because the truth is really *true*. There is one God, the Judeo-Christian God of Abraham, Isaac, and Jacob, of Joseph and Daniel, of Moses and Elijah, of Matthew, John, Paul, and Timothy, of Ruth, Esther, Priscilla, and Lydia, the one God who created all things and without whom nothing would exist. The only true and perfectly holy and infinite God who is able to hear us because He is infinite, and to be alone with us because He is personal, *is* the One who always loved us. He loved us enough to open a way to come to Him and to be accepted on the basis of the substitution of His only begotten son, the Lamb, the Messiah who came to be our substitute, to die for us. So that we might have salvation and eternal life? Yes, but also so that in this life, day by day, hour by hour, moment by moment we would have Someone always able to hear our cry, our call, our worship, our praise, our confession, our asking for direction and wisdom, our acknowledgment of weakness as we ask for an exchange of His strength. Someone with power to hear and answer.

Throughout history human beings have turned away from the one true living God, the Master of the universe, the Creator of all things, the Almighty, Invisible, Only Wise God, and have turned to a succession of other solutions, false gods, false prophets, false religions, false promises.

Today is no exception. It is extremely important to establish first of all who is there, who is the true Creator, and then how to come to Him.

The drive today for pluralism is confusing a lot of people. The general impression given in most circles is that if one has convictions concerning truth, if one believes in the God of creation as really the one God, and that the Fall of man as set forth in Genesis *is* the explanation of the abnormal universe and abnormal history, and if one believes that the Lamb was the one way given to come to Him (throughout Genesis to Malachi and then on to Revelation), then that one is "narrow" and very uninformed about history, *not* to be included in intellectual or reasonable discussion. To believe that the opposite of true is false is only permitted on exams in schools, but is excluded by many who believe a philosophic base to live on, a worldview, must allow a mixture of totally *opposite* worldviews to be equally true. This of course means that *nothing* is true.

There is a terrible danger of misunderstood pluralism. There is a realistic and present danger of feeling impelled to join with, literally or figuratively, people believing opposite things, having totally different gods, and feeling that one is having a spiritual experience by being tolerant or broad-minded. In this time of strident teaching by the New Age Movement in its many forms, there is open pressure of persuasion and subtle pressure of the astonished attitudes verbalized in such remarks as, "Well, why on earth not? What difference would it make to join with us?"

King Solomon began to practice this kind of pluralism centuries ago. We are told in 1 Kings 11:4, 5:

> As Solomon grew old, his wives turned his heart after other gods, and his heart was not fully devoted to the Lord his God, as the heart of David his father had been. He followed Ashtoreth the goddess of the Sidonians, and Molech the detestable god of the Ammonites. So Solomon did evil in the eyes of the Lord; he did not follow the Lord completely, as David his father had done. (NIV)

God spoke in this same chapter of dividing the kingdom after Solomon's death, because of this evil kind of "pluralism," that is, the forsaking of the true God by adding other gods for prayer and worship.

> I will do this because they have forsaken me and worshipped Ashtoreth the goddess of the Sidonians, Chemosh the god of the Moabites, and Molech the god of the Ammonites, and have not walked in my ways, nor done what is right in my eyes, nor kept my statutes and laws as David Solomon's father did. (1 Kings 11:33 NIV)

Turn a moment with me to the May 6, 1991, copy of *Time* magazine which I purchased on the newsstand in Vevey, Switzerland. The cover screams at passersby, "Scientology, the Cult of Greed," an important article to read to be informed about the dangers of deathly poison being fed to people in the areas of ideas. But what I want to show you is the direct relationship on page 70 of Richard Ostling's column on "Religion" to what was taking place in Solomon's life and his evil leadership in that period of history!

The article begins by describing a ceremony to mark Earth Day in Wisconsin, where people were literally *praying* to Mother Earth. It then goes on to say:

> The ceremonies were a part of a growing U.S. spiritual movement: Goddess worship, the effort to create a female-centered focus for spiritual expression. Most participants are women who seek a deity other than God the Father, and a faith less patriarchal than Judeo-Christian tradition seems to offer. Adherents claim the movement involves as many as 100,000 U.S. women.
>
> Though such ancient goddesses as Isis or Astarte are often invoked, most worship occurs in the name of a vague generic "Goddess" often depicted as Mother Earth or Gaia in line with environmental awareness. "The Goddess is not just the female version of God. She represents a different concept," says Merlin Stone, author of *When God Was a Woman*. While the Judeo-Christian God is transcendent, the Goddess is located, "within each individual and all things in nature," she says.
>
> Various groups follow a brew of Wicca (witchcraft) paganism, New Age ideas, and evocations of female power, some inspired by Native American and African traditions. Though a minority enacts malevolent spell-casting and magic (not Satanism these worshipers insist), most embrace benign beliefs, especially in harmony with nature. While some draw on ancient rituals, others invent new ones.
>
> Despite Christianity's centuries of opposition to paganism, some old-line churches are opening up to the Goddess. A witch teaches in an institute at California's Roman Catholic Holy Names College. A book by two United Methodist pastors proposes experimental Bible readings about the crucifixion that replace Jesus with Sophia (Wisdom), the divine personality used by Goddess-minded Christians.
>
> (Reported by Michael P. Harris and Elizabeth L'Hommedieu)

Human beings, ever since Adam and Eve chose to believe and act upon the advice of Lucifer rather than honoring the counsel and command of God as truth, have continually turned away from praying to, calling upon, worshiping and honoring the one true God in order to substitute worship, prayer, and the seeking of help and direction from false gods.

After King Solomon's death came a string of bad kings leading people in worship of false gods and idols.

But I want to jump to the clear confrontation at the time of Elijah, a confrontation as clear as at the time of the worship of the golden calf just before Moses came down from the mountain where God had given him the Ten Commandments.

There had been no rain for three and a half years because of the wickedness of Ahab's leading the people away from the worship of God and into the worship of Baal, the heathen god. As Ahab went to meet Elijah, he said to him:

> "Is that you, you troubler of Israel?"
> "I have not made trouble for Israel," Elijah replied. "But you and your father's family have. You have abandoned the Lord's commands and have followed Baal's. Now summon the people from all over Israel to meet me on Mount Carmel. And bring the four hundred and fifty prophets of Baal and the four hundred prophets of Asherah, who eat at Jezebel's table."
> So Ahab sent word throughout all Israel and assembled the prophets on Mount Carmel. Elijah went before the peoples and said, "How long will you waver between two opinions? If the Lord is God, follow him; but if Baal is God, follow him."
> But the people said nothing. (1 Kings 18:18-21 NIV)

This is a case of truth being examined. The Lord and Baal cannot both be God. There cannot be a tableau of Baal's prophets holding hands with Elijah and praying together in a spiritual, religious manner, simply loving each other regardless of truth, their actions signifying that "nobody is wrong because we are all *sincere.*" You know the story, but read it again. The purpose of the confrontation is so important, not just at that moment of history, but for us and our choices right now.

Then Elijah said to them, "I am the only one of the Lord's prophets left, but Baal has four hundred and fifty prophets. Get two bulls for us. Let them choose one for themselves, and let them cut it into pieces and put it on the wood but not set fire to it. I will prepare the other bull and put it on the wood but not set fire to it. Then you call on the name of your god, and I will call on the name of the Lord. The god who answers by fire—he is God."

Then all the people said, "What you say is good." (1 Kings 18:22-24 NIV)

This is a dramatically vivid confrontation to give the people who were living at that moment definite proof of the reality of the Creator being God and of His power to answer prayer. At the same time it was a moment of crystal clarity as to the lies being taught about Baal. This centers around prayer. *Who is it to whom people pray?* It *did* matter then, and it *does* matter now.

The priests of Baal cried out to their god, shouting, "O Baal, answer us." But there was no answer. Baal could not answer any more than the echoing walls of a quarry or the wild tangle of the jungle. Baal is a false god. The people's expectations were based on a lie.

After they had shouted, with no response, from early morning until noon, Elijah said sarcastically, "Shout louder. Surely he is a god. Maybe he is sleeping." So the priests began to cut themselves with knives and spears until blood flowed, as was their custom. But there was no answer. Silence.

What a picture of an empty universe where prayer is a ridiculous farce!

Then Elijah called the people to him. He repaired the altar of the Lord which was in ruins, taking twelve stones for the twelve tribes of Israel. He dug a trench around it, arranged wood on the altar, cut the bull into pieces and placed them on the wood, and then said to the people, "Fill four large jars with water and pour it over the offering and on the wood." They did this, and he asked for the same thing three times, until the water not only covered the offering and the wood, but ran down and filled the trench.

At the proper time of sacrifice, Elijah stepped forward and prayed:

> "O Lord, God of Abraham, Isaac and Israel, let it be known today that you are God in Israel and that I am your servant and have done all these things at your command. Answer me, O Lord, answer me, so these people will know that you, O Lord, are God, and that you are turning their hearts back again." (1 Kings 18:36-37 NIV)

Note that the one true God is being called to and that the motive is clearly Elijah's desire to have these people *know* the reality of who God is and that He can work in history in response to earnest prayer. The prayer is not just for the fire to fall on the sacrifice, but for a result inside people's minds and hearts, "so these people will know that you, O Lord, are God, and that you are turning their hearts back again."

Elijah's prayer was not for an exciting miracle that would be impressive, but for that which would bring the knowledge of God's existence and His hearing and responding to Elijah's prayer. Elijah was praying that the result might be a true repentance and turning back to exclusive worship of the one true living God.

> Then the fire of the Lord fell and burned up the sacrifice, the wood, the stones and the soil, and also licked up the water in the trench. When all the people saw this, they fell prostrate and cried, "The Lord—he is God! The Lord—he is God!"

Yes, many of them bowed and worshiped God, recognizing that indeed the true God had answered by fire and that He alone should be called upon, and He alone had wisdom to lead His people. Others turned away. Always there are those who turn away. Rebellion against the true God has continued through all history. The important factor is, however, that there is a true and a false and that idols and false gods *cannot hear or answer.*

We live in a time of increasing confusion, and it would be

unkind not to point out the pitfalls or the dangerous places that lead to slippery rocks and sharp cliffs! There is a search for help or guidance that brings an answer which is a very wrong answer from a very wrong source! In writing about prayer, it is essential to point out such horrible dangers leading to wrong "answers" that take people father and farther away from the true God. It is often a case of the blind leading the blind into quicksand.

Who is there to answer if it is not the living Creator God, who is all-holy and all-powerful? In the supernatural world there is the one who rebelled in the heavenlies, Satan, Lucifer, the devil, and the angels who followed his leading are the demons. Until Jesus the Messiah returns, there is a continual battle going on as Satan tries to hinder people from coming to God, even as he has through the ages.

We are clearly and fairly warned throughout the Bible to *beware*. To beware of experimenting with other sources for finding out something, or getting help, or being given guidance. The enticements of various things in the New Age Movement are really not new. As people are enticed to go to "channels" who go into a trance and speak with some other voice, giving information that is supposed to come from someone who has died, a short time ago or a long time ago, this is the same kind of temptation that was dangled before people in past centuries. This is to be totally avoided, run away from, and *not* to be tried out as an amusement or to satisfy curiosity.

We find several commands that need to be read and remembered:

> "Do not turn to mediums or seek out spiritists, for you will be defiled by them. I am the Lord your God." (Leviticus 19:31 NIV)

> "When you enter the land the Lord your God is giving you, do not learn to imitate the detestable ways of the nations there. Let no one be found among you who sacrifices his son or daughter in the fire, who practices divination or sorcery, interprets omens, engages in witchcraft, or casts spells, or who is a

medium or spiritist or who consults the dead." (Deuteronomy 18:9-11 NIV)

These practices are detestable to the Lord. This does not mean that people cannot have their eyes of understanding opened, repent and turn away from it all, and be cleansed by the atoning blood of Christ. It does mean, however, that these things are seriously wrong, because it is a search for help from the enemy of God. Whatever power there is in these things is *not* the power of God.

Isaiah says:

Here am I, and the children the Lord has given me. We are signs and symbols in Israel from the Lord Almighty, who dwells on Mount Zion. When men tell you to consult mediums and spiritists, who whisper and mutter, should not a people inquire of their God? Why consult the dead on behalf of the living? To the law and to the testimony! If they do not speak according to this word, they have no light of dawn. (Isaiah 8:18-20 NIV)

In Isaiah 30 again God strongly condemns praying to or asking for help from the wrong sources:

Woe to the rebellious children, saith the Lord, who take counsel, but not of me; and who cover with a covering, but not of my Spirit, that they may add sin to sin; who walk to go down into Egypt, and have not asked at my mouth; to strengthen themselves in the strength of Pharaoh, and to trust in the shadow of Egypt! (Isaiah 30:1-2 KJV)

Seeking help from the wrong sources, in other words, praying to supernatural sources of guidance that are not the Lord's, is pointed out as sinful, a rejection of the true holy God. In no way is it neutral. Later in that 30th chapter, verse 15, the Holy One of Israel says:

"In repentance and rest is your salvation, in quietness and trust is your strength, but you would have none of it."

After a description of their turning away to the wrong sort of help, verse 18 says:

> Yet the Lord longs to be gracious unto you; he rises to show you compassion. For the Lord is a God of justice. Blessed are all who wait for him!

It is not a trivial matter to be worshiping false gods or asking help from evil spirits. God is clear and fair in His warnings. The confrontation of truth against error, of the true God against the false gods, is strong in each part of history. Yet the compassion of God so often is demonstrated in the warnings. In Ezekiel 33, the chapter that impressed upon my husband, Francis Schaeffer, the need to make the film *How Should We Then Live?* with our son Franky, verses 10 and 11 not only gave him the title, but once more made vivid the lack of any neutrality in worship and prayer. There is no neutral place; each one must turn *away* from the false and turn *to* the one true God, the Creator of the universe, who made people in His image. The turning away is important, before the turning to can be acceptable.

> Therefore, O thou son of man, speak unto the house of Israel. Thus speak, saying, If our transgressions and our sins be upon us, and we pine away in them, how should we then live?
> Say unto them, As I live, saith the Lord God, I have no pleasure in the death of the wicked but that the wicked turn from his way and live; turn from your evil ways; for why will ye die, O house of Israel? (Ezekiel 33:10-11 KJV)

Many centuries later, Paul, after his own turning to the Messiah, was in Athens and had contemplated the myriad gods being worshiped there. As he spoke at Mars Hill, he said:

> "Men of Athens! I see that in every way you are very religious. For as I walked around and looked carefully at your objects of worship, I even found an altar with this inscription: TO AN UNKNOWN GOD. Now what you worship as something unknown I am going to proclaim to you." (Acts 17:22 NIV)

Paul goes on to make known to them the Creator who has made all things and who is the Lord of Heaven and earth. He tells of the fact that there will be a Judge who will judge the world with justice, and the proof that this is the true Judge is that He was raised from the dead!

The result of Paul's discourse and teaching was that many turned away, sneering at the idea of resurrection from the dead, but others believed.

It is just as in the time of Elijah's confrontation—some turned away, others believed. In order to emphasize just how much God our Father cares about us as individuals, the names of two, a man and a woman, were given. "A few men became followers of Paul and believed. Among them was Dionysius, a member of the Areopagus, also a woman named Damaris, and a number of others" (Acts 17:34 NIV).

It is not an empty universe. There is Somebody at home! The Creator God can be reached as you call, from any spot—in a quarry, in a jungle, in a prison, in a concentration camp, on a desert during a war, from a car you're pinned under, in a plane, sitting beside a baby's crib, in a retirement facility, in an office, in a factory. No place is out of range where the "short wave" (so to speak) does not work.

But it is not possible to walk through the maze of gods offered for worship there in Athens at Paul's time, or through the many religions offered in today's bookstores or to try out the New Age mélange and at the same time to include the Trinity—the Father, His Son the Lord Jesus Christ, and the Holy Spirit—in the mix.

"Thou shalt have no other gods before Me" speaks as strongly today to us as to the people of Israel gathered on the Sinai Desert.

There is no confusion in the absolute truth of there being one Creator God, and of the need to come to Him for help, and to come to Him in worship and praise, and to come to Him for mercy and forgiveness in and through the Lamb.

We come to the Father through the blood of the Lamb, shed for us, in the power of the Holy Spirit. Our names are written in the Lamb's Book of Life. We are known to the Infinite God who even knows the number of hairs on our heads—known to Him by name—just as thoroughly as Dionysius and Damaris were! What blasphemy to call upon a false god, an idol, or an evil spirit.

We call upon the One who really is there now, and who has been and will be for eternity.

TWO

Affliction and Prayer—
Suffering and Prayer

So much that is taught about prayer is wrong. So many promises are given which God did not give. So much is taken out of context. People become bitter, angry at God, depressed, and shattered and turn away from God when they need Him most.

"If only you have enough faith, you will be healed." "If only you pray with enough faith, your child will get well." "If only you have enough faith, you will get up out of that wheelchair and walk." "If you pray long enough, you will have no troubles." "How is it you have had an accident? You have lost your job and your home? There must be something wrong with your prayers."

The teaching that promises a perfectly healthy life, plenty of success in every way, automatically good relationships among family and friends without any difficulties, all as a result of becoming a Christian and living a life of "praying," is a false teaching and one that misses some of the deepest understanding of Biblical teaching concerning prayer and the spiritual life.

Every part of Scripture makes clear that we live in an abnormal world since the Fall and that there will be no such thing as perfection until the return of the Lord Jesus Christ and the restoration of the devastated creation. What we have now is the astounding possibility of being in communication with God. To be able to praise the Creator of all things, to be able to worship the Triune God, to be able to ask for strength, wisdom, guidance, help in many areas from the infinite, personal God, is something that was paid for with the terrible price of the suffering and death of Christ.

Had not the Son of God suffered, there would be no possibility of prayer. Had not the Trinity been separated from the time Christ took our sins upon him, there would be no possibility of anyone coming to the Father, dressed in the righteousness of Christ. Christ lived a sinless, holy, righteous life so that He could exchange His righteousness—a sparkling white linen robe of righteousness—for our filthy rags of sin. Don't forget that we are told that even our "righteousness is as filthy rags."

The very heart of prayer is the suffering of Christ. The very marvelous comfort we have in the promise "I will never leave you nor forsake you" is secure *because* Christ made that choice firmly after His struggle in the garden of Gethsemane, the choice which took Him to the cross for us. He was forsaken for us . . . so that we will never be forsaken. He cried out, "My God, my God, why hast thou forsaken me?" As God the most holy Father could not look upon sin, and our sins covered Christ like an ugly garment as he hung there, "He became sin for us." What terrible suffering! What an awful affliction He bore for us as He bore the punishment for our sin! He, who knew no sin, who had never sinned, who was perfectly holy, *became* sin for us.

He suffered and died that we might have life everlasting. He was afflicted for our transgressions that we might have forgiveness. He became the Lamb dying for us and fulfilling all the prophecies so that He could be our loving Shepherd.

But . . . there could be no prayer without the historic reality of that time on the cross. Prayer has been given to us at a terrible cost, the cost of the deep affliction and suffering of the Son of God, the Second Person of the Trinity, the Lord Jesus Christ. We cannot understand such affliction, such suffering except in tiny glimpses of suffering in our own lives.

Do some of us suffer "aloneness"? Aloneness because of separation from someone or ones we long to be with? Aloneness because of being misunderstood by those we work with or live among? Aloneness because of danger or persecution? Aloneness because of betrayal by someone formerly close? Aloneness because of a broken communication? Aloneness because of being an alien in a foreign land?

No person in history has ever been as alone as the Lord Jesus Christ on the cross.

He was separated from His Father and the Holy Spirit, not for anything He had done, but for us. He was falsely accused and did not call on the angels to come and speak for Him. He was taunted, "Come down from the cross, You are the Son of God," and He could have come down and silenced their sneering voices, but He remained there suffering that horrible affliction in our place. Had He come down, our salvation could not have taken place. Had He come down, prayer could not have been given, *no one* could have prayed, "Our Father who art in Heaven, hallowed be Thy name . . ." Had He come down, no one could have been born a child of God, able to call God "Father."

He suffered terribly; excruciating affliction was part of the Messiah's work in order to make possible that glorious invitation given in the last chapter of the Bible:

> I, Jesus, have sent mine angel to testify unto you these things in the churches. I am the root and the offspring of David, and the bright and morning star. And the Spirit and the bride say, Come. And let him that heareth say, Come . . . And whosoever will, let him take of the water of life freely. (Revelation 22:16, 17 KJV)

This invitation so close to the last verses of the Bible underlines again what John wrote in the Gospel of John:

> And, as Moses lifted up the serpent in the wilderness, even so must the Son of man be lifted up, that whosoever believeth in him should not perish but have everlasting life. For God so loved the world, that he gave his only begotten Son, that whosoever believeth in him should not perish, but have everlasting life. (John 3:14-16 KJV)

The love of God for lost human beings, the compassion of the Trinity for people pictured as lost lambs or sheep wandering along dangerous cliffs, was poured out in willingness to make an atonement for us—by Christ suffering agony for us, by His leaving

Heaven and all its glories for an alien and spoiled world, to be rejected, scorned, called a liar, and crucified so that sinners could be forgiven and cleansed and made acceptable. Such love is beyond our understanding. Our understanding is only partial.

As we bow in prayer, whether with others in church, with two or three agreed to pray together for some special time or need, whether alone on a rock on a mountainside or looking out over marshes and sea, or in a small closet, to pour out our sincere appreciation for such suffering in our place, we need to ask for help that we may increase in our sincerity of thankfulness. We need to ask that we may not be reciting words without being involved in the awareness of what we are declaring!

What I often pray with depth of earnest longing is this: *O Lord, don't let me be veneer. Please make me solid oak. If I am cut, may I be the same all through. May I be solid brass, not a coating outside. Help me to be real in my love for You. May it be solid silver that is also being refined.*

Understanding of what Jesus did for us, of what the Trinity did for us, grows throughout our lifetime and will be multiplied the day we no longer "see through a glass darkly." The full perfection paid for by the agony on the cross will not be ours until the resurrection of the body, your body and mine. Our bodies will then be perfect, and there will be no more pain or suffering or sin.

No one is perfect in this life—physically, spiritually, emotionally, intellectually—nor are we promised perfection in this life after becoming Christians. Christ's death was sufficient for each one who will ever come to Him; there is nothing that can be added to His suffering for the forgiveness of sin. The price He paid at such a cost was sufficient to open the door of communication, which is prayer. As we come having believed in Jesus, we are accepted in His name by the Father in the power of the Holy Spirit. However, the suffering that continues in this life is explained with clarity throughout the Bible. That is to say, we are not to be surprised at the continuation of afflictions, nor to feel we have not been close to the Lord when an earthquake hits or when cancer hits!

At the beginning of 2 Corinthians Paul praises God for comfort in suffering and tribulation, obviously in the midst of a life of prayer and growing closeness to the Lord. He speaks of the wonder of comfort, not of the immediate *removal* of suffering.

> Praise be to the God and Father of our Lord Jesus Christ, the Father of compassion and the God of all comfort, who comforts us in all our troubles, so that we can comfort those in any trouble with the comfort we ourselves have received from God. For just as the sufferings of Christ flow over into our lives, so also through Christ our comfort overflows. If we are distressed, it is for your comfort and salvation; if we are comforted, it is for your comfort, which *produces in you patient endurance* of the same sufferings we suffer. And our hope for you is firm, because we know that just as you share in our sufferings, so also you share in our comfort.
>
> We do not want you to be uninformed, brothers, about the hardships we suffered in the province of Asia. We were under great pressure, far beyond our ability to endure, so that we despaired even of life. Indeed, in our hearts we felt the sentence of death. But this happened that we might not rely on ourselves but on God, who raises the dead. He has delivered us from such a deadly peril, and he will deliver us. On him we have set our hope that he will continue to deliver us, as you help us by your prayers. Then many will give thanks on our behalf for the gracious favor granted us in answer to the prayers of many. (2 Corinthians 1:3-11 NIV, emphasis added)

It seems to me that there is a need for us to be aware of our suffering giving us a tiny measure of understanding of Christ's suffering.

Our prayer as we are suffering the agony of a broken shoulder, pulled ligaments, hostage captivity, postoperative pain, and so on, is to be one of thanksgiving that Christ suffered all this and so much more for us. Then we are to turn and ask for help, His strength in our miserable weakness to endure what we need to be enduring with patience (not ours but His) and to be, as well as to do, that which no one else could be. Of course we are allowed to ask for deliverance from this "round of battle," but so often we are wasting an opportunity to do and be that which we could not do or be in *any other set of circumstances*. There is an opportunity for learning more reality, not only the reality of Christ's suffering, but the reality of His strength in this particular set of weaknesses, His comfort in this particular sorrow of separation or pain, which could be missed!

Paul also points out that the prayers of the Christians for Timothy and himself not only brought relief, but they gave many others a cause to thank God for His gracious answers.

Only in this life can we know (with reality and not just academically) something by experience of what it means to share in the sufferings of Christ and to share in each other's suffering. Searching for more understanding and for more true compassion so often brings us to a place of "finding" (always only partially, but always with increasing growth) as we pray in the midst of our own suffering and affliction, or the suffering and affliction of those whom we love best, or are concerned for personally and involved with, rather than the general suffering of the world.

I so often pray, and have so often prayed through the years, *Lord, don't let me waste this opportunity to learn what You want me to learn, to be what You want me to be, to prove to Satan that I really love You, as Job did, not just the good things You give.* Have I done it perfectly? Or without wasting some of those opportunities? A thousand times no. There are always repeated needs to cry out, *Lord, forgive me for the waste of that never-to-be-repeated combination of circumstances to grow in the midst of affliction and to pray with trust before the suffering becomes a part of past history.*

Never will I forget the moment when Franky and Debby arrived in that blue and white hospital room at St. Mary's in Rochester, coming straight from the airport only hours after Fran's cancer had been diagnosed. As Debby went to her father, Franky put his hands on my shoulders firmly and said earnestly, "Mom, this is when it counts — this is when it counts. Don't blow it." It was all wrapped up in those simple sentences. Reality is at such a time.

Just hours before that, when Fran had come down from the

operating room where a lymph gland had been removed from his neck and had been pronounced malignant, he had telephoned each of his four children from his wheelchair before being put back into bed. "I want to tell each one myself, not to have them hear it from someone else." Almost the same reply, that is, in almost the same words, came from each one—Priscilla, Susan, Debby, and Franky. "Dad, thank you for teaching us so thoroughly that this is an abnormal world, that the Fall was a historic reality that does affect history. You have always prepared us for this news. For years we have been prepared."

Closeness to the Lord and being in His will does not mean the end of all disasters, sudden shocks of illness or accident, or even death. In 2 Corinthians 11, let us read again Paul's list of continued afflictions and tribulations:

> Are they servants of Christ? . . . I am more. I have worked much harder, been in prison more frequently, been flogged more severely, and been exposed to death again and again. Five times I received from the Jews the forty lashes minus one. Three times I was beaten with rods, once I was stoned, three times I was shipwrecked, I spent a night and a day in the open sea, I have been constantly on the move. I have been in danger from rivers, in danger from bandits, in danger from my own countrymen, in danger from Gentiles; in danger in the city, in danger in the country, in danger at sea; and in danger from false brothers. I have labored and toiled and have often gone without sleep; I have known hunger and thirst and have often gone without food. I have been cold and naked. Besides everything else, I face daily the pressure of my concern for all the churches. Who is weak, and I do not feel weak? Who is led into sin, and I do not inwardly burn? (2 Corinthians 11:23-29 NIV)

It is immediately after this recital of his sufferings and persecutions that Paul goes on to tell of the marvelous things he heard and saw either during a vision or actually in his body in the time he was caught up "in the third heaven." He speaks of this as something he (if he was indeed "that man") would not "boast about." If he has anything to boast about, he says, it is about his weaknesses.

Then comes that all-important passage which was a part of Paul's history in his prayer life, in his asking for something specific, which is constantly important to me and to you and to all who have read this portion in the Scripture over and over again in connection with understanding the reality of there being two kinds of answers. Both kinds of answers are important in fulfilling the victory prayer has in defeating Satan as he continually accuses Christians before God (as in Job and in Revelation 12:10, 11). Rather than your stopping to look up that Revelation passage, I'll put it right here.

> Then I heard a loud voice in heaven say: "Now have come the salvation and the power and the kingdom of our God, and the authority of his Christ. For the accuser of our brothers, who accuses them before our God day and night, has been hurled down. They overcame him by the blood of the Lamb and by the word of their testimony; they did not love their lives so much as to shrink from death." (NIV)

Paul's next account in 2 Corinthians 12:7-10 puts him into the stream of history of all those being spoken about in this Revelation passage.

Are *we* among them? It is in the times of suffering and affliction, persecution, and hardships that *we* are in a circumstance to "overcome by the blood of the Lamb." Overcome what? Overcome the temptation to waste the discovery of what God's strength in our weakness time after time is in a wide area of weaknesses; to waste the circumstances during which we can find out that His grace is really sufficient, not just for other people we read about in the Bible, *not* just as a theological concept, not just as something to read at morning prayer time and appreciate during a period of comfort, but to call for in the very midst of troubles. *O Heavenly Father, please give me the mercy of Thy sufficient grace now, sufficient grace to continue today in pain,* or *to trust You after this piece of devastating news, to love You without a break. May I overcome Satan's temptation to echo with those who would taunt me saying, 'where is thy God now?' Help me to be faithful now.*

Paul goes on to report that after his great revelations, in order to keep him from being conceited

. . . there was given me a thorn in my flesh, a messenger of Satan, to torment me. Three times I pleaded with the Lord to take it away from me. But he said to me, "My grace is sufficient for you, for my power is made perfect in weakness." Therefore I will boast all the more gladly about my weaknesses, so that Christ's power may rest on me . . . For when I am weak, then I am strong. (2 Corinthians 12:7-10 NIV)

Paul is talking about the reality of *answered* prayer. There is a great reality in having the Lord's strength given to continue whatever it is we are meant to do or be when it would be impossible in ourselves to keep on. It is in such times that we know we are not doing things because we are terribly efficient, or very clever, or physically in great condition, but because the answer to our prayer for help has been, not a changed circumstance with everything going well, not a removal of pain and suffering, but it has been instead an outpouring of His strength, to do what He would have us do or to simply have a patience (not our own) or a surge of increased trust of Him whereby we may whisper, *Lord, I don't understand this, but I love You and trust You.*

Gradually as life goes on and we go through a great diversity of difficulties, suffering and weaknesses, we come to understand that when Paul says he glories in his weaknesses so that he can know the strength he has for a task, it really is the Lord's strength and not his own. This is the very opposite of thinking that having success, health, and freedom from affliction is what it means to be a Christian and to be in God's will.

Now back to that weekend following the first tests and results showing cancer. Fran and I were in a hotel with Susan, Debby, and Franky (Priscilla came a bit later), and on Sunday we had an unrepeatable precious time in the hotel room together. It

was our private family time of worship and study together. Each
of us gave a chapter that meant a great deal to us at the time, and
we each prayed. You can't write a script for a time like that in life.
It might have been our last time together; we didn't know.
Certainly we would never experience again the same kind of
uncertainty, of waiting in the dark for the next step. The pre-
ciousness of using those hours did not have to be explained by
anyone. We felt it. What a mistake to waste such a time in simply begging God.

Oh yes, we did pray for the bad cells to be driven away—
wherever they were. We did pray for more time for Fran (if indeed
the seminars to begin so soon for *Whatever Happened to the
Human Race?* were God's will for him to do), but we spent time
asking for the present moment, for what God meant us to be to
each other, and to understand in the midst of this time, and in the
particular moment in which we each were, in our own personal
lives.

There are times in family life that are full of beauty and wonder because of walks, swims, hikes, birthday dinners, Christmas,
or whatever . . . unforgettable times. There are also times of sorrow and shock, of affliction and despair, of fear and unexpected
recognition of the imminence of what previous fear had always
pushed away. In such times, prayer in the midst of sorrow and suffering, of affliction and pain, is a sharing with each other of a deep
recognition of what Paul is talking about and what Jeremiah and
other prophets experienced. Only during such times do we come
closer to sharing in the suffering of Christ.

There is a great difference, however, in our suffering,
because that is when we come to know the comfort the Lord gives
us and when we can be glad that He never leaves us nor forsakes
us. The Lord Jesus suffered total aloneness on the cross . . . with
no answer to His cry.

Fran lived five and a half years after that. There was
chemotherapy, and in the midst of chemotherapy and an addi-
tional affliction of shingles, he was given strength a day at a time
to speak at twenty-one seminars for the film series *Whatever
Happened to the Human Race?* In addition to that reality of the

Lord's strength, we now knew that during the entire time of film-ing that film in many different locations including Israel, the tired legs and weakness Fran complained to me about at each morn-ing call, which came at 2:00 or 3:00 A.M. were due to cancer rag-ing through his system. He would say, "I can't do it," and then some minutes later say, "Well, it is only one more day, and it won't be my strength, will it? It is His strength." That film was extremely important—but the Lord did not give a freedom from affliction; He gave His strength in the midst of the affliction that was increasing.

Later when *The Great Evangelical Disaster* film was made and the book to go with it, during the last three months of his life, Fran was to go straight out of the hospital with the doctors giv-ing three blood transfusions and be present, in rapidly weaken-ing condition, to answer questions shoulder to shoulder with his son in those seminars in twelve cities.

Did we not pray? What was the matter with our faith? Oh yes, we prayed, and oh yes, prayer was answered. Fran's weak-ness was dramatically evident. Toward the last platform time, his lungs were filling up with fluid, but the strength given to continue until that piece of work was finished was also evident. Fran him-self said, "When I go down the hall of the hospital, of course there is part of me that would like to be free of cancer, but I know there are ways in which I can do more *with* cancer than I could with-out it. I am one of the gang as I talk to people there. I am not look-ing with pity from the peak of health. I am one of them myself."

It is a vivid illustration of knowing with reality the comfort that is given, and knowing what it can be to comfort others with the comfort with which we have been comforted.

This is not what Sunday school lessons are made up of; this is what the Christian life itself is made up of. We long for a real-ity of prayer in our lives. We long for a greater understanding of the Lord. Yet there is a danger of trying to abort the affliction which would bring us to the deeper place of closeness to the Lord in prayer.

As Paul writes to the Colossian church, he says he does not stop praying for them, asking that God will fill them with all spiritual understanding and wisdom. However, as you read this passage (Colossians 1:1-13), you will find that Paul prayed that they may be strengthened with all power, that they might have great endurance and patience. Now patience and endurance are needed in the midst of difficulty and troubles! He is not promising these new Christians a life of riches and ease, but a possibility of calling upon the Father in Heaven for moment-by-moment help in times of need.

As Colossians ends, Paul is asking that they pray that ". . . we may proclaim the mystery of Christ, for which I am in chains. Pray that I may proclaim it clearly as I should."

Notice he does not ask that they pray that his chains might drop off, but that he might keep on with his proclaiming of truth clearly in the *midst* of that affliction.

Does this all mean we should *ask* for afflictions? That we should seek suffering? That we should turn our faces to the wall and not look at the sunsets, the tiny new moon, the changing leaves in the autumn, the tiny violets by a path in early spring? Does it mean we should *not* enjoy richly the things God gives us to enjoy? No, of course not. It is our Heavenly Father who gives us His creation of beauty to enjoy. It is our Shepherd who leads us into green pastures beside still waters time after time and gives us the wonder of a "table prepared for us in the wilderness," who showers us with unexpected delights.

But as we pray in the midst of troubles, we are not to compare our own life with other lives and *demand*, as children so often do, "Give me what you gave her or him." "Look, it's not fair; look what he has or she has or that family has." "You don't love me . . . my life is too hard." Our prayer is to be more sensitive to the reality of history and to how our lives, our understanding of true victory over the accusations of Satan, fit into the total picture.

We are not carbon copies. Your understanding, my understanding, your prayer and mine, this chapter of your life and this chapter of mine *do* make a difference in history. No two lives are exactly alike. The staggering reality is that each of us has an opportunity to affect the battle in the unseen world, as well as what is going on in neighborhoods, villages, portions of towns and cities, states, the nation, or other parts of the world. To shrug our shoulders and say, "I don't matter," is not to be humble, but to be unfaithful to what the Lord has for us to be doing in prayer, in trusting the Lord, as well as in being what we are meant to be as an influence. It could be anywhere—in our wheelchair, our hospital bed, our cell where our captors put us, our tank, our pilot's seat on a plane, our tractor, our kitchen sink, our vegetable garden, our teaching place with a few young children or Ph.D. scholars, our "march for life" as things are being thrown at us, our adoption of a pregnant woman for a period of time or a child for a lifetime.

Can't you see the diversity?

God is able to give His comfort, His strength, His wisdom in a vast number of different situations as His children cry out for help, with trust while still in a fog, not seeing any change in sight, yet *really* living in the light of recognizing that these afflictions are not to be compared with the glories that are ahead of us.

Come with me to the English countryside and meet a couple who are among a few people who are an example to me. You are meeting Philip Mason and his wife Virginia. Phil is one of the most radiant Christians I know. I'm not just picking out an adjective; his face really radiates! His smile is beautiful, and his eyes smile as wonderfully as his lips. *What an alive person!* is your thought. Intelligence, knowledge, ideas seem to burst forth even before he speaks. You know he is keeping up with many things, not just as the fine church elder he is, but with current things that would interest the young people who come to their home and with what is going on in the world today. Current events? Oh yes, but sports, music, plays, and films as well. This is a man who also lives in the Bible and is a man of deep and faithful prayer. As you approach, you see that he is in a wheelchair, but not an electric one.

All this first hits you. Then you realize that his chin is resting on a board. He cannot hold up his head otherwise. He cannot move at all! His hands cannot move. When he writes, it must be with a stick held in his teeth touching ever so lightly an electrically sensitive computer. When he eats, it is his wife who feeds him. She also dresses him and pushes his chair.

What is his background? Not too long ago he was a splendid gymnast. All those things that make you shake your head in amazed admiration as you watch gymnasts do their double and triple somersaults, their swirls on a horse, their fine disciplined movements on the parallel bars—all these were a part of his skill which seemed natural. He was heading for an expected next chapter of greater ease and even better form.

And then came the moment! It only took a second for the slight variance in timing to bring Phil down on his head at an angle that broke his neck. Had he not done this triple somersault many times perfectly? Ah yes, but this tiny divergence in how it went was to cause a totally unexpected next chapter that was going to last for all the moments of his life, until another tiny moment comes. You have heard it sung gloriously in Handel's *Messiah;* it has thrilled you as you have sung along in your own voice. You have read it in 1 Corinthians 15:51, 52. What a very real difference it should make in your life when a moment brings about a drastic or sorrowful change. What a difference it must make in mine. Not just once, but over and over again.

> Behold, I show you a mystery; we shall not all sleep, but we shall all be changed. In a *moment*, in the twinkling of an eye, at the last trump; for the trumpet shall sound, and the dead shall be raised incorruptible, and we shall be changed.

I wish this page could suddenly sing to you with full orchestra. That would surprise you out of your chair or bed and the words would fix themselves indelibly in your memory!

We need this parallel moment that is an unbreakable promise when we are hit with a devastating moment. We need to pray as rapidly as possible, *Lord, my Father in Heaven, hallowed be Thy name. May I not sin against Thee now by complaining; may I keep loving You now, and may I truly thank You that that moment is ahead of us when the trumpet will sound, and that which is a mystery to us now will be our greatest reality forever.*

Did God throw Phil on his head so that Phil could show reality in his life? I do not think so. Did God give dear Virginia recognition of that special person imprisoned in his unmovable body, give her great love, so great that she cares for the details moment by moment, *just so that she could be an example?* I do not think so. Did God give Francis Schaeffer cancer so that he could experience God's strength in his weakness for some years before his shortened life was ended on this earth? I do not think so. Did God cause Joni Eareckson Tada to break her neck in that dive into familiar water? Oh no, no, no. The battle that has been continuing between the rebel angel Lucifer, (the devil, Satan) and God will continue until the devil is cast down. That battle is not a piece of theater. It is not a script coming out of a programmed computer. I will be going more into that in my chapter "If God Is Sovereign, Why Pray?" but in this place of considering prayer and suffering, it is very, very basic to recognize that cause-and-effect history following the Fall has a place in afflictions, suffering, and persecution, as do direct attacks of Satan against God in trying to stop His children from loving Him, (which God has made clear to us in Job).

I would like to quote some from my own book, *Affliction*, chapter 3, "A Crack in the Curtain," the chapter on Job. You see Job's friends had been railing against him, even as so many Christians rail against people who are not healed of an affliction and cruelly declare they do not have faith enough or must have sinned very much to be having such a time of suffering. It seems to me that in the midst of our considering prayer in the area of suffering affliction, this is another dimension that belongs right here.

When God speaks to Job directly, he does not chide Job for his sin, but does chide him for having a lesser view of the greatness of God than he should have had. We stand with Job as God speaks, for He speaks to us too. Do we really bow as created beings before our Creator? Do we really let God be God in our communication with other people and with God himself? We must read and reread His Word—to help keep ourselves in our

place. God is saying that Job hasn't enough knowledge to see
and understand his situation in the framework of total history.
God says if you can't know all about creation, how can you
know the most subtle things?

"Who is this that darkeneth counsel by words without
knowledge? Where wast thou when I laid the foundation of the
earth? Declare if thou hast understanding . . . Knowest thou it
because thou wast born? Or because the number of thy days is
great? Hast thou entered into the treasures of the snow? Or
hast thou seen the treasures of hail? . . . Does the hawk fly by
thy wisdom and stretch her wings toward the south?"

Job bows before God and acknowledges that he has not
enough knowledge to judge his own place in total history. God
makes clear to him that only God can judge in this final fash-
ion. Job shows that he now realizes he is completely a "creature" and that God is completely Creator. It is at this point that
God turns to the friends (although Elihu is left out) and says,
"You have not spoken of Me as Job has. You have not spoken
correctly." (pages 56-57)

Remember that Job's friends have acted as some people may
have treated us in the midst of affliction. It is important to recognize that in the midst of praying for help—help that the circumstances may be changed, help in being given God's grace and
strength to continue if the affliction is not to be removed—that
there is another dimension of prayer needed. Job is asked by God
to intercede for his friends. Job's willingness to pray for them and
the sincerity and honesty of his prayer (which only God could
have known as only God knows what is going on inside when we
pray; the attitude of heart is what matters, not just words)
brought this wonderful account of the end of Job's time of suffering in Job 42:10: "And the Lord turned the captivity of Job
when he prayed for his friends. Also God gave Job twice as much
as he had before."

Does that mean that if we pray for those who have unfairly
troubled us in the midst of our most difficult moments, if we pray
for those who pour out reproof and criticize us for lack of faith
because we have not been healed, or have not had the earthquake

miss us, or have not been prevented from having an accident, etc., that immediately the result will be similar to the blessings at the end of Job's life?

Two things need to be remembered as we follow God's teaching as to whom we should pray for. One is that our motive should be to be doing what the Lord has told us to do, not to get some sort of immediate reward! Secondly we need to continue to remember that the Lord does not do exactly the same thing for each of His people, the sheep of His pasture, His children, His disciples.

As Jesus talks to Peter after His resurrection, He makes very clear to him this important distinction. Peter is to have a sharply different life and death from John. It is not a matter of any one of God's children being loved less or more. Each person in history is distinct. The importance of each life is significant. The sufficient grace and strength given to each one in a time of need has been made possible by the tremendous price Christ paid for each of these individual victories. Answered prayer—whether by taking away affliction or by giving sufficient grace and strength to go on—both kinds of answered prayer demonstrate to Satan that the victory over his attempt to separate God's people from Him and to cancel their love and trust is a reality. Victory, looked forward to in the coming resurrection at Christ's return, will be total, complete—physically, spiritually, emotionally, intellectually. The perfection will be a complete defeat to the evil one. As we notice differences in the lives of faithful believers, however, we need to remember what Jesus said to Peter and follow Jesus, keeping our eyes truly on "the author and finisher of our faith" (Hebrews 12:2).

So when they had dined, Jesus saith to Simon Peter, Simon, son of Jonah, lovest thou me more than these? He saith unto him, Yea, Lord; thou knowest that I love thee. He saith unto him, Feed my lambs.

He saith unto him a second time, Simon, son of Jonah, lovest thou me? He saith unto him, Yea, Lord; thou knowest that I love thee. He saith unto him, Feed my sheep.

He saith unto him the third time, Simon, son of Jonah, lovest thou me? Peter was grieved because he said unto him the third time, Lovest thou me? And he said unto him, Lord, thou knowest all things; thou knowest that I love thee.

Jesus saith unto him, Feed my sheep. Verily, verily, I say unto thee, When thou wast young, thou girdest thyself, and walkest whither thou wouldest; but when thou shalt be old, thou shalt stretch forth thy hands, and another shall gird thee, and carry thee whither thou wouldst not.

Thus spoke he, signifying by what death he [Peter] should glorify God . . .

Then Peter, turning about, seeth the disciple whom Jesus loved, following; . . .

Peter, seeing him [John], saith to Jesus, Lord, and what shall this man do?

Jesus saith unto him, If I will that he tarry till I come, what is that to thee? Follow thou me. (John 21:15-21 KJV)

The next verse goes on to say that among the brethren the report went around that Jesus had said John would not die. In fact He had not said that, but that if John lived until He came back, what was that to Peter? The emphasis is strongly that we are not to compare, but to be willing to continue to do what the Lord has given us to do in the midst of hardships, without being sure whether these are direct attacks of Satan or a result of cause-and-effect history, or a special opportunity to do that which is given in Romans 5:1-5:

Therefore, since we have been justified through faith, we have peace with God through our Lord Jesus Christ, through whom we have gained access by faith into this grace in which we now stand. And we rejoice in the hope of the glory of God. Not only so, but we also rejoice in our sufferings, because we know that suffering produces perseverance; perseverance, character; and character, hope. And hope does not disappoint us, because God has poured out his love into our hearts by the Holy Spirit, whom he has given us. (NIV)

It is only in this life that we can pray in the midst of pain, disappointment, loneliness, misunderstanding, cruelty, illness, tears, sorrow. Prayer in such times, declaring our trust and love and appreciation and thanksgiving, is increasingly real. When we see the Lord face to face, instead of "through a glass darkly," that opportunity to show Him we truly love Him will be over.

To illustrate the amazing contrast of lives among the family of our Heavenly Father, I would like to tell you of two sisters in an American family, Ann Wells and Shannon Lucid, whose father and mother were missionaries in China.

At this moment of my writing you could not imagine the vast difference in where they are geographically right now. Ann is in a hospital in Oklahoma having chemotherapy for her lupus, which has not responded to any other treatment. She also is legally blind. One affliction has followed another in her life with her increased understanding of suffering and her constantly increasing understanding of prayer in the midst of these devastating circumstances.

Shannon is whirling around the earth in a space ship far out in the stratosphere discovering many new wonders, along with other astronauts. She is the only woman to have gone up for the third time. Shannon doesn't know, by her own experience, what illness is. She is married, has three children, has carried on cancer research for years, along with her active program at the Houston Space Center. Both sisters are Christians. Shannon's growing understanding of God's marvel of creation comes at moments of looking from that vantage point, of seeing the earth as a ball below somewhere. She sees incredible sights hard to explain to anyone who has always been walking in deserts, or hills, on dusty country roads, or busy city streets, bound by gravity and the time it takes to get from one location to another, even by the speediest kinds of earth transportation!

Who but God can measure what is commonly called "the quality of life," a life worthy of being lived, a life accomplishing something worthwhile in history, a life affecting other people's thinking, understanding, and behavior? Who but God can know all that will be involved in His assessment of a Christian's life when He greets them saying, "Well done, thou good and faithful servant. Enter thou into the joy of thy Lord." The perspective of our immortal, invisible, only-wise God, who is infinite, perfectly holy and personal, is a perspective that sees the value of lives in a different way.

Can we jump to conclusions? No, not in any way. God really does know and does give His Peters and Johns in history extremely differing but strategically important things to do.

Ann lives in a wee house alone, arranged so that she can avoid bumping into things, avoid burning herself at the stove, and "see" with special equipment that enlarges words on a page—a long process for reading, but better than nothing. This is really a "house of prayer." I am not romantically designating it as that; Ann is really faithful day by day to take long blocks of time for prayer and to pray systematically for people and needs, works she feels impressed to take responsibility for, as well as workers. She prays for understanding and growth, wisdom and strength for prayer, for herself as well as for other people and situations. Is this a life work? There is no doubt about it; the answer is yes. I seriously believe that one day we will see what has been different in history because of Ann's prayer. I really am sure that she has done as much work in a diversity of locations as the people who have traveled by plane or boat or camel or jeep to get to these locations in person. It is the serious faithfulness that counts. Prayer taken this seriously and recognized as important is so often not recognized by others; therefore, there is not appreciation of the work, which is difficult, needs concentration, and the willpower to get down to it, just as other work does. But God does know. He is the one who has said, "He that is faithful in the least . . ." making it clear that if we are faithful in the little things, it will make a difference to our Father who is aware of what is taking place as we trust Him and love Him.

Ann does another thing people might think not so important. She goes twice a week to a hospital to rock, gently and lovingly, crack babies who have been abandoned. She feels there is response at times in these babies. It is an important compassion. When Jesus says that He will one day speak to us and say, "When

I was sick, you visited me . . ." it is only in clothing, feeding, visiting in prison or hospitals "the least of these" that we can be truly doing something directly for Him. He puts it within our reach in different times of our lives, in different places, to different people in need. Mother Teresa comes to mind, and Amy Carmichael, but there are unknown people caring for people within their own reach—faithfully and prayerfully. It is all a part of the importance and significance of each one in history.

John's time of writing while confined on the Isle of Patmos would certainly—at times—have been gladly exchanged for the life shortened by the martyr's death of Peter. We each at times look up with our eyes of imagination at our loved ones who are a part of the cloud of witnesses now and wonder what it would be like to be through with the battle or the race that we are to run patiently until we reach the end of the course!

So I am in no way suggesting in my contrast of two sisters that Shanon does not first of all have very difficult responsibilities and the suffering that goes with wanting to be in two places at one time. Nor would I suggest that one needs to be walled in with a body that cannot move, such as Phil's in his wheelchair or Ann's with her constant pain and limitations, in order to pray. No, we are admonished to pray in all kinds of places and situations. To be up there in the stratosphere is not necessarily to be closer to God, nor is it to be farther away from Him. I am sure that Shanon prays in thanksgiving and worship, but also for help and strength, even as the Christian astronomer does in his research, as the Christian surgeon does with all the instant choices and decisions to be made in the operating room, as the Christian artist does in attempting to do really good art work, and as the Christian composer does who composes symphonies or jazz. There is a kind of suffering and tribulation wound up with our lives which needs a more clear understanding that these are *not* strange things, but a part of living in a fallen world. We must also realize that we are *meant* to be praying for guidance and help, for strength and endurance. We need to know that Christ's suffering paid the price to make this kind of asking both possible and essential.

"What difference does it make to pray?" you may be muttering right here. "If God is sovereign, what difference could it possibly make?" That I will go into in another chapter, but suffice it to say here that the Word of God has made clear that prayer makes a *tremendous* difference. It is also clear that through centuries some have been giving their lives to a work of prayer.

At the beginning of L'Abri there were about twenty people who on their own volition asked to be the Praying Family and promised to pray a certain length of time each day for L'Abri. Among these was my mother, who sat in a rocking chair with her Bible and notebook, faithfully praying for individual people and needs day by day. Monday was the L'Abri day of prayer, and each Monday my mother would take the day for fasting and prayer, staying in the rocking chair with her Bible and the notebook in which she would write names and needs. In a nearby town a county clerk prayed early each morning before work, took her noontime for prayer, and set Monday aside as a special day of fasting and prayer. Her friend, Jane Mitchell, a housewife, arranged her time in the same way. Half a world away in Manchuria, Bertha Byrum, a missionary doctor, was in solitary confinement in a prison camp for a long time. She had her Bible with her, but was not allowed her pen. During that long time, she read and prayed, read and prayed and, using a hairpin to mix saliva with dirt from the floor, she made a kind of "ink" which could be read years later. Dr. Byrum told the Lord during that difficult but very real school of prayer that if she ever got free, she would give three hours a day to prayer for two different works, in addition to her regular prayer. When the release took place, she did not go back on her promise. She seriously prayed as to which works she should give these daily sections of time to, and wrote to us that L'Abri had been impressed on her mind as one of the two.

Dr. Byrum prayed very earnestly for the people who went to L'Abri and for the people of God's choice to get there without hindrance. Among so many others, her own grandson was one who came and to whom that period made a great difference.

I often think of Dr. Byrum's understanding of loneliness and suffering in that cell as something like Ann's loneliness; Phil's "cell" of his paralyzed body; the loneliness of Blake as years went on since his mother, father, and brother were killed in a plane crash . . . and all the other lonely, suffering people in a great variety of hard, even excruciating circumstances.

God's grace *has been* and *is* sufficient, and His strength was and is being made "perfect in weakness." The reality of answered prayer has gone on through centuries with two kinds of answers being equally spiritual.

Please come to two places that need to be reviewed frequently—by me, also by you. We are *not* to be ashamed of our God no matter what difficulty we are in the midst of. We are to keep trusting Him with deep loyalty as to a friend whom at the moment we don't understand, but we stand up for that friend, trust his knowledge, his compassion, his wisdom. Our friend is not perfect; he or she makes mistakes. But we know God *is* perfect, which is all the more reason to display our trust. We do this in prayer. Come to Psalm 25:1-6, 20, 21 as David prays:

> Unto thee, O Lord, do I lift up my soul. O my God, I trust in thee; let me not be ashamed . . . . let them be ashamed who transgress without cause. Show me thy ways, O Lord; teach me thy paths. Lead me in thy truth, and teach me; for thou art the God of my salvation; on thee do I wait all the day. Remember, O Lord, thy tender mercies and thy lovingkindnesses; for they have been ever of old . . .
>
> Oh, keep my soul, and deliver me; let me not be ashamed; for I put my trust in thee. Let integrity and uprightness preserve me; for I wait on thee. (KJV)

David comes in the midst of many afflictions, surrounded by enemies, as he prays for God's mercy and lovingkindness and asks to be led in truth and taught. He speaks of *waiting* on the Lord all day. He does not expect instantaneous removal of the difficulties, many of which he has recognized he brought about by his own sin. Yet he asks that he will not be ashamed.

I think of this Psalm in the light of Daniel facing the lions' den and the three men facing the fiery furnace. The gist of their declaration to men and their prayer at those times was, "Our God is able . . . but if not, we trust Him and will worship only Him." They did not approach the awful moment being ashamed of God.

Paul, as he preaches to the Romans in Romans 1, has suffered terrible things (which of course are related earlier in this chapter). When he says in verses 15-17:

> So, as much as in me is, I am ready to preach the gospel to you that are at Rome also. For I am not ashamed of the gospel of Christ; for it is the power of God unto salvation to every one that believeth; to the Jew first, and also to the Greek. For in it is the righteousness of God revealed from faith to faith; as it is written, The just shall live by faith. (KJV)

Paul is not ashamed of preaching an unpopular message of truth, declaring it has been true through the ages and that all human beings should have recognized the Creator from His creation and should have glorified Him as God. Not only is Paul not ashamed to preach this message as truth, and not as another religion among religions, but he is not ashamed of the persecution that he is at that time living through and which comes to those who believe.

Yes, God does give amazing answers to prayer, and of course Daniel was glad and thrilled when the lions' mouths were shut supernaturally. God is able to do all things, but too often people feel ashamed if their troubles have continued, or new afflictions have hit them, right in the midst of a time of taking a new step of trust and of spending more time in real worship and prayer. We are to ask the Lord for His help to be not ashamed at such times, no matter how we are taunted by other people, either believers or unbelievers.

As I was writing this, the telephone rang, and it was Franz Mohr from New York asking me to pray especially for Stephen Griffith and his family. A most unusual affliction had hit them— not a flood nor an earthquake, but an invasion of bats! Hundreds of bats had invaded their house in North Carolina, and they were told by an exterminating firm that it is against the law for them to exterminate them. This story does not have an ending yet. But I felt it belonged right here. Steve's wife has left the house with the two youngest children. Steve is there trying to edit a book, and his teenage daughter is staying too. Franz and I prayed together on the phone. You may be sure Steve and his family and other friends are praying too. But what about the people who will make rude remarks? People who may sarcastically ask, "Where is your God now?"

Jesus suffered that awful persecution as people shouted, "Come down from the cross if You are the Son of God!" The difference is that He willingly stayed there and suffered all that sarcasm for us.

Yes, we have an open door to our Father in Heaven to ask for a sudden change—the bats to go as suddenly as they came, the operation to be a success, the pain to be relieved, the house to be re-constructed, the money to be supplied, the strength to flow into our exhausted bodies in time for the task.

But in this chapter we are dwelling on prayer that is given the other answer, the answer given to Paul when he cried for the thorn in the flesh to be removed: "My grace is sufficient for thee; My strength is made perfect in weakness."

Hebrews 11 reviews history for us in speaking briefly of God's people who lived lives of trusting Him, of acting upon their faith to do what He gave them to do, to take steps based on faith. Remember that it tells what faith is and gives many examples. Read the chapter again, but I will give a few excerpts:

> But without faith it is impossible to please him; for he that cometh to God must believe that he is, and that he is a rewarder of them that diligently seek him. By faith Abraham, when he was called to go out into a place which he should after receive for an inheritance, obeyed; and he went out, not knowing where he went. . . . (Hebrews 11:6, 8 KJV)

The chapter goes into the faith of Noah, of Sarah (Abraham's wife), of Isaac, of Jacob, of Joseph, of Moses, of Rahab the harlot, of Gideon, of Samson, of David. One by one, people are commended for their faith, for their prayer answered with amazing provision and guidance and care. But before the chapter ends, there is a list of the kinds of persecution and martyrdom people of God suffered.

And others had trial of cruel mockings and scourgings, yea, moreover, of bonds and imprisonment; they were stoned, they were sawn asunder, were tempted, were slain with the sword; they wandered about in sheepskins and goatskins; being destitute, afflicted, tormented. (Hebrews 11:36, 37 KJV)

Verse 39, "These all having obtained a good report through faith," refers to those who had tremendous answers to prayer, such as Noah seeing the wonder of the animals coming to be on the ark to be saved from the flood and his seeing the first rainbow; or Joshua seeing the walls of Jericho fall down; or Gideon marveling at the Midianites being conquered with such a tiny number of soldiers and strange equipment . . . But equally those who were tortured and killed, who were not given a last moment reprieve, a sudden opening of prison doors—these *equally* "obtained a good report through faith." What they had was sufficient grace for each moment of need.

To go back now to verses 39 and 40 of Hebrews 11 and quote them in full:

And these all, having obtained a good report through faith, received not the promise, God having provided some better thing for us, that they without us should not be made perfect.

This excites me very much. It held more meaning as various people whom I knew well died—my father and mother, Hans Rookmaaker, Anne Bates, families of other L'Abri workers, the fathers, or mothers, or wives, husbands, children of other people precious to me. As I thought about people suddenly "being absent from the body and present with the Lord," which Paul says is far better, I began to think more and more about this phrase: "that they without us should not be made perfect."

What is it that they are waiting for and that we are waiting for too?

There is something we are all going to experience in one fell swoop. God is going to give us all the greatest surprise, the most fabulous experience in one moment of time. No one will be ahead of anyone else in this incredible moment of history, this fabulous pulling back of the curtain . . . as *the resurrection of the body takes place.*

Christ will return, we are told, and the dead in Christ will arise, and those who are still alive at that time will be changed, and in a moment, in a twinkling of an eye, we will have perfect bodies. We will make this discovery together. We will discover what perfection is like in our resurrected bodies at the same time as Abraham, Isaac, Joseph, Moses, Peter, Paul and *everyone* who has gone before us!

We fall on our faces before our Father in Heaven, our Savior, the Lord Jesus Christ, our Comforter, the Holy Spirit with a crescendo of praise and thanksgiving for such a plan, for such a HOPE. How can we fail to trust Him and love Him and worship Him with a growing realization of His love. Oh, we must not be ashamed of Him.

But come back to verse 16 of Hebrews 11. This is where He tells all people through history that He is *not* ashamed to be called the God of those who suffer as well as of those who are delivered. "But now they desire a better country, that is, an heavenly; wherefore, God is not ashamed to be called their God; for he hath prepared for them a city."

All the people referred to in Hebrews 11 and all the people they represent right up to scattered people in today's world are ones regarding whom God has declared, "I am not ashamed to be called their God."

Yes, the promises are sure. We can trust God who has given them with clarity. There is coming a time as definite a part of history as Christ's first birth in a geographic location was. He is coming back, and what is ahead is so completely perfect for each one that God is able to say to Peter and to John and to Phil in his wheelchair and to Paul Wylie flying over the ice in his figure skating—to each one of His children in whichever state they are and in whichever kind of answer their prayer is having:

> "I am not ashamed to be called your God,
> because I have prepared for you a city."

THREE

Helps in Being Real in Prayer

Do you feel awkward in talking to some people and yet immediately relaxed with others? Do you have a sudden "kindred-spirit feeling" with someone and realize that you are being understood even before you finish a sentence? Rare! It happens from time to time in life unexpectedly. But it only takes place if you have been listening, *really listening,* to the other person and finding out that communication is truly taking place, gradually finding out who that other person is.

Last summer Priscilla and I were sitting at her kitchen table in their little Chalet Tzi No talking about communication as well as other things. She picked up her pen to show me what she had been doing as a help to herself. You see, so often some of us who have a lot to tell in the area of ideas or of things we have been doing can forget how time flies, and we use up all the discussion time or communicating time without letting the other person get a word in "edgewise." There is a tremendous *need* to have a two-way time of talking if we are really going to have good communication and get to know the other person better.

Priscilla took her pen in her right hand and, stretching her left thumb out, followed that little crease at the base of her thumb a bit, making an ink line, and then made another tiny line, forming an L. Yes, an L hidden by her thumb when she closed her hand but available for herself to look at. Why to look at? As a reminder that she needs to check up on herself. "Have I been listening?" I needed that a lot, as that is my weakness—going on too long with stories or ideas without leaving time for the other person. OK, it has been a help. L for listen, unobtrusively hiding at the base of the left thumb. "Don't forget," my brain tells me. "Look at your little reminder and remember that talk you and Prisca had looking out at the skyline of the alps against that blue sky and hearing the village clock ring its bells for noon." You may be in New York, or Minnesota, or Tennessee, or Colorado, but don't forget to remind yourself to listen. If you want communication to develop, if you want to have a relationship, it takes listening, as well as talking. It takes looking at each other's artistic offerings, thinking about each other's ideas, considering each other's needs, hearing what the other person is saying.

With human beings, listening surely helps, but every person you meet is not going to develop into a friend just because you listen. Nevertheless, whether it is your business partners, someone you work with daily, relatives, your spouse—whomever you are complaining about as not communicating with you—there needs to be a checkup on whether or not you really take time and interest and thought to listen. That L is a good idea if we honestly want relationships to improve.

PRAYER IS COMMUNICATION. Prayer needs to be a two-way communication. We need to spend time listening to God our Father, the Creator of all things, and to Jesus His Son described in Isaiah 9:6: "For unto us a child is born, unto us a son is given, and the government shall be upon his shoulder; and his name shall be called Wonderful, Counselor, The Mighty God, The Everlasting Father, The Prince of Peace."

We cannot grow in our knowledge of God, our understanding of Him, in our love of Him, and in the sincerity of our worship of Him without listening to what He says to us in His Word, the Bible.

Yes, the Bible is to be read for history, for knowledge of how we are meant to live in God's sight. It is to be read to help us understand what sin is and how far we fall short of being what we are meant to be. It is to be read to understand something about the time we live in, something about human beings, and to have some knowledge about the future. It is God's revelation. He has not been silent, but has spoken. Yes, we need correct teaching and

preaching, but we have been given God's communication to read
. . . and to have continually as His word to listen to, to hear.

In other words, one needs to read and pray, read and pray.
To pray in the context of reading God's Word is to have a devel-
oping relationship with God our Father and with Jesus Christ our
Shepherd. The Holy Spirit is our promised help in this.

Where do you start? Where do I start? In the Psalms, in
Isaiah, in so many places in the Old Testament, then later in the
New. It depends on how much time we are taking day by day, and
we soon find we need a whole day, or at least a long block of time
to put aside other things and listen and pray without hurry. I put
little marks in my Bible. They are some of my response, my reply,
as I listen. I put them on a separate piece of paper or in a notebook or in the margin. Thanksgiving is so overwhelming for me
as I read, I need to write it; or confession to the Lord is too much
to just think in my mind or to whisper. But this is a personal communication, and as I read and pray, I will stop at different places
to worship in my own words or in the words of a verse, to praise
and to worship or to make a request.

We wait in hope for the Lord;
    he is our help and our shield.
In him our hearts rejoice,
    for we trust in his holy name.
May your unfailing love rest upon us,
    O Lord, even as we put our hope in you.
                         (Psalm 33:20-22 NIV)

*Thank you, our Heavenly Father, for Your unfailing love.
May the reality of our waiting upon You and waiting for You
show You our trust. Forgive our lack of trust. Please increase my
trust today and my recognition of Your love resting upon me.*

Then one can go on and pray for each person especially on
his or her heart, for the increase of "waiting in hope" and of trust,
for each one by name.

Trust in the Lord and do good;
    dwell in the land and enjoy safe pasture.

Delight yourself in the Lord
>   and he will give you the desires of your heart.
Commit your way to the Lord;
>   trust in him and he will do this:
He will make your righteousness shine like the dawn,
>   the justice of your cause like the noonday sun.
Be still before the Lord and wait patiently for him;
>   do not fret when men succeed in their ways,
>   when they carry out their wicked schemes.
Refrain from anger and turn from wrath;
>   do not fret—it leads only to evil.
For evil men will be cut off,
>   but those who hope in the Lord will inherit the land . . .
The salvation of the righteous comes from the Lord;
>   he is their stronghold in time of trouble.
The Lord helps them and delivers them;
>   he delivers them from the wicked and saves them,
>   because they take refuge in him.

>   (Psalm 37:3-9, 39, 40 NIV)

What does it mean, Lord, to delight in You? I do delight in Your creation, the new moon and light on the snow, the dark trees against the sunset, the wings of that butterfly, and the amazing way You gave animals instinct—dogs, swallows, salmon, and trout. I delight in Your communication that is so rich. Oh please, Father in Heaven, help me to delight in You more and more. O Father in Heaven, may my committing my way to You be so real that the righteousness You have provided through Christ will really shine through me in a way that would please You. I ask this now for (and I name each one for whom I am praying that day).

Psalm 51 has so many markings in it—I'm asking that God in His unfailing love would wash me from my sin and prepare me for prayer. Come to verse 10:

Create in me a pure heart, O God, and renew a steadfast spirit within me. (NIV)

Create in me a clean heart O God, and renew a right spirit within me. (KJV)

Restore to me the joy of your salvation and grant me a willing spirit, to sustain me. (v. 12 NIV)

Yes, Lord, give me, give each one for whom I am praying, joy today—the kind of joy You mean us to have.

As we read and pray the day we come to Psalm 56, we may take courage to plead for help in the midst of whatever form of attack has come upon us. It may be from people similar to David's enemies, but attacking in quite another form.

Be merciful to me, O God, for men hotly
     pursue me;
  all day long they press their attack.
My slanderers pursue me all day long;
  many are attacking me in their pride.
When I am afraid,
  I will trust in you.
In God whose word I praise,
  in God I trust; I will not be afraid.
What can mortal man do to me?
All day long they twist my words;
  they are always plotting to harm me.
They conspire, they lurk,
  they watch my steps,
  eager to take my life.
                    (Psalm 56:1-6 NIV)

It may be in the midst of an intense board meeting these words will come to you again; it may be in the midst of a business deal, or a university situation, or in medical research or scientific research, or a political situation. It may be in the kitchen as a young mother hears untrue gossip. Memory of this passage will send you back to your Bible at prayer time or will cause you to go to a spot in the middle of the night to read it and pray again,

the words of the Psalmist as they apply to your situation or the
situation of a close friend or family member.

*Help me, Lord, my Father. I am afraid. Help me to not be
afraid, to stop trembling, and to trust You to be ABLE to enter
into this situation.*

When we prayed together that day in Rochester as a family,
reading and bringing various portions of the Bible, we were waiting for the final report the next day of the extent of the cancer
cells in Fran's bone marrow. I've spoken about it in the previous
chapter. Psalm 71 was the Psalm I read in that room and spoke
about. You need to read it all and intersperse listening to the Lord
with praying, realizing that for centuries God's people have come
to Him in this kind of distress. We pray in a stream of history. We
are not alone. We pray with those who are God's people through
the ages.

Just a few verses here of Psalm 71:

> Be not far from me, O God;
>> come quickly, O my God, to help me . . .
>> I will come and proclaim your mighty acts, O Sovereign
>>> Lord;
>> I will proclaim your righteousness, yours alone.
> Since my youth, O God, you have taught me,
>> and to this day I declare your marvelous deeds.
> Even when I am old and gray,
>> do not forsake me, O God,
> till I declare your power to the next generation,
>> your might to all who are to come.
> Your righteousness reaches to the skies, O God,
>> you who have done great things.
>> Who, O God, is like you?
> Though you have made me see troubles, many and bitter,
>> you will restore my life again;
> from the depths of the earth
>> you will again bring me up,
> You will increase my honor and comfort me once again.
>   (Psalm 71:12, 16-21 NIV)

We asked that morning that there might be more time to "declare" the truth of the Creator to "the next generation." Grandchildren and great-grandchildren in mind? Yes, but the immediate thing before us all was that the film *Whatever Happened to the Human Race?* had just been finished, and there were to be twenty-two seminars all over the states and then others in England. It seemed there was a tremendous need to finish this piece of work. We called for restoration for this piece of history directly ahead of us. The film was not yet edited. In between our waiting for results from the tests and praying earnestly, Franky and Jim arranged to show Fran the beautiful portions of the film made in Israel so that at least he could see the unedited shots.

Even that hard waiting time became a time of special communication with each other and with the Lord in prayer. The intensity of uncertainty seems to make minutes and hours more precious. Also one realizes with fresh reality the utter dependence one has on God.

I have discovered that it is in times of intense need, such as Franky's polio, the floods and avalanches that nearly carried our chalet away, the edict telling us to leave our home and village in six weeks, the need for a private plane to take Fran (on a stretcher) out to Mayo in Rochester (five and a half years after the Sunday I describe above)—it is in such times that one realizes that prayer is the central reality.

What do I mean by central reality?

It is when there is *nothing* one can do in one's own strength, or one's own wisdom, or one's own cleverness of planning that it becomes so true and real that God has said, "Call on me." One realizes that it is immediately important to fast and pray, to get up in the night while others sleep, and pray, to reach for the Bible and listen and pray, to ask for all sin and hindrances to be removed. The central reality of God's existence, of His availability through Christ in the power of the Spirit, is not pushed into some prescribed time or a proper place; one prays in the hospital beside the bed, also in the hall, or the bathroom. One prays in the early dawn or all night beside a child's bed. A Christian general prays for the God who never slumbers nor sleeps to care for his troops when he simply must get four hours. One prays with real urgency shutting out other things.

Coming to know who God is, more about His compassion, His presence, His holding our hand in our deepest fear and distress cannot be turned on and off like a little list of how-to's, a list of ways to pray more fervently! So often if we pray for reality, we enter into a dark period. We are not handed a script for a play and told to work up reality; it simply grows in the midst of real life.

To go back to that prayer time in Rochester . . . results seemed definite; we felt certain it was right to stay and have Dr. Petitt be Fran's doctor and start chemotherapy. Yes, he did have five and a half more years to go on "declaring God's power to the next generation" in various ways. Not five easy years, but time, and a reality of "sufficient grace and strength" for the variety of work needing to be done, all the while never knowing how much longer there would be.

Did we pray more properly than others who have had another answer in the same kind of circumstances? No, a thousand times, no. Last year Avis and Bob Dieseth's daughter-in-law, Gloria, a young mother of a four-year-old daughter, went to the doctor for what she thought to be a small problem. In a few hours she was in the cancer department of a Minneapolis hospital having chemotherapy and many other things done to her for a rapidly progressing form of cancer. It did not seem possible that she was so soon in intensive care and that the case seemed so hopeless and time so short.

Although I had a speaking schedule and was traveling, I was able to call my good friend Avis as she and the family spent much time in the hospital. Our prayer together, two agreeing to pray together, was a comfort. What passages did I read over the phone? For listening to the Lord is excruciatingly important at such a time. Of course we read, or I read to her in this case, many passages from Isaiah, among other things:

"To whom will you compare me? Or who is my equal?"
    says the Holy One.

Lift up your eyes and look to the heavens:
    Who created all these?
He who brings out the starry host one by one,
    and calls them each by name.
Because of his great power and mighty strength,
    not one of them is missing.
Why do you say, O Jacob, and complain, O Israel,
"My way is hidden from the Lord;
    my cause is disregarded by my God"?
Do you not know? Have you not heard?
    The Lord is the everlasting God,
    the Creator of the ends of the earth.
    He will not grow tired or weary,
and his understanding no one can fathom.
    He gives strength to the weary
    and increases the power of the weak.
Even youths grow tired and weary, and young men
       stumble and fall;
    but those who hope in [wait upon] the Lord will
       renew their strength.
They will soar on wings like eagles,
    they will run and not grow weary,
    they will walk and not be faint.

                              (Isaiah 40:25-31 NIV)

Oh, how I prayed for Gloria to be made better and for her husband John, for the little girl, and the rest of the family! Many in that northern Minnesota town were praying. Many people had loved Gloria for the quiet way she went about helping people in need—old people and mothers who needed their babies cared for. Oh yes, many were praying.

    I turned to the next portions of Isaiah. If you could see the margins, you'd see my dates and little cries of intercession. Beside "So do not fear, for I am with you. I have chosen you and have not rejected you" I jotted down "June '85, send Janine telegram, son's suicide . . ." but prayed for her, which sent help before the telegram could get there.

    But then with Avis we went on to Isaiah 43:1-2a:

But now, this is what the Lord says—
   he who created you, O Jacob,
   he who formed you, O Israel:
"Fear not, for I have redeemed you;
I have summoned you by name; you are mine.
When you pass through the waters,
   I will be with you; . . .

Then I prayed with her:

Dear Heavenly Father, thank You for Your comforting promises. Please be with each one there in that waiting room and in intensive care. Hold the hand of each one right now. You have said You write the name of each believer in the Lamb's Book of Life. We thank You for the Messiah, the Lamb of God, who died to have a victory over death itself. We thank You that Jesus wept at the tomb of Lazarus and that He said that the last enemy that will be destroyed is death itself. Please give the needed grace sufficient for now to that dear couple as they are alone and Your strength in their weakness for the need of now.

Yes, Gloria died. It seemed impossible that there had been so little time. Yet, when John, her husband, talked with his mother and father, he said that Gloria had been so aware of what was taking place. She had chosen Scripture and hymns for a memorial service in their church. She had been thinking of what she wanted her mother and father, as well as her little girl, to hear. She also arranged for a copy to be kept for her daughter when she would be older.

Grace sufficient? Amazingly sufficient grace and amazing strength—the Lord's strength in her all-consuming weakness. It was a demonstration to many in that town of the reality of what Gloria believed.

What then? Do we need to say rather coldly, without the passion of hate for death that Jesus showed at Lazarus' grave, that it was all for the best? Are we to smile sweetly at the dear little girl and say, "God took your mother to Heaven because he needed her there"?

Oh no. We are to be sure the little girl knows as much as she can about the abnormal history that has continued since the Fall. We are to remind each other that we are in a battle that Lucifer started with his coup in the heavenlies, as he gathered angels around him to attempt to be equal with God. We need to continue throughout our lives and our own times of terrible struggle to remind each other that there are things we do *not* understand, but we are to keep trusting God who does understand.

As a part of our listening and praying with trust and growing love for God, we are to remember that:

- After the Fall there is a cause-and-effect history that results from all the changes which came from the curse affecting all creation.

- As we see in Job and Revelation, after Satan and the fallen angels were thrown out of Heaven, they continued to attack and to try to separate people from God.

- There are times when what seems to be a defeat, whether Paul's thorn in the flesh or ours, turns into an amazing new chapter of victories because of sufficient grace given in an unchanging circumstance.

Yes, for each other at such times and for the little ones, we are to remember that we are to weep with those who weep, as well as to rejoice with those who rejoice. Jesus wept, not just to demonstrate compassion, but with real anger and hate for death. He came to bring life, but because of the historic reality of the Fall and all its results, and because of the sin passed down in the chromosomes and genes from Adam and Eve, there was no way of giving forgiveness of sin, mercy that we each need . . . except through His own death. Yes, death can be hated, and Satan can be hated.

What does the Lord SAY to us, that we need to listen to? God told Ezekiel to speak to the house of Israel, saying:

> If our transgressions and our sins be upon us, and we pine away in them, how should we then live? Say unto them, as I live, saith the Lord God, I have no pleasure in the death of the wicked, but that the wicked turn from his way and live; turn ye, turn ye from your evil ways; for why will ye die, O house of Israel? (Ezekiel 33:10b, 11 KJV)

The compassion of God is shown in the Old Testament. Over and over again it is clearly said that death is a result of the Fall, the choice made by Eve and Adam when tempted to believe Satan's lie. The compassion of the Trinity opened the way for that sin to be paid for by the death of the Son of God. But as death has not yet been destroyed, it is a sorrow for now, along with the great hope we have that one day death itself will be destroyed!

As we listen to what God says in one portion or another of His Word and pray in the midst of life with all its disappointments and joys, with growing understanding, our love, trust, faith, adoration, and awe grows.

To go back to my husband's continued life in the midst of continued cancer—yes, he did go on in the Lord's strength in his increasing weakness. He finished his last book, *The Great Evangelical Disaster*, in the hospital, over the phone with his editor, Lane Dennis. And as he went with Franky and Jim (I learned to give Fran heparin injections needed along the way) to answer questions from the platform for twelve seminars all over the country, the clear supernatural reality was not a healing, but the Lord's strength being given day after day.

So very soon after that, only a couple of days before he died, he quoted, "from strength to strength" and whispered, "Keep on." Psalm 84 is where this occurs, and it was as if he were giving that to each of us in the family to listen to. It is God's pointing us to the Psalmist's prayer as a help, not just in that extreme moment, but time after time as our lives go on. The wonderful thing about the Bible is that we can read it privately and talk to the Lord in secret, praying in secret many, many times. It is a private two-way conversation. Yet for so many generations, God has put it into the hands of people so that they may know Him.

> How lovely is your dwelling place,
>   O Lord Almighty!
> My soul yearns, even faints,
>   for the courts of the Lord;
> my heart and my flesh cry out
>   for the living God.

Even the sparrow has found a home,
    and the swallow a nest for herself,
    where she may have her young—
a place near your altar,
    O Lord Almighty, my King and my God.
Blessed are those who dwell in your house;
    they are ever praising you.
Blessed are those whose strength is in you,
    who have set their hearts on pilgrimage.
As they pass through the Valley of Baca,
    they make it a place of springs;
    the autumn rains also cover it with pools.
They go from strength to strength,
    till each appears before God in Zion.
Hear my prayer, O Lord God Almighty;
    listen to me, O God of Jacob.
Look upon our shield, O God;
    look with favor on your anointed one.
Better is one day in your courts
    than a thousand elsewhere;
I would rather be a doorkeeper in the house
    of my God than dwell in the tents of the wicked.
For the Lord God is a sun and shield;
    the Lord bestows favor and honor;
no good thing does he withhold
    from those whose walk is blameless.
O Lord Almighty,
    blessed is the man who trusts in you.

                  (Psalm 84 NIV)

This Psalm has had many markings and dates, with prayer for each family member in 1980 that each might "dwell in the Lord's house," remembering that God tells us that HE is our "habitation" in another place, and also that the Holy Spirit dwells in us. We are then reminded of our need to be overwhelmed at times that we have a need to pray for the cleansing of this dwelling place. Yes, of course as I read it in 1984 that May day before Fran's death, I thought of Heaven as God's dwelling place and the place He is preparing for us. I thanked God we will *all* dwell there in the future and that Fran soon would. But as one reads and listens in the midst of this Psalm, one prays with longing to really yearn for Him here. We ask for a realistic fervency, for His strength spiritually to help us to trust Him more now. Yes, to pray for the possibility of going on in life "from strength to strength" at that time was also a part of day-by-day prayer for my next chapter of life.

I have a note in the margin: "N.Y. April 5, 1986. Please bless my book *Forever Music* as it comes out, and may it bring forth much understanding among musicians."

Another Psalm we could go through verse by verse, a Psalm in which I have so frequently spent time in listening, is Psalm 119. As it has 176 verses it, along with so very much else, needs to be simply referred to.

> Your word is a lamp to my feet
>   and a light for my path.
> I have taken an oath and confirmed it,
>   that I will follow your righteous laws.
> I have suffered much;
>   preserve my life, O Lord, according to your word.
> Accept, O Lord, the willing praise of my mouth,
>   and teach me your laws.
>
> (vv. 105-108 NIV)

Proverbs spurs us on to sincerely and honestly seek for wisdom and discipline. Proverbs 1:7 states that "The fear of the Lord is the beginning of knowledge, but fools despise wisdom and instruction." This word *fear* is not the word meaning to be afraid or terrified, but to have proper awe, respect, and honor for the perfect holy God.

We read that and pray, *Forgive me for my lack of respect to You, O Heavenly Father. You have said we may come boldly to the throne of grace, and we thank You. We are grateful for Your mercy, but right now I do want to ask for the kind of worship in my mind and heart that I should have. Help me in this, please.*

Consider also Proverbs 1:8, 9;

Listen, my son, to your father's instruction
   and do not forsake your mother's teaching.
They will be a garland to grace your head
   and a chain to adorn your neck. (NIV)

The *King James Version* puts it this way:

My son, hear the instruction of thy father, and forsake not the law of thy mother.

Children, both sons and daughters, are clearly to value both father and mother as sources of instruction and guidance, but this is preceded by the strong statement that "the fear of the Lord is the beginning of knowledge." The wisdom and knowledge that is to be searched for is the Lord's knowledge, not the independent ideas of any of us as parents who think that a few years of life have given us so much wisdom that we don't need to search for it any more.

That both generations, and of course the generations to come, are to search for knowledge and wisdom from the Lord is made vivid in Proverbs 2:1-6:

My son, if you accept my words
   and store up my commands within you,
turning your ear to wisdom
   and applying your heart to understanding,
and if you call out for insight
   and cry aloud for understanding,
and if you look for it as for silver
   and search for it as for hidden treasure,
then you will understand the fear of the Lord
   and find the knowledge of God.
For the Lord gives wisdom,
   and from his mouth come knowledge
     and understanding.

                          (NIV)

God speaks to mothers and fathers, sons and daughters, from generation to generation, of the importance of seeking for wisdom and understanding. Parents are meant to seek for wisdom and understanding, as are children! We are never to think that we have arrived and that we have enough education to stop studying and searching for fresh understanding. That is true of our general knowledge. We need to keep reading history, literature, philosophy, science, poetry, and books of all sorts to gain a wider knowledge of what has taken place in the past and of what is going on today. When it comes to the wisdom, knowledge, and understanding God is speaking of, never do we have a final degree so that we can stop searching "as for silver and hidden treasures." The treasures to be discovered are endless!

How do we search?

That is what prayer is all about. We continue to pray for further understanding, for wisdom in making choices and decisions, for discernment, for fresh perspective, for the words to make clear the need for a base for moral choices in the area of ethics in business, in medicine, or in law. Whether we are standing in front of a seminar of some sort, or sitting with one or two of our own children, or with a friend who is a kindred spirit, we still cannot charge ahead without asking for wisdom and understanding. We can so easily be a hindrance rather than a help if we fail to have this particular kind of two-way communication with the Lord. We need to put an L in the crook of our thumb as we pray in the context of these strong sentences in Proverbs so that we apply what the Lord is saying to ourselves, rather than nodding with approval while thinking, *That is what so and so should do.*

When we are praying as we read in Proverbs, we need at times to turn to James. Perhaps you have written, as I have often, a request for sincerity in the search for wisdom and understanding, honesty in asking for hindrances to be removed, for real repentance where needed. Then it is good sometimes to turn to James 1:2-8:

> Consider it pure joy, my brothers, whenever you face trials of many kinds, because you know that the testing of your faith develops perseverance. Perseverance must finish its work so that you may be mature and complete, not lacking anything. If

any of you lacks wisdom, he should ask God, who gives generously to all without finding fault, and it will be given to him. (vv. 2-5 NIV)

Suddenly I can't go on—maybe you could—but I stop to pray. *O Father in Heaven, perfect in Your wisdom, thank You for Your grace and mercy in giving such an answer in our search for knowledge and wisdom. Thank You for the continuity in Your Word that gives such fantastic encouragement to our hope of having a drop of wisdom right now, when we are so far from perfect, when our knowledge and wisdom are so inadequate in the face of THIS present problem, this present choice. Oh, how we lack wisdom, Lord. We are the ones You are speaking to. Please give wisdom for this particular need in the light of this promise.*
Then I read on:

But when he asks, he must believe and not doubt, because he who doubts is like a wave of the sea, blown and tossed by the wind. That man should not think he will receive anything from the Lord; he is a double-minded man, unstable in all he does. (vv. 6-8 NIV)

I read this twice, listening, and go on with prayer: *Holy Father and Creator, how marvelous Your works are—the blue-green waters of the sea piled up in frothy waves, catching the morning sunrise. How perfectly You use the creation of Your hands to give us a penetrating illustration of what You mean us to understand clearly. We suddenly see a boat, tossed in the wind, its sails almost dipping in the sea, or a rowboat on the sea of Galilee, pitching and tossing in a way that made the disciples fearful.* (If someone has never seen a sea or even a lake, the blowing of wind on a stream or even a small pond or puddle, blowing leaves or bits of wood out of control, comes to memory.) *O God, my Father through Christ, please forgive me for saying one thing to You and having an opposite thought in my mind at the same time. Please may I not be double-minded and pretend, even to myself, that I never falter. I do ask now, in addition to asking for wisdom, to be cleansed from any double-mindedness, to be given more reality and consistency in my belief that You are able to do all things. Father, You know that not one of us is ever perfect. You have said we will be made perfect when Jesus comes back, but please may I at this time really fulfill what You mean me to be in asking now for wisdom, truly believing.*

I then go on praying for each one who is especially on my heart—my children, grandchildren (those whom they have married are my children too) and others who are close to me, and those I have adopted, a friend or a kindred spirit, in the context of both Proverbs and James, asking for wisdom and understanding in each of their needs at the very hour I am praying, wherever they are in the world. If I am aware of a need at the time, I am very specific; if not, I ask knowing the Lord can translate my request. Even as I have need for not being "tossed by waves of doubt" or for no double-mindedness in my very requests for them, so I also ask for each one for whom I am praying, help from the Lord to be filled with fresh trust and cleansed of any double-mindedness.

Does this mean that every day one follows an exact formula? What I am relating here is a continual reading and praying. It takes time to go through the Psalms; it takes time to go through Isaiah. Of course we go back and drink from places that have been refreshing to our thirst, as we hunger and thirst after righteousness and long for the Water of Life that flows from the Bible when we are in a dry and dusty desert spot. But there is no end to a lifetime of two-way communication with our Heavenly Father to whom we may come through the door He has given, that is, Jesus, the One who has said, "I am the door."

"But," you may say in dismay, "what you have been telling would take hours or at any rate much time. Can't there be short times? Can't one ask for wisdom and understanding briefly?"

As I was writing this, I had an early telephone call from Sandy, a nurse at St. Mary's Hospital across the street where she is assigned to the Intensive Care Heart Unit. Of course this means dealing with patients who have had sudden attacks, always unexpectedly, and with family members who are full of fear and anxieties. It is not an easy place for a nurse who needs to be alert and constantly aware of what she must do, but who also has deep concern for the people she is in contact with. Sandy is a Christian and really cares.

Her conversation went something like this: "Hope I'm not calling too early, but I just came off duty. I worked from seven to seven, and last night seven serious cases came in. It has been a hard night, but I wanted to tell you what a help your praying with me yesterday was. It helped me to remember that it was important to ask briefly right in the middle of a need, instead of waiting for time to be alone when I could pray and read undisturbed. My night went so differently, and I wanted to thank you. I didn't rely on myself and my own wisdom, but found I could so quickly and quietly just ask, *Lord, please give me Your wisdom for this . . . Father in Heaven, give me the words to tell this to the husband . . .* I really found a difference because of asking God for help right when I needed it. You know it is so hard to tell parents or families waiting when things are not going well."

As we talk about being real in prayer, it needs to be in the midst of *real* needs. A brief call following the Lord's speaking to us and saying in Psalm 50:14, 15: "Offer unto God thanksgiving and pay thy vows unto the Most High, and call upon me in the day of trouble; I will deliver thee, and thou shalt glorify me," can be made in the moment of trouble and need. We are meant, however, to have longer times of thanksgiving, as well as listening, so that we are ready in the moments of emergency. Whether as a nurse or doctor needing help asking for wisdom, or as an artist needing help with a deadline for producing a composition, music, film, painting, sculpture, architectural plan, book, or play, or as a government person making a snap decision, or a businessman, or a student writing an editorial for the school newspaper, or an athlete training for the Olympics—whatever our sudden need for help is—a brief call for help will be answered by our Heavenly Father whom we have been listening to. We may not think it perfect, but we will have a growing reality of two-way communication as we continue to grow in our love and trust and desire to do what He asks us to do, rather than simply ask for benefits and gifts.

Of course when your child suddenly has a high fever, or you rush your husband or wife to the hospital emergency entrance, you don't take time to have an hour of reading and praying in between each verse. Of course you should feel free to "come boldly to the throne of grace," being assured of God your Father's mercy and grace, knowing He will hear, not because you have done everything perfectly up to that point, but because of His mercy, the grace is real. Real mercy and real grace. Read Hebrews 4:14-16. (This is the NIV; *boldly* is used in the *King James*.)

> Therefore, since we have a great high priest who has gone through the heavens, Jesus the Son of God, let us hold firmly to the faith we profess. For we do not have a high priest who is unable to sympathize with our weaknesses, but we have one who has been tempted in every way, just as we are—yet was without sin. Let us then approach the throne of grace with confidence, so that we may receive mercy and find grace to help us in our time of need.

Yes, as we call, cry out, whisper, or plead in a brief moment of time, *Help me . . . O Father in Heaven, have mercy on me . . . Please give me Your words in my mouth; I don't know how to speak to this person . . . This, O Great Shepherd, is my moment of deep need . . . please do what is necessary for me now.* Whether we are in a hospital or a factory, on a farm or in a university, on a battlefield or a football field, in an airplane or on a bicycle, in a tossing ship at sea or on a truck in the desert, kneeling by a sick child's bed or helping at the scene of an accident . . . it doesn't matter. In all the urgent times of sudden need, we can be just as immediately in the presence of the Creator of the universe, and He can meet the need whatever it is.

Yes, in horizontal human communication, as you grow closer to someone you love and come to understand more and more, the longer times of listening carefully as well as talking bring results of such a growing closeness that when urgency of sudden need or unexpected trouble arrives, only a few words are needed to bring immediate help from that finite human being, even if he or she is limited.

We need to save time, protect periods of time, plan for a half-day or an hour at other times, and review our use of hours and days, weeks and months to check up on ourselves as to whether we are giving enough time to listening to the Lord, reading and praying with growing understanding. As I was reading in Isaiah 50 today, reviewing verses I talk about in another place in this book, and praying that I might rely more on Him, I read and reread verse 2, thinking it belonged in the end of this chapter on the two-way communication. The chapter starts with: "This is what the Lord says . . ." Then verse 2 says, "When I came, why was there no one? When I called, why was there no one to answer?"

God is speaking here and although it is to Israel, it also is to us, His people, through the Lamb. There is the recurring possibility of you, of me, not answering when He is calling. It is possible to be so full of our own requests, our own troubles, our own needs, our own desires that we don't hear His call to us. Are we conscious of the need to have *time* to read and listen to His Word and to respond and answer Him?

Or are we always absorbed with wanting an answer from Him without listening and responding to His call?

"When I called, why was there no one to answer?"

FOUR
Fasting and Prayer
Part One

As Fran and I mailed that letter resigning from our mission board in early June 1955, we looked at each other with a measure of dismay! In the letter we said we were going to live by prayer. We were going to set forth to answer honest questions with honest answers, insofar as God would give us wisdom and His help. We would not try to get people to come; we would not ask for money for food and expenses. We wanted to demonstrate God's existence, not only by showing the logic of truth being true, but also by His provision in the simple and observable things of everyday life.

What had we done? There was Priscilla at the University of Lausanne. True, Swiss universities do not cost more than a few dollars, and she was scrimping on food. There was Susan in bed with rheumatic fever and working on a correspondence course from Calvert School. There was Debby in school, just nine, and Franky, two and a half, just starting to get back to walking after polio. What had we set out to do anyway? How serious were we about prayer? Would there be a difference in using time? We knew we had been clearly brought to this particular place, not just geographically but also in our seriousness about not wanting to "sell Christianity as one would cornflakes." We wanted a real work that would not be our wisdom, but wisdom and knowledge given by God as to the next step. What would we do?

"Mummy," said Susan as I took her lunch tray into her room and sat on the edge of the bed (which took up the whole narrow room), "Mummy, let's have every Monday be a day of prayer. Look, I've made a chart with the hours divided up from seven in the morning until seven in the evening. You have to work, cooking and washing clothes and taking care of Franky and everything, and no one of us can pray *all day right now*. But if we are going to live by prayer, don't we have to pray more? Let's have twelve hours of prayer every Monday, but divided up so that we pray one after another!"

"Good idea," I said, and from that week on, Monday became our "day of prayer." I printed, by hand, a sheet of paper with verses that had helped me to have that two-way communication. I then wrote some spiritual requests, some material requests, some requests for each of us and whoever had come to be with us that day in areas of physical need and need for strength and direction. We made that sheet, a Bible, a notebook, and a pencil available so that each one could add something he or she wanted the rest of us to pray for. We stayed in the room praying until someone came to relieve us, feeling like a watchman on a wall! We were not in the room at the same time, but the feeling of togetherness and taking responsibility was very real. Perfect? No. But real.

About twenty-two people in America had asked if they could take responsibility to pray for us as we were now alone— to pray for the people of God's choice to come, people who would need help in their search for answers, search for truth, search for understanding. These praying people received copies of what we then called the prayer list, which they read and prayed over, read and prayed over with us. Of course, they continued to read also in their own Bibles and to listen to God. We wrote them, "Dear Praying Family," and I do believe that only God knows who did the most effective work, because intercession is *work*. Each member of the Praying Family promised (all of their own volition) to pray on Mondays, as long a block of time as each one could, and to pray for a half-hour or hour each day for L'Abri.

A few weeks passed, and we were deluged. No electrical appliances worked; everything had to be done by hand. Fran was clearing refuse out from under hedges and digging a vegetable garden. We came to feel that we needed something more than our Monday of divided time and our own personal times of prayer, the prayer in our Sunday services, and our family prayer times. We felt a great need for something more. What could that be?

Only one thing—a day of fasting and prayer with all of us taking part.

There is a wonderful passage in Ezra telling about the people of Israel preparing to go back to Jerusalem. King Artaxerxes had let them go and was making it possible for them to go back to worship "the God of Israel whose dwelling is in Israel." In Ezra 8:21 comes this (Ezra speaking):

> There, by the Ahava Canal, I proclaimed a fast, so that we might humble ourselves before our God and ask him for a safe journey for us and our children, with all our possessions. I was ashamed to ask the king for soldiers and horsemen to protect us from enemies on the road, because we had told the king, "The gracious hand of our God is on everyone who looks to him, but his great anger is against all who forsake him." So we fasted and petitioned our God about this, and he answered our prayer. (NIV)

This serious fasting and prayer, bowing humbly before God with repentance and concern for His mercy, took place in the context of practical need—for protection and guidance, for help in choices and for the supply of material things. This day of fasting and prayer was not separated as a kind of retreat aimed at achieving a spiritual high; it was a part of the warp and woof of a hard time in family life. It was an intensely important time in the next step of Ezra's responsibilities.

They asked for a safe journey with their children and with all their possessions. The asking was to be a demonstration of their trust that God could do it and that they were not going to the king for help. (This fits in with the command of God to NOT go "to Egypt" for help.)

Is fasting ever a bribe to get God to pay more attention to the petitions? No, a thousand times no. It is simply a way of making clear that we sufficiently reverence the amazing opportunity to ask help from the everlasting God, the Creator of the universe, to choose to put everything else aside and concentrate on worshiping, asking for forgiveness, and making our requests known—considering his help more important than anything we could do ourselves in our own strength and with our own ideas.

When the news of the breaking down of the walls of Jerusalem and of the suffering of the remnant in captivity came to Nehemiah, he responded with sorrow and fasting and prayer.

And it came to pass when I heard these words, that I sat down and wept, and mourned certain days, and fasted, and prayed before the God of heaven, and said, I beseech thee, O Lord God of heaven, the great and terrible God [or awesome God], who keepeth covenant and mercy for them who love him and observe his commandments: Let thine ear now be attentive, and thine eyes open, that thou mayest hear the prayer of thy servant, which I pray before thee now, day and night, for the children of Israel, thy servants, and confess the sins of the children of Israel, which we have sinned against thee; both I and my father's house have sinned. We have dealt very corruptly against thee, and have not kept the commandments, nor the statutes, nor the judgments, which thou commandest thy servant, Moses. Remember, I beseech thee, the word that thou commandest thy servant, Moses, saying, If ye transgress, I will scatter you abroad among the nations; But if ye turn unto me, and keep my commandments, and do them, though there were of you cast out unto the uttermost part of the heaven, yet will I gather them from thence, and will bring them unto the place that I have chosen to set my name. Now these are thy servants and thy people, whom thou hast redeemed by thy great power, and by thy strong hand. O Lord, I beseech thee, let now thine ear be attentive to the prayer of thy servant, and to the prayer of thy servants, who desire to fear thy name; and prosper, I pray thee, thy servant this day, and grant him mercy in the sight of this man. For I was the king's cupbearer. (Nehemiah 1:4-11 KJV)

Nehemiah has first fasted and prayed for some days, obviously including others with him in this intercession, in preparation for going to the king with his request to rebuild the walls of Jerusalem. He takes a long time of prayer and fasting, confessing sin, and preparing for the Lord's answer, which he expects. It reminds us of the Lord's telling Joshua to have the people sanctify themselves in preparation to see the Lord's answer to their entering Jericho. It is a solemn thing, an awesome thing, an overwhelming thing to ask and then receive an answer, whether the answer is sufficient grace to go on in the midst of affliction, or whether that answer is a fantastic opening up of a path in the wilderness in some form.

Fasting along with prayer is meant to be a means of seriously asking for cleansing, not only in the Old Testament, but also after Christ's death has cleansed us. We need to realize that although we come to God our Father, in the name of Jesus Christ who told us to come this way, we ourselves need to ask for preparation to make requests. Sometimes that preparation should be in the midst of fasting; other times we call out to Him as we are dropping in a parachute, scuba diving, rolling in a car down a snowy embankment, sitting all night by a baby who has croup, or waiting for word from the operating room. There are moments of extreme need when we can scarcely form words, let alone sentences—moments of crisis, moments of impending tragedy, or sudden fear. At such times only a brief prayer can be lifted in a cry or a whisper, *Lord, Your mercy and Your strength, please.*

It needs to be pointed out that some people have diabetes and need proper amounts of food every two hours; others have low blood sugar for other reasons or get severe headaches if they go without food or juice or a hot drink at set times. Of course, any who have these problems need to provide food to take along with them if they are going into the woods to pray for a whole day or if they work in the hospital as nurses or doctors. Also those who are anorexic need to be urged to eat and pray as an important help in their reluctance to eat for one reason or another. At L'Abri through the years I have prepared a picnic of some small sandwiches, an apple, some biscuits for ones whom I felt needed to eat and pray on the day of fasting and prayer. In every day of fasting and prayer we would assign someone to put out soup and bread so that people could quietly come and take something if they felt faint or could not concentrate because of a headache.

However, we asked (ahead of time of course) that no one linger and talk at that time. The food was there between one hour and another which had been announced, a simple soup and bread, and could be taken away to eat.

These are simply practical notes for those who might feel they have failed to do "the right thing" because of a need for food. It is good to re-read that portion of Revelation in which Jesus says, "Behold, I stand at the door and knock. If any one opens the door, I will come in and sup with him." This speaks to the unsaved as an invitation, but also to the Lord's people who would in a very real sense pray quietly as they eat alone.

Back to Nehemiah. After he is in the presence of the king, the king asks, "For what dost thou make thy request?" Nehemiah prayed to his God in Heaven and then answered the king. He does not stop calling on God at the end of the days of fasting and prayer. His communication is natural and has a continuity of faith and trust.

As you read on through to the end of the sixth chapter, you will see that prayer was a basic part of the rebuilding of the wall, but prayer did not replace hard work, nor did it replace being prepared to fight the onslaught of the enemy with weapons. The reality of continued prayer and trust that God would fight for them did not remove the need to blow the trumpet on the wall to ask for others to come and help at a particularly dangerous place, at a particularly dangerous time. Trusting God to answer our intercessions and requests does not make it wrong to call for help as the floods rise, the earthquake hits, the fire burns our barn, or hail ruins a field of crops. There is a lifelong lesson to be learned, over and over again, that we are not self-sufficient. We need God's help. We also need to accept and give "servant-like" help to each other, as well as to work hard and to fight "the enemy" who is attempting to break down the wall *we* are building.

Yes, of course moral and cultural breakdown and the difficulty of finding an absolute that could roll back the multiplying and terrifying results is troubling people. Rebuilding, repairing the broken walls in these areas will take hard work accompanied by very serious fasting and prayer by individuals as well as the gathering of some to intercede together. It requires a combination of prayer, slogging work, calling each other to help at some point on the wall, and then doing what is needed in the way of fighting when attacked.

Yes, they were told to have *weapons* as well as trowels with which to put the stones together with mortar. It is a very definite combination of hard work, prayer that our God will fight for us, calling to others for help, and keeping our swords by our sides. Read Nehemiah 4:17-20:

> They who built on the wall, and they who bore burdens, with those that laded, everyone with one of his hands wrought in the work, and with the other hand held a weapon. For the builders, everyone had his sword girded by his side, and so builded. And he who sounded the trumpet was by me. And I said unto the nobles, and to the rulers, and to the rest of the people, The work is great and large, and we are separated upon the wall, one far from another. In whatever place ye hear the sound of the trumpet, resort ye thither unto us. Our God shall fight for us. (KJV)

God's fighting for us does not exclude the responsibility to be prepared for battle both in the area of strategy and in equipment. Trusting God completely in prayer, believing that He is able to do all things, does not remove the need to pray for His strength in our weakness and then to do, to take action in His strength to accomplish what He has prepared us to do! We are to do what He is unfolding for us to do, fulfilling what God is giving us strength to do, acknowledging that it is His strength and not ours. It is a truly active passivity, not a false whining humbleness that says, "I can't do anything; I'm too weak."

Day by day we face local, national, and international battles. The battles need a balanced involvement. We need to fight the killing of the unborn who would be the next generation; we need to fight the spoiling of the land and be God's stewards whether by planting more trees or purifying the air in other ways. We are faced with scandals on every side in medicine, government, business, sports—increase of crime or the removal of any moral base for the teaching in schools. The battle for truth is not simply someone else's business, but something we need to pray about as to what the Living God, our Heavenly Father, would have us do.

Yes, we are to turn the other cheek as people do things to harm us personally. But in injustices internationally, nationally, and in our towns and villages, we need to be brave enough to fight for the protection of the weak, to fight for liberty for others, and for the next generation. To fast and pray in the midst of considering what we are meant to do in a practical way, today, tomorrow, this week, this month in the now of history is important indeed.

It is not always another organization that is needed, with a big name and offices and vast buildings. Sometimes we must be willing to "pray in the closet alone," to go out into the mountains or woods, fields, or parks, by streams or lakes, or into a woodshed or empty kitchen and really pray for courage, direction, and willingness to be where He would have us be. That place may not be visibly a part of anything other people may observe. It may be a willingness to go on filling teeth as a dentist; cooking and scrubbing clothing and floors and reading aloud to children as a mother; painting, drawing, or sculpting as an artist; doing what we do well, with excellence, to be beside the person who needs us to say the right word. What person? The patient, the client, the actor, the cameraman, the woman cleaning the washroom, the driver of a taxi. Who is going to be in our place "on the wall" if we are not there? That is what being a light not hidden under a bushel is all about. There are no bright lights announcing that our place today is the most important place in the whole piece of today's history. We are to be serving each other as servants, as if we were serving the Lord, knowing He is perfectly fair and just.

We need to read Ephesians in the midst of Nehemiah's building and preparation for battle. As we listen to the Lord as we read the whole of this epistle during our days of fasting and prayer or at other times, we see, as in a mirror, our sins and shortcomings, realizing our need of prayer for help.

Finally, my brethren, be strong in the Lord, and in the power of his might. Put on the whole armor of God, that ye may be able to stand against the wiles [schemes] of the devil. For we wrestle not against flesh and blood, but against principalities, against powers, against the rulers of the darkness of this world, against spiritual wickedness in high places [against rulers, against authorities, against the powers of this dark world, and against the spiritual forces of evil in the heavenly realms]. Wherefore, take unto you the whole armor of God, that ye may be able to withstand in the evil day, and having done all, to stand. Stand therefore, having your loins girt about with truth, and having on the breastplate of righteousness, and your feet shod with the preparation of the gospel of peace; above all, taking the shield of faith, where with ye shall be able to quench all the fiery darts of the wicked. And take the helmet of salvation, and the sword of the Spirit, which is the word of God. (Ephesians 6:10-17 KJV)

Clearly what is outlined here is an ongoing battle. It is the conflict of the ages, of all the centuries since Lucifer rebelled against God and gathered other angels to rebel under his leadership. It is a conflict, a battle, which will not end until the Lord Jesus Christ returns to have the final victory, to defeat death itself, for the last enemy to be destroyed will be death. Yes, we are in the midst of battle, and whether we are persecuted and killed for the sake of the truth of the gospel, as were the martyrs through the ages and present-day martyrs, still we are to stand firm, working hard to build the wall with a trowel in our hands.

Even as prayer is stressed in Nehemiah and the statement is made there, "our God will fight for us," so Paul goes on in this passage to unfold to us our responsibility and plural responsibilities! Yes, fighting, calling to each other for help, building, and prayer. "Praying always with all prayer and supplication in the Spirit, and watching thereunto with all perseverance and supplication for all saints" (Ephesians 6:18 KJV). This is very, very strong. It is a command. It is an unfolding in practical terms of the command to "pray without ceasing," which we will talk about later. "Praying always . . . all prayer and supplication . . .

all perseverance and supplication . . . for all saints" does not leave much out!

Prayer is an essential part of the practical fighting in the ongoing battle in which we all are involved—the battle for truth when the very existence of truth is being denied!

As in any day of history, prayer has to be interwoven into every part of the day and week and month. But we, as well as people in past ages, need a whole day of fasting and prayer at times. We cannot have any unbroken time otherwise; we cannot have freedom to read and think, to consider our own sin in the light of Ephesians 4:26-32:

> Do not let the sun go down while you are still angry . . . Get rid of all bitterness, rage and anger, brawling and slander, along with every form of malice. Be kind and compassionate to one another, forgiving each other, just as in Christ God forgave you. (NIV)

We need a long period of time, either fasting from conversation and food preparation and eating, or fasting from sleep and other good normal parts of life, to be able to search our memories and our consciences to ask forgiveness for our sin. We are not to blithely make a list of requests without having time to prepare for prayer. In our reading and praying, this follows along very strongly. A central place must be considered for unbroken times of prayer, as well as for the snatched moments.

Ephesians 6 goes on with Paul asking for intercession for himself:

> Pray also for me, that whenever I open my mouth, words may be given me so that I will fearlessly make known the mystery of the gospel, for which I am an ambassador in chains. Pray that I may declare it fearlessly, as I should. (vv. 19-20 NIV)

Paul does not ask prayer that the chains may be removed; he asks prayer that he would declare the mystery of the gospel fearlessly. He is already in chains for doing that very thing, but he is asking prayer for courage and persistence in continuing without fear of what might happen to him. He is asking that the truth of what he is communicating may not be hindered by any hesitancy in his speaking. In the *King James Version* the word used is *boldly*: "Pray . . . that I may open my mouth boldly as I ought to speak." His call is for help in continuing the battle.

The battle does continue. The immediate focus changes as history goes on. The need to pick up the stones out of the dust and carefully place them again in "the wall" continues all through every change of history. Russian Christians have a new freedom to worship and to receive Bibles openly as the amazing change has come in the overturn of the power of communism. The Baltic countries have a new measure of freedom also. But as for these people in having a worldview which will give them a base for formulating new laws and a new pattern of life, it is evident there is much building to be done.

In the battle for teaching and living on the basis of right rather than wrong, truth rather than lies, there is now and always will be opposition. Anyone rebuilding the shattered stones and giving a base for morals and ethics will be attacked. Understanding that an attack may come from two sides at once is very important in living practically in our present-day undertakings that are similar to Nehemiah's restoration of the wall of Jerusalem.

What do I mean?

Keith Saltzman went as an official delegate to a medical ethics seminar in Washington, D.C., as a representative of his military hospital in the South. As papers were read and discussion took place, he had an opportunity to point out that no one had given any base for their ideas of ethics. In other words any declaration regarding right and wrong made by people who do not believe that there is a God, an unchanging absolute that determines right and wrong, is a declaration that gives no answers. As Keith and other believing doctors speak to these issues, there is need to pray they will be heard but also that the fierce opposition that arises may not become the norm for rules and regulations governing the practices of the medical profession. Whether the issue is euthanasia, or genetic engineering, or infanticide, or the definition of the quality of life, these battles are not theoretical, but very practical, and affect many people now and in days to come.

In facing the rapid changes in many parts of our children's world, we have responsibility to pray for a wider number of people, our doctors—the believing doctors we know and the medical people and scientists who struggle with choices and decisions. We cannot simply criticize without praying seriously and doing some practical things to help.

Abortion is another practical place where we need to be involved in some way. Marches, rallies, voicing objections in various ways to the disregard of human life? Yes, but also to have true compassion and desire to help people who need help during the months of waiting for a baby. Young girls? Yes, but also mothers who need help with an unexpected pregnancy. When someone feels she is being criticized, disapproved of, and in a desperately impossible situation, she needs human compassion, someone to "rush to that place on the wall" with some warmth of pitching in to help. But also there are false "helps" being offered, being insisted upon, being pushed, being whispered into ears, being flashed on a screen, being suggested as the only way to rid yourself of a problem. "Friends" or medical people or family members may be saying that there is no absolute. There is no right and wrong, because everything is relative anyway, and this collection of molecules is not a human being. We cannot do everything that needs to be done in this world at this time, but whatever area we ask God to give us strength to be involved in needs prayer, positive building, fighting the enemy, and blowing the trumpet to get others to come to this spot where we are being hindered or attacked in putting the dusty stones of "ideas" back in place again. Some are needed on a hot line, others to open their homes, others to start a crisis pregnancy home.

Yes, we usually take a day of fasting and prayer in the midst of urgent needs in our personal and family lives, in the midst of our work. It is often taken when there is an enormous question mark about what comes next. On such a day, we also need to give serious attention to sorting out what issues and areas we want to involve ourselves in in our private prayer, what practical ways we can help, which battles we must be willing to serve in! As we serve each other in our lives, sometimes that will mean aiding each other in a battle as someone's attempt at putting the stones of correct ideas into place is being fiercely attacked, and the enemy seems to be overpowering! *Lord, give me a sensitive ear to hear the trumpet being blown for help.*

There is also the kind of need that people have when they are caught up in something that they really want to get out of, but find the desire to remain in it is stronger. Such a one needs help intensely. A believer who reads the Bible daily and prays often and goes to a believing church does have a measure of help. Very great weakness needs a calling, a blowing of the trumpet, for someone who understands to come to that one's place "on the wall" with a comprehensive insight of the struggle going on, encouragement that what seems impossible is possible, and a willingness to help, to spend energy and time to be available when needed. What am I talking about? Alcoholism, drugs, the gay life style, and other areas of need not so frequently recognized.

I have recently talked with a charming artistic fellow who was gay and who has discovered a Christian group that meets in a nearby city once a week. This has been started to be a support and help to those who have taken the firm decision to abstain from practicing homosexuality, which they have come to believe is contrary to Biblical teaching. It is a battle that comes from two fronts. First, there is the urging on the part of individuals who are not Christians to come back into the active gay life style. Then there is the declaration of a certain grouping of gay Christians that it is all right and that what is needed is gay churches and gay weddings (called "holy matrimony"). All temptations need to be fought by prayer and fasting, but it is important for us to know that such groups exist to help people in their particular place on the broken wall, to be able to faithfully put the "stones" back in place, even when opposition is tearing these out with an attack that threatens to discourage any more trying.

This fellow told me of a fine international conference for gays who want to abstain and go on with a new life style, held recently in Toronto, Canada. It is an encouragement to have such specific seminars and lectures as well as prayer. However, I think that for those of us for whom this is not a problem, we are responsible for praying for these groups and for the help they need. There are local groups in various cities which give counseling, prayer, and loving help to those who are seeking help with a desire to have a change in life style. Just as in AA where it is a help to have others facing the same battles and to know from others that it is possible to have human encouragement to abstain, as well as to ask the Lord for His strength in fighting this temptation, so it is with people tempted in other ways to live or dip into sin God clearly points out to us as sin.

We are finite and limited in our time for fasting and prayer. Even when we take a whole day of prayer or a night of prayer, the hours slip by, and we find we have not covered everything we wanted to pray about. However, just as we are admonished to bear one another's burdens, so we are clearly told to pray for one another. In our time of fasting and prayer, when we have a longer periods of time, a *part* of that time should be spent in really praying for any we know who are struggling with their own temptations or difficulties or for some who are sacrificially giving time to helping others in some area of struggle. We can't just shrug our shoulders and pull away from involvement.

So often people in the deepest sort of struggle and depression are facing temptation from two sides at once. It is as if they are standing in the middle of arrows being shot from two sides; turning from one side is to face the other.

Think of someone in a wheelchair, unable to walk and perhaps also unable to use hands and arms. Think of another with the dreaded news of cancer and someone else who is blind, but with another disease which is very painful. The arrow on the *left* comes from someone who is sneering, "Hah! Where is your God? Why don't you just read one of those books on how to commit suicide? Why go on? There is no purpose in a life with no quality. Just kill yourself." The arrow on the *right* comes from people in the church, shaking their heads, saying, "If only you had enough faith, you could get up and walk." "If only you had enough faith, you could see again." "If only you had enough faith, you wouldn't have any pain." "If your family had faith, if your husband only had enough faith, if your friends only had enough faith . . . all this paralysis, and pain, and blindness would disappear. God doesn't want you to be this way." "It's your fault."

The arrow from the left stings with a buzz of temptation. The arrow from the right tears the flesh near the other one and brings with it a stab of doubt, a wave of anger, and then a cold fog of depression.

The arrows multiply. From the left comes the hissing whisper, "There isn't any God." From the right comes, "If only you were more spiritual, you wouldn't be having any physical illness or disablement."

In our times of fasting and prayer we need to pray for our own victory from the double arrows, but also to pray for others we know in hospitals, or in especially difficult times with chemotherapy, or with frustrations because of limitations. This kind of concentrated prayer is the reality of bearing one another's burdens.

The double-arrow attack is the same for homosexuals who are really struggling, striving, working hard on living a changed life style of abstinence, filling their lives with wonderfully creative things in music, design, painting, landscape gardening, as well as studying the Bible, praying, and spending time with others who are being helpful. Then—just as with the disabled person—the arrows whiz from left and right. The left is an arrow full of pressure. "Come on back, live with me, join the rest of us. You're crazy. You're spoiling your life." The arrow from the right is labeled with the name of one or another Christian denomination, an arrow full of equal pressure. "God made you this way. You can't help having a different preference. This desire is good. Come join us. You can make a vow to live with one person all your life, even adopt a baby. This is just a different life style. God made diversity."

The point of placing these two sorts of beleaguered people badgered from both sides beside each other in this illustration of the arrows is to help us to see the need to take serious prayer responsibility, rather than just to argue.

Whether it is doctors struggling as to what is ethical, businessmen struggling over ethics, pregnant women being urged to abort for one reason or another, or any other of the flood of changing worldviews coming from the media, we need to take times of fasting and prayer *seriously*, to pray for those whose decisions and choices are being attacked. And we should get ready for that time of prayer with honest preparation in the context of God's Word.

FIVE
Fasting and Prayer
Part Two

So often my husband would say, "Christ must be the Lord of all our life." He meant that everything we do is to be done in the light of the reality of our being the people of God, a part of His flock, the ones He has told to be light and salt in society. We can't wiggle out of that responsibility by pointing to our many hours of prayer or occasional days of fasting and prayer. We are to grow in understanding of what the Word of God teaches us as to what is meant to be happening in our day by day living, and we are meant to be seeing growth in the reality of our actions measuring up!

In Hebrews 4:12, 13 we are reminded strongly that reading the Bible will make us aware of how far we fall short of being what we are meant to be:

> For the word of God is quick [living and active] and powerful, and sharper than any two-edged sword, piercing [or penetrating] even to the dividing asunder of soul and spirit, and of joints and marrow, and is a discerner of the thoughts and intents of the heart. Neither is there any creature that is not manifest in his sight [nothing in all creation is hidden from God's sight]: but all things are naked and opened unto the eyes of him with whom we have to do. (KJV)

The rest of that chapter we will come to later, but this is talking about each one of us. We, you and I, are included among the ones who must give an account to this most holy God.

Now come back to Isaiah where Jehovah speaks in a penetrating way:

> Cry aloud, spare not, lift up thy voice like a trumpet, and shew
> my people their transgression, and the house of Jacob their sins.
> Yet they seek me daily, and delight to know my ways, as a
> nation that did righteousness, and forsook not the ordinance of
> their God: they ask of me the ordinances of justice; they take
> delight in approaching to God. (Isaiah 58:1, 2 KJV)

But they are praying, aren't they? They are even delighting
in knowing God. They sound so spiritual . . . so what is wrong?
Read further:

> 'Why have we fasted,' they say, 'and you have not seen it? Why
> have we humbled ourselves, and you have not noticed?' (v. 3a
> NIV)

They have been fasting and praying and have humbled
themselves with sackcloth and ashes. Isn't this a picture of a
pious, spiritual group of faithful people? What have they left out?
Let us go on carefully, thoughtfully reading:

> "Yet on the day of your fasting, you do as you please and
> exploit all your workers." (v. 3b NIV)

But aren't they sitting on sackcloth with ashes on their
heads? Where are these "workers"? This is speaking to any person with others working under him or her. When we are praying,
workers under us—out in a field half the world away or someone
in the hospital half the city away or secretaries, gardeners, factory
workers, any employees—are at the same time being exploited if
we are being unfair. God's sharp two-edged sword goes on to out-
line what is wrong with this fasting and prayer:

> "Your fasting ends in quarreling and strife,
>   and in striking each other with wicked fists.
> You cannot fast as you do today

and expect your voice to be heard on high.
Is this the kind of fast I have chosen,
only a day for a man to humble himself?
Is it only for bowing one's head like a reed
and for lying on sackcloth and ashes?
Is that what you call a fast,
a day acceptable to the Lord?"

(Isaiah 58:4, 5 NIV)

Obviously, if we are carefully listening and absorbing the question, we know this is not the definition of a fast that pleases the Lord. As I have said before, God is not bribed by our going without lunch, or breakfast, or giving some evidence of humbleness. This does not cause us to walk into His presence with a proper preparation for a long time of worship and communication, a time of bringing our needs and the needs of others to Him in a satisfactory way.

Has His Word pierced us in our own private time before Him, the One before whom our ideas and thoughts are naked, as well as our actions? As God speaks through Isaiah, He points to eight things as really demonstrating in *action* that there is a reality of preparation inside us, in hidden places, for fasting and prayer. These eight things apply to us today as much as to His people living in Isaiah's time. They are not hidden from the eyes of at least a few other human beings, nor of course are they hidden from the eyes of God.

"Is not this the kind of fasting I have chosen:"
1) "To loose the chains of injustice."
Am I doing that for someone or for many? Have I done it on a small scale, for a child in school, for my own child, a neighbor's child? Have I helped a person in an accident who was unjustly kept from receiving the proper insurance and had no one to search for witnesses and so on? Have I tried to do anything in my town or state about injustice in various areas? Is there something nationally I can vote for or march for? Is there something internationally I can help in some way? "To loose the chains of injustice" covers a great many kinds of things.

Wait a minute. We are finite and limited. I am finite and limited. I cannot, you cannot, we cannot unloose all the chains of injustice nor can we follow every possibility of doing something in that area of need. But because we can't do *every*thing does not mean we cannot do *some*thing. We need to check up on ourselves frequently, asking God for wisdom and His help in choosing what to do to help break some of the chains of injustice!

2) "Untie the cords of the yoke [undo heavy burdens]."

The passage refers to some specific yokes, but people in our cities, towns, villages, neighborhoods are caught under heavy burdens of a variety of kinds. Drugs, alcohol, promiscuous sex, stealing or cheating under coercion by a gang, as well as burdens of overwork or care of elderly or handicapped people in the home. We are told in the New Testament to "share one another's burdens and so fulfill the law of Christ." It seems to tie in with this kind of "fasting" that God speaks of in Isaiah. Undoing burdens, helping to carry the "yoke" so that the person can really throw it off, takes a lot of forms, not to mention time, energy, imagination, and creativity.

This is not a far-fetched connection with fasting and praying. Also, let me repeat for those who are too introspective, we can't do everything; we are finite and limited, but we must consider what is given us to aim for. Some never are bothered by the need to grow in the knowledge of the Lord's Word and the need to grow in behavior and action in doing.

3) "To set the oppressed free."

This idea does go with the phrase above, but can be separated in the undoing of *some* heavy burdens. There are oppressions placed on people by dictatorships, whether of a school superintendent in a town or of a political head of a country. These oppressions are indeed burdens, but are of a different sort, needing another set of actions, depending on where we live, what is going on in this moment of history that we can do something about. So often people look back over history and exclaim, "How could they sit by and do nothing?" Terry Waite did do something! And there have been heroes in many moments of history who have made a big difference. Not only have the names we know had an effect, but there have been those willing to speak out against oppression of various kinds. There are lawyers who are willing to risk a lot to speak against oppression that seeks to prevent Christmas carols being sung in American schools, just when Marxist countries are allowing open teaching and celebration of Christmas for the first time this year after seventy years! There are courageous people in unknown places making it possible for *some* of the oppressed to go free.

This comes under the heading of a fast that God has chosen. It hits me that at times it is a fasting from safety, which ties in with "he that is willing to lose his life for my sake and the gospel . . . shall find his life" . . . but that needs to be dealt with later.

4) "Break every yoke."

Again, it comes in the same sentence but connects with the reality of having Jesus as Lord and Savior of the whole of our lives. That is not a slogan but needs constant translation into reality day by day.

What kind of a yoke is meant here? A yoke ties together two oxen pulling a plow. A yoke ties people together, joining them in a relationship. If one is "tied" or "yoked" with a person, or a project, or a false religion, or a crime ring, or a mafia string of gambling houses, brothels, or pornographic stores, one needs help in breaking that yoke. The breaking of the yoke, even if it is a yoke hidden from the eyes of other people, is what Isaiah is stressing. God is saying that these negative things need to be cared for, to be put aside, to not be a part of a person's life, before a day of fasting and prayer is acceptable!

5) "Is it not to share your food with the hungry?"

This is extremely practical in having any reality of obedience in our day by day lives. In the Old Testament it is always stressed that grain is to be left to be gathered by the gleaners, or grapes at the edge of the vineyards are purposely to be left. This was a sharing of crops with people who had no crops. At no time in history have there *not* been hungry people, and God is saying to those who are complaining that He is not listening to their prayers as they humble themselves before Him, "I have chosen a more practical fast that needs to be a part of your lives." We are to do something about caring for hungry people, friends, family— locally, in our states, in this country, and internationally. Can we do everything? No, not one of us could. We are finite in every way, limited in every way, but we are to do something, something practical to share our bread.

Six and seven are strong commands:

6) "To provide the poor wanderer with shelter."

In the *King James* it is: "Bring the poor that are cast out to thy house."

7) "When you see the naked, to clothe him."

Are these a picture of the many homeless in our own countries? The orphans in Romania and other places, the starving in famine countries, the ones without homes after fires, floods, or earthquakes? Disaster areas seem to multiply, and the call for help is on every side of us. What are we doing?

There is energy, time, money, or ideas to spend on whatever God would have us do. Does that mean all of us should quit being dentists, doctors, makers of musical instruments, film makers, pilots, teachers (from kindergarten to universities), government workers, authors, farmers, building contractors, bus drivers, engineers, nurses, soldiers—is each of us to stop all else to go to all the disaster spots of the world? Oh, no. But we are meant to be involved in some way. God is giving through Isaiah a description of the kind of fasting He has chosen so that the Lord might really be Lord in all of our lives. And so that we might understand in a growing way what satisfactory prayer is composed of. Prayer cannot be separated from the reality of our attempts to be obedient in the areas that have been explained to us so carefully, if we are to be solid wood and not veneer.

Please consider Matthew 25:31, 34-40:

"When the Son of Man comes in his glory, and all the angels with him, he will sit on his throne in heavenly glory . . . . Then the King will say to those on his right, 'Come, you who are blessed by my Father; take your inheritance, the kingdom prepared for you since the creation of the world. For I was hungry and you gave me something to eat, I was thirsty and you gave me something to drink, I was a stranger and you invited me in, I needed clothes and you clothed me, I was sick and you looked after me, I was in prison and you came to visit me.'

"Then the righteous will answer him, 'Lord, when did we see you hungry and feed you, or thirsty and give you something to drink? When did we see you a stranger and invite you in, or needing clothes and clothe you? When did we see you sick or in prison and go to visit you?'

"The King will reply, 'I tell you the truth, whatever you did for one of the least of these brothers of mine, you did for me.'" (NIV)

As we read and study this—and truly think about it—we are seeing a fantastic word picture. A fabulous view in the midst of a long walk in the woods suddenly opens up like a huge window with clear glass, and the curtains pulled back with perfect lighting allow us to see a vivid picture of a moment in the future. This is not fantasy. This is reality of the most definite and certain kind. We are being told that this will take place.

All the things given so many centuries before for Isaiah to tell to the people wanting to fast and pray are the same sort of practical things Jesus wants us to do and accept as done directly for him. The food given to the homeless, the bowl of soup taken to the sick lady, the visits in prison, the visits in the hospital, the care of people in disaster areas, the hospitality given to people in need, the cup of cold water, the pot of tea—this is the only way we can give these things directly to the Lord.

What is the difference between giving a dinner party for people who will invite you in return or having the family for Christmas, and the deeds spoken of in Isaiah and by the Lord in Matthew? The difference is that this kind of energy spent, money spent, time spent, creative ideas spent will not be returned to us. It is not business entertaining. It is not simply a social exchange. This kind of involvement, of being kind and human to other people, done quietly with a desire to take care of the Lord is not simply a part of an organized response to an organized appeal; it is to be as natural as breathing.

In a very real sense one might say it is to be our preparation for prayer without ceasing. That is, we are to be ready any moment for prayer because of this kind of fasting, the fasting God is describing through Isaiah.

8) "And not to turn away from your own flesh and blood." Who are our flesh and blood? These are those who literally have the same genes and chromosomes, i.e., our family circle for whom we have a measure of responsibility. The youngest members of the family are the unborn children, conceived, growing in the safety of the womb, but not yet in the world to breathe the air and eat the food, to be clothed and cared for by the family. Abortion is a turning away in the most drastic form. Abortion is snuffing out life before there is any opportunity to provide clothing, food, or violin lessons!

Another form of turning away from one's "own flesh and blood" is being taught in how-to books and TV lectures and debates. In the December 1991 issue of *Commentary* there is an article by Leon R. Kass, "Suicide Made Easy," in which he reviews books such as a recent bestseller, *Final Exit: The Practicalities of Self-Deliverance and Assisted Suicide for the Dying* by Derek Humphry. Leon Kass says wisely:

> I do not want you to read it. It never should have been written, and it does not deserve to be dignified with a review, let alone with an article. Yet it stares out at us from nearly every bookstore window, beckoning us to learn how to achieve the final solution—for ourselves or for those we (allegedly) love so much that we will help them to kill themselves. Says the Lord High Executioner, Derek Humphry, prophet of Hemlock: "I have set before thee life and death; therefore, choose death." "Courageous," bleat the media, "Timely," "Rational," "Humane." Is there no one who will call evil by its proper name?
>
> This is not the usual and notorious evil of malicious intent or violent manner; this is humanitarian evil, evil with a smile: well-meaning, gentle, and rational, especially rational. For this reason it is both harder to recognize as evil and harder to combat. Yet, also for this reason, it deserves our most vigilant atten-

tion, for it is an exquisite model of modern rationalism gone wrong, while looking so right.

Bravo to Leon R. Kass and to *Commentary* for presenting this and other very important current issues we need to be made aware of! This article is a must for reading, but it is not necessary to read the book.

Isaiah pours out these requirements God has given for the people to hear and do in preparation for fasting and prayer. Yes, we need to ask for mercy and grace for our own wrong actions and thoughts and to pray for the current spread of evil to be recognized, discerned for what it is. In Isaiah God certainly calls for our vigilant attention to the current smog choking the thinking of people who attempt to talk about ethics without considering the absolute base given.

Isaiah 59:7-11, 14-16a describes our own period of history as well as that time so vividly. We need to read this during an unbroken time of prayer preparation or on a day of prayer itself:

Their feet rush into sin;
   they are swift to shed innocent blood.
Their thoughts are evil thoughts;
   ruin and destruction mark their ways.
The way of peace they do not know;
   there is no justice in their paths.
They have turned them into crooked roads;
   no one who walks in them will know peace.
                                             (NIV)

Abortion, euthanasia, helps to suicide!

So justice is far from us,
   and righteousness does not reach us,
We look for light, but all is darkness;
   for brightness, but we walk in deep shadows.
Like the blind we grope along the wall,
   feeling our way like men without eyes.

> At midday we stumble as if it were twilight;
> > among the strong, we are like the dead.
> We all growl like bears, we moan mournfully like doves.
> We look for justice, but find none;
> > for deliverance, but it is far away . . .
> So justice is driven back,
> > and righteousness stands at a distance;
> Truth has stumbled in the streets,
> > honesty cannot enter.
> Truth is nowhere to be found,
> > and whoever shuns evil becomes a prey.
> The Lord looked and was displeased that there was
> > no justice.
> He saw that there was no one, and he was appalled
> > that there was no one to intervene.
>
> > > > > > > (NIV)

That has always struck me with a terrific force. He, the Lord, saw that there was no one to intervene, and He was appalled. Paul gives instruction that is to be seriously followed, which underlines this for us, in 1 Timothy 2:1:

> I urge, then, first of all, that requests, prayers, intercession and thanksgiving be made for everyone—for kings and all those in authority, that we may live peaceful and quiet lives in all godliness and holiness. This is good, and pleases God our Savior, who wants all men to be saved and to come to a knowledge of the truth. (NIV)

I wonder about our, your, my seriousness about our commission to intercede for people living in our moment of time. Are we serious enough to review what Isaiah 58 might say to stir us up into doing something more that has been outlined as preparation for true fasting and communication with the Lord?

Our Father, who art in Heaven, please may I not be among those described in Ezekiel 33:31, 32:

My people come to you, as they usually do, and sit before you to listen to your words, but they do not put them into practice. With their mouths they express devotion, but their hearts are greedy for unjust gain. Indeed, to them you are nothing more than one who sings love songs with a beautiful voice and plays an instrument well, for they hear your words, but do not put them into practice. (NIV)

Have mercy on me and forgive me for what has been only expressed by my mouth when something else has not measured up to the words. May the words of my mouth and the meditations of my heart be acceptable to You, Lord. Please show me which of Your directions for my life I have neglected to "put into practice." May I take more responsibility to intercede for people who are tempted by one or another of today's arrows being shot by the Evil One. Help me to make a difference by growing in trust and in deeds based on faith.

Now we need to return to Isaiah 58 and read on, letting it sink in:

"Then your light will break forth like the dawn,
    and your healing will quickly appear;
then your righteousness will go before you,
    and the glory of the Lord will be your rear guard.
Then you will call, and the Lord will answer;
    you will cry for help, and he will say: Here am I.
If you do away with the yoke of oppression,
    with the pointing finger and malicious talk,
and if you spend yourselves in behalf of the hungry
    and satisfy the needs of the oppressed,
then your light will rise in the darkness,
    and your night will become like the noonday.
The Lord will guide you always;
    he will satisfy your needs in a sun-scorched land
    and will strengthen your frame.
You will be like a well-watered garden,
    like a spring whose waters never fail.
Your people will rebuild the ancient ruins

and will raise up the age-old foundations;
you will be called Repairer of Broken Walls,
Restorer of Streets with Dwellings.
If you keep your feet from breaking the Sabbath
and from doing as you please on my holy day,
if you call the Sabbath a delight
and the Lord's holy day honorable,
and if you honor it by not going your own way
and not doing as you please or speaking idle words,
then you will find your joy in the Lord,
and I will cause you to ride on the heights of the land
and to feast on the inheritance of your father Jacob."
The mouth of the Lord has spoken.

(NIV)

Remember this was all in answer to the question: "Why have we fasted and you have not seen it? Why have we humbled ourselves and you have not noticed?"

As we go back to Hebrews 4 now, we can deeply agree that the Word of God is living and active and penetrates us deeply with pain, the pain of realizing how far short we fall from being what God wants us to be and do as His people.

Could we ever be perfect? No, not until Jesus comes back and we are changed in a twinkling of an eye to be like Him. But we are meant to be learning more all the time and acting upon what we learn. We are not meant to be feeding on nothing but milk, but on solid food, so that we can understand gradually more and more about the teachings of righteousness.

If we needed to be perfect before we could pray or take a day of praying and fasting, then not one of us could do so. The next verses in Hebrews 4, after the ones speaking about the Word being like a sword, go on to encourage us to come to our Father in Heaven through Christ asking for help in all we have talked about.

Therefore, since we have a great high priest who has gone through the heavens, Jesus the Son of God, let us hold firmly to the faith we profess. For we do not have a high priest who is unable to sympathize with our weaknesses, but we have one who has been tempted in every way, just as we are—yet was without sin. Let us then approach the throne of grace with confidence, so that we may receive mercy and find grace to help us in our time of need. (Hebrews 4:14-16 NIV)

The High Priest offered up the sacrifices. It was he who brought the lamb to the altar, asking forgiveness on the basis of the death of the lamb, for the people's sins and for his own. When Jesus died, He died as the Lamb for all who would come to Him. He became the sacrifice for us, He who had no sin became sin for us, and He gives us His righteousness in exchange—a costly gift, a powerful miracle of the atonement for sin. Jesus became the High Priest, as well as the Lamb. It is so beautiful that He also became the shepherd seeking His lambs! We can approach Him with confidence because His substitution was complete, and He has told us we may come in His name.

The thief on the cross who turned to Jesus, believing and calling on him, was that day to die and to go to Paradise. He had no time for learning more, being active in doing God's Word in a growing way, and praying with worship and intercession. You and I, however, did not die the day we first believed and accepted that sacrifice of Christ in our place. Our salvation is complete, but our sanctification is to be a daily reality of continued studying, learning, and acting upon what we are discovering.

Each life is like a weaving, a tapestry of various threads arranged in parallel lines on a loom—threads consisting of work, creativity, talents, drudgery, dreams, weaknesses, longings, failures, successes, satisfying achievements, moments of reality, frustrating failures, fresh ideas, surprises of joy, spurts of energy, disappointing weariness, deadlines met in time, hindrances cutting into work seeming to go well. Prayer is woven in (in this picture I see) helping day by day to turn the threads into a fabric with a pattern that brings forth what your life and mine could be. As history moves on, the history of your life and mine, prayer is the thread that helps us find out what God wants us to know from His Word and moment by moment to ask for His guidance in the practical next step of doing it, as well as really depending on His strength to enable us to run and not be weary.

In beginning to recognize how important prayer is, we may see how much we need to have the thread of the woof to make a firm whole of the more or less loose threads on the loom (called the warp). The Christian worldview is complex. If we have come to know the truth of the created universe being not chance, but the creation of the Creator, we affirm a complexity that, along with the myriad threads of our lives in practical areas, needs the moment-by-moment weaving together by the woof thread of prayer.

SIX

When Pray?
Where Pray?

When we were in Hong Kong in 1972, I was speaking to a group of single Chinese office girls about prayer and creativity. I spun a lovely picture of the need of being alone with the Lord in a "closet," in a corner of a room, in a bathroom to be private, or in a park. In the portion on creativity I talked about drawing conversation together. This could be done by placing a bowl of leaves or arranging some stones on a table center to bring a feeling of togetherness to those eating. My real topic was communication—with the Lord, yes, but also on the horizontal level with other human beings. How do we shut out distractions and bring a quietness into the atmosphere when we're shut alone into a small space with the Lord? Or when we're shut into a prepared space, an atmosphere with some beauty and quiet, to eat and talk with our family, a friend, a number of roommates?

Questions came as a bomb blast to me! Oh, the voices were soft and shy. The questions were a bit hesitant, but the general response was one of bewilderment. "I live in a two-room place with eleven people. There is a tiny bathroom and no proper kitchen. We have no place to serve a meal anyway. We buy a bowl of rice and things to eat at street stalls and eat out there or go to tea houses which are very crowded and noisy with chairs and tables close together. Only very rich people have more space. There is no place to read the Bible and pray alone in the house at all—maybe a rare time when everyone is out or in the night when others are asleep.

This description of crowded life came from each one. One girl said, "We keep adding people to the little apartment when

someone swims across from the mainland and makes it! How can
we say, 'No room'?" Others nodded and told similar tales. The
problem was a basic one of finite limitedness in a circumstance
that was very real. The questions were honest with a desire for an
answer that would be practical. "Where and when can I find a
place to communicate alone with the Lord, away from the chaos
of too many people in too small a place?" "Where and when can
I prepare any kind of atmosphere conducive to deep and real horizontal communication, let alone thoughtful questions about the
problems of life?" "Where is there any possibility for creativity
of any kind? Or privacy to read, pray, and think?"

At another time in that same year, I stood before a gathering of missionary women in Kenya, having responded to a plea
for help. Women missionaries from different missions had gathered together enough money to send a ticket that brought me
from the Chalet les Mélèzes kitchen one afternoon, as supper was
being prepared, to the Geneva airport, and on to Rome where I
called during a three-hour wait to find out how Franky was and
whether the supper had turned out okay. It seemed more like
falling through Alice's rabbit hole than flying, but after seeing
desert and unfamiliar trees from time to time under us, I finally
stepped out into furnace heat to go through immigration and
finally to be met by two eager missionaries. Zebras and giraffes
delighted me as we drove to our destination. Was it all real? Was
I having visions of things not there? Contrast struck my senses,
contrast of sounds and sights. It was all so very different from
Switzerland, yet also different from what I had imagined.

But when I stood in front of the hopeful women who had
come long distances to listen and to ask questions, the questions
came with the same sense of bewilderment, evidence of disap-
pointed expectations. Faces were discouraged, and tiredness
showed up in eyes and little frown lines. After the first lecture
came the questions. "But where can I pray and read my Bible? I
came expecting it to be so much more a spiritual work—being a
missionary. I expected to be closer to God. But with the time it
takes to wash and fix food, to keep clothing clean, dispense
aspirin and give shots, to clean wounds and bandage sores, I find

I never am really alone in my hut, never in a place of privacy where I can read the Bible and pray. I feel so dry." It came over and over again. "Where can I pray?" "Where can I pray?"

When pray?

There is much we are told as we follow God's Word, the Bible, and the history of God's people through the centuries.

> But I call to God, and the Lord saves me. Evening, morning and noon I cry out in distress, and he hears my voice. (Psalm 55:16, 17 NIV)

Here David speaks of his regular faithful prayer three times a day. Daniel prayed faithfully three times a day at regular times. Pray first when awakening:

> O Lord my God, in thee do I put my trust; save me from all them that persecute me, and deliver me. (Psalm 7:1 KJV)

> O Lord, our Lord, how excellent is thy name in all the earth, who has set thy glory above the heavens! (Psalm 8:1 KJV)

> I will bless the Lord at all times; his praise shall continually be in my mouth. (Psalm 34:1 KJV)

> Have mercy upon me, O God, according to thy lovingkindness; according unto the multitude of thy tender mercies blot out my transgressions. (Psalm 51:1 KJV)

> Be merciful unto me, O God, be merciful unto me; for my soul trusteth in thee. Yea, in the shadow of thy wings will I make my refuge, until these calamities be overpast. (Psalm 57:1 KJV)

> Hear my cry, O God; attend unto my prayer. From the end of the earth will I cry unto thee, when my heart is overwhelmed; lead me to the rock that is higher than I. For thou hast been a shelter for me, and a strong tower from the enemy. I will abide in thy tabernacle forever; I will trust in the covert of thy wings. Selah. (Psalm 61:1-4 KJV)

Praying along with David in these prayers of his for mercy, forgiveness, and protection under the shadow of God's wings is not necessarily a long time alone nor in an atmosphere that makes prayer easy.

O God, thou art my God, early will I seek thee; my soul thirsteth for thee, my flesh longeth for thee in a dry and thirsty land, where no water is. (Psalm 63:1 KJV)

Wherever and whenever we waken—in a desert, on the street, in a crowded Hong Kong room, in a hut, in a palace, in a farmhouse, in a trailer, in a city apartment, in a hospital, chained to a wall—our prayer for forgiveness in God's mercy, our cry for help, our praise of His marvelous works, and our thanksgiving for His opening the door to Himself in communication through the Lamb can be made without our voices being heard by anyone else in our room, our "space." It is possible to talk to God our Father, through the Lord Jesus Christ, in the power of the Spirit, without *anyone* overhearing us, wherever we might be immediately after awakening. The urgent needs of God's children as well as the worship of God's people do not change from century to century, as the results of the Fall are upon all history! Of course some lives are more oppressed and difficult than others, but we have available a privacy inside our brains, our minds, our hearts that does not depend on our outward location or even on the press of the people about us.

Our Creator made us in His image, made us with amazing brains where myriad ideas can follow one another, among which choices can be made in all the areas of our lives. Silently, within people's brains, music is composed, buildings are designed, new businesses are planned, gardens are landscaped, houses are restored, skating and dancing are choreographed, boats are built, wood is selected for musical instruments, food is combined for new recipes, poems are written, paintings and sculpture take shape, roads are mapped out, plays and films are planned and clearly seen as if on a screen, sports of a great variety are given new designs or twists. Our brains can silently invent *many* things, but can also silently communicate with the living God, can silently confess our sins and weaknesses to Him, can silently call for His strength in our terrible weaknesses, can silently call for His help in times of temptation.

Our place of privacy can be invaded by torture and brain-washing of cruel sorts, but martyrs through the ages of history and recent ones who have been chained to walls in darkness in these past years have taught us breathtaking things concerning the reality of the moment-by-moment availability of the Lord as He was called upon in prayer—in prisons as well as in countries where there was (or is now) no freedom to pray openly.

A place where there is privacy and a time that is protected should be treasured as precious gifts by those who have them. If we have to get up earlier than usual, if we have to plan and pro-tect a midday break, if we have to work at having a time alone somewhere in the evening, we should be thankful. Some people have no freedom to find a place alone with a Bible, to find unhindered time for prayer, even for a few moments, in a regular man-ner. Therefore, we should not let these periods of time and these private places be carelessly set aside or easily exchanged for something else.

Of course, if a doctor is called to come for an emergency, if a nurse's beeper goes off, if a child is in great need, or if we need to be a Good Samaritan to an unknown person in distress, we must leave the private place and shift the time to take care of the interruption. Each morning I do pray, *Lord make me sensitive to Your interruptions. May I not be rigid in my schedule and inflex-ible to what You would insert into my time. But please help me to be disciplined to do what is important to do and not to turn easily aside.*

We need to go into the command to pray without ceasing which needs our growing understanding as life goes on. It does not, however, cancel the need to have a discipline during the twenty-four-hour days of stopping what we would be doing to read something from the Bible and to come consciously into the presence of the most holy God with thanksgiving and with a recognition of our danger of letting time slide by without worshiping and praising the Lord. Praying before we eat a meal—whether at home, on a plane, in a restaurant, or on a picnic—is a means of praying with regularity at set times too. The carefully observed set times of prayer are as important to our growing spiritual life as set times of sleeping and eating. Again I would say there are important exceptions, whether it is fasting from sleep or food to have long unbroken times of prayer, or whether our drive to meet a deadline in one or another kind of work means we must continue working through normal sleeping times or mealtimes. The exceptions cannot be exceptions unless there is a basic pattern that we have decided is to be unbroken—*except* for exceptions!

Back to Hong Kong and Africa . . . and to many other places in the earth's geography where the questions of when and where are a daily problem.

What we are talking about is praying alone, privately. Prayer with other people is something else again. My suggestion to those who have to snatch moments and places is to take a small copy of the New Testament and the Psalms in a pocket or a paperback copy of one of the Gospels or a prayer book in a pocket. If even that is too much to take along through the day, copy by hand (or with a copier) that which would be most helpful for a time of prayer and slip it in a pocket. When to read and pray in the context of these verses or portions prepared? When you are walking to work, or across a courtyard to the hospital, or on the other side of a tree during a short break, on a subway, commuter train, or bus. There are minutes allowed during a workday for a coffee break or to use the washroom. A peculiar idea? Not really. If you are desperate enough, eager enough to find time to have a time apart from other human beings, separated from other ideas, to clear your thoughts and to give proper attention to the most holy God our Father who has given such a costly gift—His only begotten Son that we might not perish—it is not strange or peculiar to prepare an opportunity to be alone to both listen and to express thankfulness and make requests before the day is over. The determination to pray, the sincerity and earnestness of worship, the honest humbleness to bow before God as a sinful creature before the perfect holy Creator can take place anywhere.

In Luke 18, Jesus spoke a parable to illustrate this:

> Two men went up into the temple to pray; the one a Pharisee, and the other a publican. The Pharisee stood and prayed thus with himself, God, I thank thee that I am not as other men are, extortioners, unjust, adulterers, or even as this publican. I fast twice in the week; I give tithes of all that I possess. And the publican, standing afar off, would not lift up so much as his eyes unto heaven, but smote upon his breast, saying, God be merciful to me a sinner. I tell you, this man went down to his house justified rather than the other; for everyone that exalteth himself shall be abased; and he that humbleth himself shall be exalted. (Luke 18:10-14 KJV)

It seems clear to me that it was not the place, the physical place, that made the difference, but the place of that man's mind and heart in recognizing the holiness of God and his own unworthiness as he pled for mercy.

Elizabeth and Franz Mohr had me in their home for a week as I was interviewing Franz for the book *Forever Music.* Each morning I ran for the early morning Long Island commuter train in the dark cold of February. Now Franz had already had a short time of prayer in his cellar, which is his custom at five o'clock, but each day as we found seats or stood in the swaying aisle, Franz reached into his briefcase and pulled out his Bible, turning to the place where he was in his daily reading. During the hour's commute to Steinway in Manhattan each day, Franz, the master technician, uses the hour there and the hour back to spend "alone"—alone in a swaying train, alone in the crush of unsmiling, tired people on the way to work, alone as thoroughly as if in a meadow or woods, sitting on a rock in the sunrise. This was not an ideal place, nor was it magically transformed into beauty as far as anyone could see. But the beauty of the Lord God, Master of Heaven, could be thought about and listened to as the Bible was being read and thought about, and as prayer was taking place silently and worshipfully.

Recently I was sitting outside the Denver airport, waiting. Al had walked a long distance to search for his car. As I waited, quietly praying, I turned to look at someone on the other end of the bench. There was a man with an open Bible on his lap, engrossed in reading it, obviously very carefully. He had his foot on the first rung of his cart. It was a large cart full of brooms, mops, a pail, and thick cloths, a spray can of cleaning fluid, and Windex in a bottle beside it. There was a half-eaten apple in his hand and from time to time he took a bite.

As he leaned over to the cart to put the apple core in a waste can, he turned and said, "Hello." I "helloed" back and then asked if that was a Bible. "Yes, ma'am," he responded, "I don't have time to read much in the day if I don't read in the lunch break. It's too noisy in there, so I come outside where it is quieter. I'm reading Ephesians."

This lovely black fellow who keeps the portion of the airport that is his responsibility clean went on to tell me something about how he became a believer and then said he thought it was so important to *make* time to read, which was more important than going to lunch. The desire to really worship, to be in communication with the Lord, to "feed upon the Word of God," is a desire that takes some attention and the putting aside of casually letting time slide through the hour glass without notice. He finished his portion of Ephesians, looked at his watch, and hurriedly took the brake off his cart saying in a friendly as well as polite manner, "Good-bye and God bless you."

The sun was setting, the sky above the car park was streaked with apricot, but this was far from an ideally prepared place for worship and prayer. Obviously, however, this was a regular time and place of faithful prayer! Whether King David, Daniel, Elisha, or the man who cleans the Denver airport, it is the discipline of guarding uses of time, the faithful carrying out of a resolve, that makes these times of prayer a framework for the day and a base for life.

Not only do no two people have exactly the same difficulties and obstacles to private times to read and pray, but also for many of us no two days may be alike; certainly no two weeks are alike. Interruptions, whether major tragedies like a car crash, a heart attack, being taken hostage, having the house burn down in the middle of the night, a hurricane, an earthquake, an avalanche that sweeps away hikers or skiers, or even the more mundane of interruptions such as a person arriving in need at the door, a phone call asking for some kind of help, a baby not sleeping during the expected free time of his or her nap, children sick and home from school and needing care, needing to be read to, needing a memory later in life of loving imagination provided for them at that time—all these interruptions throw off the whole schedule of where and when to pray that day. We cannot plan ahead for the interruptions, whether we are mothers, businessmen, "shepherds of the flock" for whom we are available, missionaries, or football players, tennis pros, or swimming coaches. We need to start our day's schedule with a prayer, after praising our Creator and thanking Him: *Please help me to recognize Your interruptions and to turn away from other hindrances to being faithful in regular times of prayer.*

In the church, men like St. Benedict and St. Basil the Great earnestly sought uninterrupted times of prayer and reading God's Word, and a rocky retreat in one place or another became places where men gave their lives completely to prayer. But even in these places and times of preparation for uninterrupted prayer and meditation on God's Word there was a recognition of the reality of the Lord in the whole of life, being honored and praised and glorified by work well done. As St. Benedict in the fifth century put such emphasis on growing vegetables and fruit, on supplying physical needs by hard and faithful physical work, on the importance of beauty and works of art, we realize that prayer without ceasing was something that needed to be understood with the Lord's help, then, in the time of Paul and Timothy, and now.

No matter how free we are to choose an ideal time and place to pray during the day, no matter how careful we are with the content of our prayer times, giving a balance to worship, praise, asking forgiveness, thanking God for His mercy, and making requests, we still need to ask for a constantly growing understanding of what is meant by praying always, praying without ceasing. Not one of us will come to know this constant communication with God perfectly, but there is to be a measure of growing daily in trust and praise, in love and adoration, which it seems to me should have a growing expression in words and action.

In searching for a measure of praying without ceasing, we need to recognize that the *place* is to be everywhere we are, the *time* is to be always! 1 Timothy 2:8 speaks of everywhere: "I will therefore that men pray everywhere, lifting up holy hands, without wrath and doubting" (KJV). Everywhere means walking down the Hong Kong street, standing and examining the eyes of throngs coming to a clinic in Africa, scrubbing the floor in one's kitchen, feeding a baby, editing a film script, shoveling snow, or cutting grass. Everywhere is a succession of places! Everywhere is not a nonplace; it is a word denoting myriad places, too many places throughout history to ever describe. Since I am finite, and so are you, we can only be in one place at one time, right? If I succeed in a tiny measure to pray everywhere, it means I am praying only in one place at a time, even if I am walking along a road, up a mountain path, along a beach, or riding a bicycle, either stationary or on a bicycle path in Holland. Everywhere for a finite person has to be one place in one moment even for a skater skimming over the ice or a runner racing against time. Everywhere includes the commuters' train, the Hong Kong office or tea shop, the tractor in the field and the barn, as well as the grocery store and the food packaging company preparing barrels of flour or drums of orange juice to send across the world. There isn't anywhere that is not covered by everywhere!

Thinking of time, we turn to Philemon 4: "I thank my God, making mention of thee always in my prayers" (KJV). Paul is writing to Philemon and assuring him that he always makes mention of him in his prayers. Being finite we are also *limited*. Just as we can only be in one place at any one time, we can only pray for one person or speak of one sin we are asking forgiveness and mercy for, mention one glorious attribute of God we want to praise Him for in any one second or minute. Minute by minute, time unfolds. A grain of sand goes through the hour glass measuring time, one grain falling rapidly after another. Always is made up of a succession of seconds. Being limited in our humanness, we cannot do everything at once or pray for everybody at once or for every diversity of need at once. Choice is needed in our use of time as to whom we pray for, even when we are promising to pray always and attempting to do it with honesty and sincerity. When the Lord Jesus Christ intercedes for us, as truly God, He intercedes to the Father. The Trinity is infinite and unlimited, so that there is a tremendous difference between the infinite, unlimited Son of God, praying, interceding to the Father in our behalf on the basis of His own death for us, in the power of the Third Person of the Trinity, the Holy Spirit.

We need to be realistic and honest when we say, "I'll pray for you always," or "I'll pray for you without ceasing," as well as when we say, "O God, I want to praise You continually."

At the end of this short letter to Philemon, Paul writes: "But withal prepare me also lodging; for I trust that through your prayers I shall be given unto you" (v. 22 KJV). In addition to talking much about his desire that these people in the church he is writing to will take good care of his "son" Onesimus (a young man he must have loved greatly, having led him to Christ) and receive him as a brother, beloved to Paul but also now to them, Paul goes on to add that he expects an answer to their prayers that he himself will return soon. This expectation is so certain that he wants them to get a place ready for him, a place to eat and live. This preparation would be an action, a specific action based on trust that God would answer that prayer for Paul.

Yes, constant prayer is set before us as a thing to strive for as we seek righteousness and reality in our living as God would have us live, but interwoven with that is a trust in God's making known to us over and over again that prayer is heard when we ask specific requests and that history *will* be different because we prayed with trust for our "Paul" in a moment of need for hindrances to be removed and a result that would be different because of continual prayer, now in this century, in this opportunity to trust the unchanging Creator, our Father.

In 1 Peter 5:7 Peter directs believers in the midst of urging

vigilance and watchfulness in our growing lives: "Casting all
your care upon him, for he careth for you" (KJV). *All* is a
sweeping word needing the other words *continually* and *without ceasing* to be accomplished! True isn't it, that if you attempt
on Monday to cast your cares upon the Lord, Tuesday you will
have some new mail, an unexpected phone call, a tax bill, news
of a friend's accident. Tuesday has some new cares or burdens,
troubles or anxieties. In Tuesday's prayer, time must be again
taken to cast verbally these specific persecutions or attacks or
troubles on the Lord. Let me quote the context of this admonition, 1 Peter 5:6-11:

> Humble yourselves, therefore, under the mighty hand of God,
> that he may exalt you in due time, casting all your care upon
> him; for he careth for you. Be sober, be vigilant, because your
> adversary, the devil, like a roaring lion walketh about, seeking
> whom he may devour; Whom resist steadfast in the faith,
> knowing that the same afflictions are accomplished in your
> brethren that are in the world. But the God of all grace, who
> hath called us unto his eternal glory by Christ Jesus, after that
> ye have suffered awhile, make you perfect, stablish, strengthen,
> settle you. To him be glory and dominion forever and ever.
> Amen. (KJV)

There is no promise woven in here that suddenly all of life
will be easy and without afflictions and sorrow. There is no
promise that if we only cast on God all our care, with trust and
unceasing prayer, no more troubles will come and that the devil
will stop roaring and attempting to devour us with troubles and
temptations.

Peter, who had experienced looking down and being terrified at the waves as he walked on the water toward Jesus, knew
all too well how easy it was to stop midway in trusting and to be
swept with doubts and fears. His teaching as he goes on in the second epistle gives us tremendous impetus to keep on keeping on in
our attempts to pray without ceasing with a growing measure of
reality as our lives go on.

As we read that first chapter (do it now if you have a Bible nearby) and go over this small list a few times, we are over-whelmed by how far short we fall from being what we are called to be.

> Whereby are given unto us exceeding great and precious promises, that by these ye might be partakers of the divine nature, having escaped the corruption that is in the world through lust. And beside this, giving all diligence, add to your faith, virtue; and to virtue, knowledge; and to knowledge, tem-perance; and to temperance, patience; and to patience, godli-ness; and to godliness, brotherly kindness; and to brotherly kindness, love. For if these things be in you, and abound, they make you that ye shall neither be barren nor unfruitful in the knowledge of our Lord Jesus Christ. (2 Peter 1:4-8 KJV)

You, I, we have a possibility—not of being perfect in this land of the living but of not being barren and unfruitful either!

How can we possibly make any progress in this list of adding? By continually praying, praying for virtue, knowledge, temperance, patience, godliness, kindness, love. By recognizing our failures and confessing them to the Lord, by praying, inter-ceding for this list we have been given as a measure of growth for our beloved people, best friend, husband, wife, children, nieces, nephews, the people we work with and care about in a special way. It takes a measure of unceasing thought for the reality of fruitful and productive lives for ourselves and people we are responsible for. Can we pray for everyone in the world? Can we pray for all believers in the world with diligence and personal love and compassionate thoughtfulness? Not in our finiteness and lim-itedness. But we cannot simply come to God with a grocery list of requests and never spend time on the things we have been strongly taught are desired by our God and Father in His children, throughout His Word.

> Blessed is the man who walketh not in the counsel of the ungodly, nor standeth in the way of sinners, nor sitteth in the seat of the scornful. But his delight is in the law of the Lord; and in his law doth he meditate day and night. And he shall be

like a tree planted by the rivers of water, that bringeth forth its
fruit in its season; its leaf also shall not wither; and whatsoever
he doeth shall prosper. (Psalm 1:1-3 KJV)

The beauty of a green tree during a time of drought amid
brownness all around gives a picture of what the Lord means His
people to be. A well-watered tree with fresh green leaves, buds,
flowers. A fruit-producing tree, healthy, not blighted or dying,
beckons hikers to cross a dry field to sit under the shade and rest,
to eat some of the fruit and be refreshed. We who are the Lord's
people are meant to be like such a tree.

You remember the parable Jesus told of the sower sowing
seed? There was the seed that fell upon rock: "and as soon as it
was sprung up, it withered away, because it lacked moisture"
(Luke 8:6 KJV).

Where does the moisture come from? What is the river that
feeds roots? How can our "ground" be well-watered? How can
we keep from being withered?

We are to meditate day and night on His law and to delight
in the law of the Lord. This is speaking of His Word, the Bible,
the Word of God. God's Word is to be our water; our "roots" are
to be watered by filling the "water bucket" of our minds and
thoughts at the well of His Word. This isn't talking about quot-
ing verses to other people. This is private, being obedient to an
instruction from God as to how to stay alive, as a plant or tree in
the midst of a polluted atmosphere. The words that hit our ears
in the workplace can be like a withering blast of destructive hot
wind. In the middle of that destructive atmosphere, we are told
to fill our minds, to consider, to reflect, to think about, to ponder
over, to concentrate, to meditate on God's law, on God's expla-
nations, on God's instructions, on God's Word. When? "Day and
night." Day and night fits in with always, continually, without
ceasing!

The two-way conversation of reading and thinking about,
meditating upon some portion of God's Word, and then praying
in the context of that, is the teaching we are strongly given as to

how to keep our leaves a fresh green, how to not wither, how to be a fruit-producing tree.

When Joshua was being called upon to be strong and of good courage, to go on and take Moses' place, and was told that the Lord would be with him wherever he went, it was with a command to do something faithfully.

> This book of the law shall not depart out of thy mouth, but thou shalt meditate therein day and night, that thou mayest observe to do according to all that is written therein; for then thou shalt make thy way prosperous, and then thou shalt have good success. (Joshua 1:8 KJV)

"Day and night." "Always." "Continually." "Without ceasing." These rather total phrases leave no time in between. If we meditate on God's Word day and night, if His word is continually in our mouths, when do we do honest work with our own hands and care for the land, the ground we are meant to care for? If we are praying continually, when do we care for our own households, cook, wash feet, give cups of cold water, and serve others with love, do excellently our daily work?

First of all, what is told us is not to be ignored. We are given a goal of perfection when we are told, "Be ye, therefore, perfect, even as your Father, who is in heaven, is perfect" (Matthew 5:48 KJV). Jesus puts forth perfection as the standard. But no person will be perfect until at one moment we will all be changed to be like Christ at the Second Coming of Christ. John in his first epistle, 1 John 2:1, writes: "My little children, these things write I unto you, that ye sin not. And if any man sin, we have an advocate with the Father, Jesus Christ the righteous" (KJV). And 1 John 1:9 says, "If we confess our sins, he is faithful and just to forgive us our sins and to cleanse us from all unrighteousness."

If we were to be acceptable before the most holy God on the basis of our own moment-by-moment consistency, always resisting temptation, never doubting, never lacking trust, loving God with all our hearts, never deviating in humbleness, having only kind thoughts and deeds, always being merciful to others, always being meek and longsuffering, we each know that we could not come to Him. We come to Him on the basis that Christ who lived a perfect life for us as well as dying for us as He took our sins upon Him and became our substitute, our atonement, has covered us with His righteousness. After we bow before Him with true repentance for our sins and accept Him as our Savior, then God the Father will mercifully allow us to come into His presence with our praise, thanksgiving, adoration, and requests for help, wisdom, guidance, and special needs.

We could never pray at any time or place if we could not be accepted. Our own goodness would never be enough to give us entrance.

Please let us reflect deeply, think about this seriously. Jesus really did tell us to be perfect! Yet, He made it clear that only by His own death in our place could sin be removed. Then John's epistle urges Christians to "sin not." He also quickly gives the practical answer that IF any of us sin, Jesus is our lawyer, our righteous lawyer, pleading His own blood in our behalf.

Does this mean that we shrug our shoulders and stop battling against our own most difficult temptations? Does this mean that we toss our heads and push aside all need to grow in sensitivity to our own weaknesses and faults? Oh no, not at all. We are to grow. Paul, as he writes to the Ephesians, speaks through the centuries to us. We need to read the whole book as we prepare for prayer. The fourth chapter tells so specifically of the things that need changing in us, as in verse 14 we are warned not to be tossed to and fro by crafty people waiting to deceive us and so on. Then follows verse 15 as a contrast: "But, speaking the truth in love, [we] may grow up into him in all things, who is the head, even Christ" (KJV).

We are to grow steadily, but not always with the same rapidity, even as plants in the garden. If weather, sun, rain, and soil are just right, the growth can be spectacular, but when hail comes and breaks the leaves or sprouts, time and tender care are needed to gently repair the damage and to see signs of life and growth again. We are to help one another in times of falling or weakness, not with pride but with recognition that each of us needs that help and forgiveness. With all this, the standard is still perfection and we are to continue until we step out of our bodies into His presence or until Christ comes back. We are to continue to ask forgiveness for what we did an hour ago, a minute ago, or a day ago, and ask for help, time after time, yet realizing that there has been growth over the last months!

What has that to do with the admonitions to pray always, without ceasing, continually, day and night? A lot.

Just as our gradual sanctification, that is, our gradually growing closer to what we are told to *be* and to *do*, so our understanding and practicing praying, not just three times a day, or six times a day, or nine times a day, but with fewer and fewer breaks in between, is to be throughout our lives closer to what we are given as a standard. This standard is not to be ignored, but worked on, attempted in various ways. It is something private, however, between you and the Trinity or between me and the Trinity. The call to be humble warns us not to talk about much praying, but to do it.

Is it imperative to climb a mountain, go into a cell, live as a monk, to give ourselves to prayer alone? Is that the only possible way of having a true attempt at praying constantly, always, day and night?

It seems to me that the answer is no. The instruction in Ephesians is to all the church, and the word about prayer is to do something in the midst of everyday life.

Praying always with all prayer and supplication in the Spirit, and watching thereunto with all perseverance and supplication for all saints; And for me, that utterance may be given unto me, that I may open my mouth boldly to make known the mystery of the gospel, for which I am an ambassador in bonds; that in this I may speak boldly, as I ought to speak. (Ephesians 6:18-20 KJV)

This is clearly a part of what is to be done. Perfectly? No, of course not, but actually and literally insofar as it is possible in the midst of finiteness and limitedness and in the midst of weakness, imperfection, and sin. We are to try to grow in understanding and practice of prayer through the days of our lives, with shorter breaks in between.

We need to examine the possibilities in our own days and nights. There are waiting times—for buses, trains, trams, planes, red lights. There may be a moment during a walk to work, or to a store, or out to a field to bring in the corn or potatoes. These times can be used to pray in the words of a remembered Psalm, or a hymn, or in asking for mercy and forgiveness, or in thanking God for His blessings, or in praying for someone who is on our mind. We need also to discover times when our work includes minutes when our hands or feet are occupied, but our minds are free to think about the wonders of God's creation and to thank Him for creating rivers, trees, mountains, the diversity of food we are able to have, and for opening the way for us, for each of us personally to really approach such a magnificent, holy Creator. Prayer is not always asking for something, but bringing our appreciation and worship in very real ways in the in-between times, very naturally.

As we tie a shoe, we silently thank God for the earnestness of a small boy's eyes and the freckles on his nose. As we brush a little girl's hair, we thank Him for the beauty of shiny hair and small hands so soft yet so tough. We marvel and praise Him for the bird songs at twilight in a thicket as we walk and for swooping gulls over a lake or sea or the first fat robin in the spring announcing the bursting forth of crocuses. In thanking Him and loving Him for the perfection of His creation which has been so spoiled by the Fall, we thrill with a bursting bubble of thanks when we notice the "left-over beauty," not only of a scientist's brain and a great pianist's concert, but of a tiny baby's toenails and the wonder of eyelashes and ears. Communicating our recognition of our great Creator's myriad details in every area of His creation, it seems to me, is a response that takes place very truly, though silently, throughout the waking hours.

You may say, "I can't thank Him for a baby's smile—I don't have one." But there is a baby in the park or in a cart whose smile you can notice. You may say, "I can't be thankful for the new moon and stars—I'm in a city of dirt and confusion." But the sky is visible somewhere, and the sunset reflected in skyscrapers' marble or glass walls can capture something of the sunset's glow in the mountains. Even a puddle can reflect a light or float a leaf! Of course there are prison bars, chains on a captive's feet, destroyed places and destroyed people which need to be prayed *for* when we see documentaries or films or are ourselves in the midst of such areas of the world. But even there, there are things to thank God for in that He remains accessible and will give us wisdom as to what to do, as we ask Him.

This is all a practical unfolding of thoughts as to what prayer always, communication with the Lord, thanksgiving to Him can be in snatches of time in the midst of everyday life.

There are set times and places where we can pray alone, if such places can be found in our homes or surroundings. There are set times when we pray with others in church or gather together with two or three others or a group of people for an evening or day of prayer. In such set-apart times when we have agreed to put aside other things to pray, we will still discover that choices have to be made as to the use of time in praying for situations, needs, people in tragic situations, people in desperate need, and for each one we have promised to "always pray for." In China, when I was a little girl, the people praying in church for different requests all prayed out loud at the same time. Confusion? No, they were accustomed to studying aloud at school, each person occupied with what he or she was saying. This seemed to me an economy in the use of time; so many people and subjects were covered in the same hours. But of course this is not the Western manner of agreeing to pray together for some special needs, for a suffering child, someone at sea, or for work for someone who needs a job.

We are silent as one person prays aloud, but the idea is that we join in inside our minds and concentrate on the same needs or person or request inside our minds. We are given examples of groups of people agreeing to pray in the account of the early Christians in Acts 1:13,14:

And when they were come in, they went up into an upper room where abode Peter and James, and John, and Andrew, Philip,

and Thomas, Bartholomew, and Matthew, James, the son of
Alphaeus, and Simon Zelotes, and Judas, the brother of James.
These all continued with one accord in prayer and supplication,
with the women, and Mary, the mother of Jesus, and with his
brethren. (KJV)

Of course this was a very special time of prayer for guidance
in choosing the man to be the twelfth apostle. But along with
other examples of several banding together with one accord in
agreement to pray for the Lord's guidance, His wisdom to be
shown, His help in a moment when a decision needs to be made,
is Matthew 18:19, 20. The two or three are to be in agreement as
they pray together with a request for direction, for help, for the
Lord's will to be unfolded, for courage to make a choice.

Praying together need not take place in the same geographic
spot. We need not be in the same spot in the fields, the same boat,
the same rock on a mountainside, the same church building, the
same house, the same bench. We can, in this day of communication systems, be together on a telephone—from Nepal to
England, from Finland to Boston, from Colorado to Minnesota,
from New York to Rochester, from Texas to the island of Elba in
Italy.

When Mary Crowley was having radium treatment, shut
into a glassed-in space away from visitors for a length of time, she
asked me to please telephone her and pray with her in that place
of isolation. She gave me an exact time, and I was in Elba, without a telephone in the rooms on a hill where I was staying for a
rest with Debby and Udo. I arranged to take the family, including the children, down to Portoferraio for supper in an old hotel
by the ferry. The hour would be right for calling; a telephone
booth was in the lobby. Easy? No, it took lots of "pronto, pronto,
prontos," lots of asking for help from the young hotel manager
who became interested in this hospital call across the world, and
finally came Mary's voice, full of appreciation as well as pain, and
pleasure mixed with suffering. "Oh, you did get through. I needed
you; your prayer with me and your friendship makes so much difference right now."

Couldn't I pray alone on the beach or up under the euca-
lyptus trees in early morning on the hill and have an effectual, fervent time of prayer for her? Of course. I did that too, but to pray
WITH a person or persons is a different answer to the questions
"When pray? Where pray?" The voice in the ear across the miles,
of another human being, a friend, agreeing to pray for and with
one in a time of extreme need of one variety or another is a dimension we have been *given*. Horizontal oneness in the presence of
the most holy God, our Father and Creator, ushered in by our
Shepherd and Savior Jesus Christ in whose name we come, in the
power of the indwelling Holy Spirit who gives us His power, is a
part of what we have been richly given in a growing prayer life.
We may come alone, we may come with the church, we may come
secretly with no one but the Lord hearing our whispers, we may
come with a dozen others, we may come with one person who
needs to hear our voice or whose voice we need to hear—recognizing the spiritual aspect of what God meant (in part, that is, we
never understand perfectly) when He declared, "It is not good for
man to dwell, or be, alone." The stark isolation of an intensive
care glass-and-chrome prison can be suddenly a place of TWO
human beings, friends, together entering the living God's presence
and finding the double comfort of human togetherness, oneness
in God's family, and closeness to the Lord Himself, two human
beings half the world away!

This is not fantasy, but reality.

However, please remember that every human being is finite
and limited.

Every choice to pray a great deal for one person is a choice
not to use the hour, or minutes, to be praying for someone else
(at that time). Every choice to pray together on a walk or on a
phone with one person is a choice not to be either praying or
doing something with or for another person or persons. I had to
leave the table to make that phone call. It took over an hour to
get a line through from Italy to the Texas hospital. By the time I
returned, the meal was more than half over. Could the time be
reused? No. But the choice had been made very specifically. Yet
one must reflect deeply upon this fact—every positive choice in

use of time, and energy, and thought, and response to any one person or need is in a very real way a negative choice in putting aside some other person or need for which we might use that time and energy.

This is where we have to be realistic when we talk about our determination to follow our *intention* to be faithful in the battle we are told about in Ephesians 6:18. We are meant to really DO something about following that series of instructions or admonitions as to how to live and not be overcome by the "wiles" or "schemes of the devil." "Praying always with all prayer and supplication in the Spirit, and watching thereunto with all perseverance and supplication for all saints." "Always . . . all . . . all . . . all."

How much time does "always" take? Forgetting that we need to sleep and do other things to fulfill our promises to our patients as doctors and nurses, to fulfill our contracts to build or to put out a newspaper on time, forgetting that area of limitation or finiteness—even if we were in a monastic cell on the side of a cliff—our finiteness requires us to choose WHOM we are going to pray for this hour, this ten minutes, this thirty seconds, this second.

We can make a sweeping request and pray for "all the sailors on the sea," for "all the men and women in government," for "all the students in universities," for "all the Romanians in the midst of this change," for "all the athletes in the Olympics," for "all those in prisons," for "all the hungry people of the world"— and there is a place for such prayer—but we need to take responsibility to care very personally for individuals, our own families, friends, those whom the Lord brings to our minds and hearts to pray for, those for whom we have promised to pray. Paul gives us his example, declaring that he prays for those in Philippi "always in every prayer of mine for you all making request with joy." Yes, we DO have responsibility for specific prayer for a number of individuals and a great responsibility to keep promises to pray. Yet we are finite, limited, and must ask God's wisdom to be given us in using our time.

When pray? It seems to me that when we make a promise

in a letter, "I will pray for you," before writing the next sentence it is imperative to stop and pray for a minute for that person and the specific needs! When on the phone I say, "I'll pray for you," it seems important to me to pray *right then,* even if briefly. To treat that phrase as a kind of spoken friendliness or evidence of interest is a kind of falseness hurtful to the one making the promise.

As we come asking God's mercy and forgiveness as we pray early in the morning, we need to review and ask for forgiveness for false promises we have made, as well as for the other sins we have committed.

A growing understanding of God's promise, "I will never leave you nor forsake you," means we can speak to Him in the depths of "the pit" as Jeremiah did, or in the midst of a storm at sea, or when we are sitting beside a baby with croup or an asthma attack. Our prayer without ceasing, it seems to me, is a growing recognition that He is with us without ceasing, so that a whisper, a small word, "Do Thou for me, Lord," asking for help without being able to verbalize a request, "Do thou for him, for her," is a natural part of our growing awareness of our Father's presence.

Prayer without ceasing, it seems to me, is like having an oxygen tank for exploring the depths under water. How long can we swim under water without oxygen? What happens in the depths if oxygen is cut off? We need spiritually to be able to breathe, to be confident that we are connected. The scuba diver is absorbed in the fantastic plants he is seeing, in the astounding discovery of the beauty of the fish, in exploring a wrecked ship. His or her thoughts are filled with the joy of creativity, with a piece of work to be accomplished scientifically, with photography to be satisfying. Meanwhile, the breathing goes on naturally enabling the person to go on with his or her work or pleasure. Just so—as we pay attention and give thought to doing what we are doing with excellence, desiring that our work and pleasures, our creative ideas and excitements, all bring our thanksgiving and praise to our Creator, we are connected with the Source of our spiritual oxygen. We breathe quite naturally, aware that we could not go on without being truly connected to Him.

The gaps occur when we think we can do it—whatever it may be—in our own zip and vigor, in our own clever ideas and plans, and we ignore our dependence upon the "spiritual oxygen." The gaps occur when we fall into despair and cease to breathe or to call upon the Lord for help. The gap occurred for Peter when he stopped keeping his eyes on Jesus and turned them down to the fearsome waves. As life goes on, the gaps should be narrower, shorter in length, and our awareness that God is with us as our Father and Shepherd, our Rock and our High Tower, our Home within the wilderness, our Comforter without ceasing should make a turning to Him in prayer, in communication, in praise, in calling for help, in asking for forgiveness, in interceding for someone so constantly on our minds or in our hearts, like taking a deep breath, like natural and life-sustaining breathing!

Can we arrive at being perfect as our Father in Heaven is perfect? Can we arrive at the place of praying without ceasing? No, not until the Messiah returns the second time, not until the Lord Jesus Christ comes back, not until "in a moment, in a twinkling of an eye" the dead shall rise, and we who are alive are changed to be like Him, for we shall see Him as He is. But we are meant to have these standards of perfection as our goal, and we are truly meant to see satisfying real growth as we look back. We can grow because His grace is sufficient for us, and His strength is made perfect in our weakness, and He is with us without ceasing.

SEVEN
Continuity of Prayer Through Centuries
Part One

O Lord, our Lord, how excellent is thy *name* in all the earth. (Psalm 8:1 KJV)

And God said unto Moses, I AM THAT I AM: and he said, Thus shalt thou say unto the children of Israel, I AM hath sent me unto you. And God said moreover unto Moses, Thus shalt thou say unto the children of Israel, the Lord God of your fathers, the God of Abraham, the God of Isaac, and the God of Jacob, hath sent me unto you; this is my *name* forever, and this is my memorial unto all generations. (Exodus 3:14, 15 KJV)

The name of the Creator God, the most holy God of Abraham, Isaac, and Jacob is our never-changing continuity through all generations. "I AM" is ever-present, not past, not future, *ever* present, always present, continually present, unceasingly present.

Now know I that the Lord saveth his anointed; he will hear him from his holy heaven with the saving strength of his right hand. Some trust in chariots, and some in horses; but we will remember the *name* of the Lord our God. They are brought down and fallen; but we are risen, and stand upright. Save, Lord; let the king hear us when we call. (Psalm 20:6-9 KJV)

I will declare thy *name* unto my brethren; in the midst of the congregation will I praise thee. Ye who fear the Lord, praise him; all ye, the seed of Jacob, glorify him; and fear him, all ye, the seed of Israel. (Psalm 22:22, 23 KJV)

For thy *name's* sake, O Lord, pardon mine iniquity; for it is great. . . . Look upon mine affliction and my pain, and forgive all my sins. . . . Oh, keep my soul, and deliver me; let me not be ashamed; for I put my trust in thee. (Psalm 25:11, 18, 20 KJV)

Bow down thine ear to me; deliver me speedily. Be thou my strong rock, for an house of defense to save me. For thou art my rock and my fortress; therefore, for thy *name's* sake lead me, and guide me. (Psalm 31:2, 3 KJV)

Praise ye the Lord. I will praise the Lord with my whole heart, in the assembly of the upright, and in the congregation. . . . He hath made his wonderful works to be remembered; the Lord is gracious and full of compassion. . . . He hath shown his people the power of his works, that he may give them the heritage of the heathen. . . . He sent redemption unto his people; he hath commanded his covenant forever; holy and reverend is his *name*. (Psalm 111:1, 4, 6, 9 KJV)

Not unto us, O Lord, not unto us, but unto thy *name* give glory, for thy mercy, and for thy truth's sake. Wherefore should the heathen say, Where is now their God? (Psalm 115:1, 2 KJV)

All those centuries ago, David not only honored and revered the holy name of God, but prayed that answers to prayer would be glorifying to God's name. Time after time the plea comes, "Do this, O Lord, for *thy name's* sake." Through the centuries there is a measure of understanding among God's people, when people are deeply honest and sincere, truly longing to honor God, that answers to prayer demonstrate a fulfillment of His promises and bring honor to His wonderful name.

In Proverbs we have an impressive contrast that helps us to appreciate what it can mean to us to honor God's name. "The name of the Lord is a strong tower; the righteous runneth into it, and is safe" (Proverbs 18:10 KJV). What a protection we are offered here as we need a safe place to run to. *Our Father which art in Heaven, hallowed be Thy name,* we pray, and we have run into the strong tower of His *name.* Yes, our time of prayer so often can be a running into that strong tower!

Then the next verse gives the contrast: "The rich man's wealth is *his strong city,* and as a high wall in his own conceit" (Proverbs 18:11 KJV). Or in the NIV version: "The wealth of the rich is their fortified city; they imagine it an unscalable wall." This is not saying a rich person cannot pray when in trouble, nor does it say every rich person ceases to trust and honor the name of the holy God and *never* runs to "the strong tower" of His name in prayer. But it is a warning not to trust in riches, not to feel protected by riches, to the danger of regarding riches as a thick protective wall against any invasion of sorrows or pain or enemies!

For each of us the name of the Lord is our only strong tower. Each of us, as with David in Psalm 55, can relate to his description:

Fearfulness and trembling are come upon me, and horror hath overwhelmed me. And I said, Oh, that I had wings like a dove! For then would I fly away, and be at rest. (vv. 5, 6 KJV)

In this time of history, as with David in his moment, we need to go on and pray specifically running to "the strong tower."

As for me, I will call upon God, and the Lord shall save me. . . .
Cast thy burden upon the Lord, and he shall sustain thee; he shall never suffer the righteous to be moved. (vv. 16, 22 KJV)

The name of the Lord carries with it His glory and honor and majesty. In Isaiah 9:6 we have that prophecy of the coming of the Messiah which emphasizes what His name is to be—this Second Person of the Trinity, this One who was to say later to the Pharisees that he was "I AM," that He was everlasting.

For unto us a child is born, unto us a son is given, and the government shall be upon his shoulder; and his name shall be called Wonderful, Counselor, The mighty God, The Everlasting Father, The Prince of Peace. (KJV)

I am the Lord: that is my name; and my glory will I not give to another, neither my praise to graven images. (Isaiah 42:8 KJV)

Thus saith the Lord, thy redeemer, and he who formed thee from the womb: I am the Lord who maketh all things; who stretcheth forth the heavens alone; who spreadeth abroad the earth by myself. (Isaiah 44:24 KJV)

Jeremiah in his time called out in praise to God: "Forasmuch as there is none like unto thee, O Lord; thou art great, and thy *name* is great in might" (Jeremiah 10:6 KJV). As the Lord speaks of a future time in Zechariah 10:12, the importance of His name is emphasized: "And I will strengthen them in the Lord; and they shall walk up and down in his *name*, saith the Lord" (KJV).

The importance of honoring and hallowing the name of God is stressed throughout the Bible. The third commandment, that we are not to misuse the name of the Lord, needs to be woven into our thoughts as we come directly to Him in the stream of history. That is, as we look into the continuity of prayer, communication with God through *centuries* of time, it is really breathtaking to contemplate imperfect people being given the possibility of honoring God, of bringing acceptable worship and praise to Him, of bringing thanksgiving to Him, and of truly loving Him.

One afternoon about thirty years ago, a twenty-year-old man burst into the Chalet les Mélèzes kitchen with flushed cheeks and starry eyes. "I've just had the most exciting time in my life; I've been talking to the Creator of the universe." He had accepted Christ as his Savior a few short hours before.

Do we ever lose that excitement, that sheer wonder, that astonishment that we have really been accepted into the presence of the most holy God because He really prepared the way to come to Him at tremendous cost and that that "door" has remained the same door through centuries?

That excitement should be translated into an intense desire to ask Him for help in honoring His name, to trust Him with a growing trust that makes known our love to Him.

In coming toward the end of the Old Testament, two places cause me to bow and ask to be cleansed from sin and be truly repentant and in the right place before the Lord. How easy, it seems to me, it has been through centuries of time for people to speak words with their lips and yet not be real in their hearts. It is so easy to put on a mask, to hide behind right words, but no one can hide from God the truth of what we really are or of what our minds are full of.

The first of these two places is Zechariah 13:9:

And I will bring the third part through the fire, and will refine them as silver is refined, and will try them as gold is tried; they shall call on my name, and I will hear them. I will say, It is my people; and they shall say, The Lord is my God. (KJV)

The second place is in the last book of the Old Testament, Malachi 3:16, 17:

Then they that feared the Lord spoke often one to another; and the Lord hearkened, and heard it, and a book of remembrance was written before him for them that feared the Lord, and that thought upon his name. And they shall be mine, saith the Lord of hosts, in that day when I make up my jewels; and I will spare them, as a man spareth his own son that serveth him. (KJV)

Awesome thought! The Lord has a book of remembrance in which the names of all those who fear Him (that is, reverence Him and honor Him) and who really think about Him, think upon His name, are written, and these are precious to Him. These are His jewels!

Near the end of the Old Testament the time of the second coming of Christ is looked forward to, though it was confusing to those who lived before the Messiah's first coming. However, the name of the Lord and the importance of honoring that precious name are spoken of right up into the last few verses.

But unto you that fear my name shall the Sun of righteousness arise with healing in his wings. (Malachi 4:2 KJV)

But for you who revere my name, the sun of righteousness will rise with healing in its wings. (NIV)

When we call people whom we love and are eager to have a conversation with, whom we desire to have respond to our questions, whom we look to for help in our ideas, whom we think might give us some advice on an important decision, whom we genuinely trust and respect, we call on them by name, the name they have asked us to call them, the name that indicates some understanding and knowledge of who they are. We don't go to a best friend and use an insulting name to start a warm communication.

What we have just read from the Bible in these few verses gives us some idea of the way God's people, the ones who have come to Him through the ages in His given manner, have respected the holiness of His name, showing that they have some understanding of His perfection, His infinite holiness and might as well as His compassion and mercy.

When Jesus taught the disciples how to pray, these people had a background of knowing that the name of God was to be revered. The Lord's Prayer fits in with David's prayers in the Psalms, as David cried out to the most holy God and as he declared His name to the congregation. Jesus teaches that this reverence is as important today in our coming to the Lord in prayer as it was through the centuries.

After this manner therefore pray ye:
Our Father, who art in heaven,
    Hallowed be thy name.
    Thy kingdom come,
    Thy will be done in earth,
    as it is in heaven.
    Give us this day our daily bread.
    And forgive us our debts
    as we forgive our debtors.

> And lead us not into temptation,
>   but deliver us from evil.
> For thine is the kingdom, and the power,
>   and the glory, forever. Amen.
>
> (Matthew 6:9-13 KJV)

How many times have we prayed with these words, yet a lifetime is not long enough to sufficiently hallow His name! If we were trying to fill up a silver cup of reverence to the most holy name of our Father God whom we can call Father because of the active obedience of Jesus Christ as well as because of His death, that cup would *never* spill over. The infinite God, perfect in holiness . . . can He receive something real by our glorifying His precious name as we pray with these words? There must be a growing inward reality of our love and desire to honor Him. There must be a growing appreciation of being in His presence, which makes the words come alive in a way a mechanical voice— a phonograph record, a tape, or a disc—cannot.

For a human being the presence of a beloved friend speaking with a voice full of true desire to communicate, enhanced by expression in the eyes, underlined by some facial expressions or movements of hands, cannot be compared to the mere repetition of the same words on an expressionless machine. Even a telephone conversation, with an attempt to communicate appreciation, is very different from a canned message, a "singing card" intoning happy birthday over and over again.

Tibetan prayer wheels, with papers fixed in certain places, the thought being that each time the wheel turns the prayer is being said, display very forcefully what Jesus is speaking about when He precedes the giving of the Lord's Prayer with this warning: "When ye pray, use not vain repetitions, as the heathen do; for they think they shall be heard for their much speaking." Not only are they praying to false gods, but the very mindless, thoughtless manner of praying by mechanically turning a wheel blots out the significance of the personality of the person praying and of the one to whom that person is praying.

Our Father—Jesus' Father and the Father of each one who

comes through Jesus the Lamb—is being addressed as the same
One who has made clear in the whole Bible that His name is to
be reverenced, adored.

Our Father who art in Heaven—Asaph's prayer in Psalm
73:23-28 is made to God whom he understands to be in Heaven.
Centuries before our time, he calls out to the Lord God in
Heaven:

> Nevertheless, I am continually with thee; thou hast held me by
> my right hand. Thou shalt guide me with thy counsel, and after-
> ward receive me to glory. Whom have I in heaven but thee?
> And there is none upon earth that I desire beside thee. My flesh
> and my heart faileth but God is the strength of my heart, and
> my portion forever. For, lo, they that are far from thee shall
> perish; thou hast destroyed all those who go a whoring from
> thee. But it is good for me to draw near to God; I have put my
> trust in the Lord God, that I may declare all thy works. (KJV)

Jesus teaches us to go on in the continuity of prayer with
David and God's people who have had comfort and help, practical answers given through the ages. Who else is there to whom
we may come with praise and bring honor, but the Lord God in
Heaven?

Hallowed be Thy name needs to come with the feeling of a
swelling crescendo of unseen voices added to ours. Thousands
join unseen by us, voices not speaking mere repetition but with
adoration and praise—they join us in saying with deep meaning,
"Hallowed be Thy name." God knows each one by name. He
knows our names and has called us by name, we are told, one by
one. Not a nameless mob are praising Him through the centuries,
but significant human beings, born into His family by faith, by
trust in the truth of His Word. These all, in some very real and
growing measure, are praying, *Hallowed be Thy name. Thy
Kingdom come, Thy will be done in earth as it is in Heaven.*

We are meant to pray for the coming of God's Kingdom.
Although we are clearly told in the Gospels that no one knows
when Jesus will triumphantly return, we are told to pray for His
coming.

But of that day and that hour knoweth no man, no, not the angels who are in heaven, neither the Son, but the Father. Take heed, watch and pray; for ye know not when the time is. (Mark 13:32, 33 KJV)

We are being given very specific and careful instructions about what to do as we mourn over the wickedness in the world, as we cry over the suffering in so many places, as we look into the eyes of tragic people in darkness without hope. We are to have compassion on those for whom we are meant to be light and salt, but also we are to continue with all who have prayed for centuries, praying, *Thy Kingdom come.* We are to watch and pray!

For the Son of man is like a man taking a far journey, who left his house, and gave authority to his servants, and to every man his work, and commanded the porter to watch. Watch ye, therefore; for ye know not when the master of the house cometh, at even, or at midnight, or at the cockcrowing, or in the morning; Lest, coming suddenly, he find you sleeping. And what I say unto you I say unto all, Watch. (Mark 13:34-37 KJV)

Watching properly as the Lord tells us to watch for the coming of Jesus, for the coming Kingdom, for the perfection of the resurrection does not consist of sitting on a stone wall or a mountaintop or a wonderful rail fence, looking at the view, gazing up into the sky. We are the servants of the living God, and we have work to do. We have creative work, the work also of caring for people, showing forth love in practical ways, showing compassion by giving the cup of cold water in specific ways, over and over again. We are to be concerned about constant needs of people and the importance of doing our work well while we are praying for the Lord's coming.

As we pray for the Lord's will to be done on earth, we realize that there is a battle going on and that the enemy, Satan, continues to scheme as he seeks whom he may devour. Our earnestness in asking that the Lord's will be done on earth should be accompanied by a personal cry after the Lord's prayer, *Please give me Thy direction and strength and wisdom to do Thy will today.*

Jesus instructs us to pray day after day for our daily bread. This in no way cancels out the wonderful portion of Jesus' teaching in Matthew 6 where he tells us to look at the way God has clothed the flowers of the field and fed the birds of the air, telling us to not worry about how we shall be fed or clothed. "But seek ye first the kingdom of God, and his righteousness, and all these things shall be added unto you" (Matthew 6:33 KJV). In the *New International Version* of the Bible, the next verse is translated this way: "Therefore do not worry about tomorrow, for tomorrow will worry about itself. Each day has enough trouble of its own" (Matthew 6:34).

Clearly seeking righteousness, seeking the Kingdom of God, bringing honor to His most holy name comes first, but we are told to pray daily, one day at a time, for our bread. Our Heavenly Father desires us to ask that He might meet our needs. Day by day we are to ask, recognizing that He is the giver, and we are to ask a moment at a time for the needed wisdom, courage, and strength to continue in this life even as we pray, *Thy Kingdom come.*

Forgive us our debts, as we forgive our debtors. This is part of the prayer Jesus instructs His people to pray. A lifetime of praying these words does not remove from us the need to ask forgiveness for our sin of harboring unforgiveness in our minds and hearts. What can it mean?

Jesus goes on to emphasize what this means:

> For if ye forgive men their trespasses, your heavenly Father will also forgive you; But if ye forgive not men their trespasses, neither will your father forgive your trespasses. (Matthew 6:14, 15 KJV)

Is not our sin paid for by Christ becoming sin for us and dying in our place? Oh yes, there is no other way to come to the Father except through the cross.

However, our lives are meant to demonstrate a reality of change, of growth, inwardly and outwardly. Isaiah 58, which we read together in studying fasting and prayer, makes very sharp the admonition of God to those who were covered in sackcloth and ashes and fasting as they prayed. The command to them was to treat their workers properly, to care for their own families, to provide food for the poor. Through the centuries God has admonished His people to come to prayer with a growing measure of realistic preparation to show that it is not just words that matter.

As we fearfully pray, *Forgive us our debts as we . . .* we need to say with David in Psalm 51:

Have mercy upon me, O God, according to thy lovingkindness; according unto the multitude of thy tender mercies, blot out my transgressions. (v. 1 KJV)

And again with David in Psalm 61:1, 2:

Hear my cry, O God; attend unto my prayer. From the end of the earth will I cry unto thee, when my heart is overwhelmed; lead me to the rock that is higher than I. (KJV)

How comforting to remember as we continue in prayer with all those who have seriously prayed through the centuries that David said in Psalm 103:13, 14, 17:

Like as a father pitieth his children, so the Lord pitieth them that fear him. For he knoweth our frame; he remembereth that we are dust. . . . . But the mercy of the Lord is from everlasting to everlasting upon those who fear him, and his righteousness unto children's children. (KJV)

Lead us not into temptation, but deliver us from the evil one. We are to realize that this is of constant importance, prayer against the darts of the evil one. We need always to be asking for protection and victory in the ongoing battle, which will not be over until the Lord's return.

For Thine is the Kingdom, and the power, and the glory forever. Amen. Praise and adoration of our Father in Heaven conclude this prayer. How great is our need to bow before Him, to be filled with thanksgiving that indeed it is true that the Kingdom is His, that power and glory are His and will continue forever! The victory in that battle with the evil one is to be a final victory— forever. But we are to continue in prayer along with all those who have gone before.

So many instances of prayer for specific events or desires are recorded throughout the Bible to encourage us and to help us remember that these people are like us. We follow in the stream of history with them.

Remember Hannah in 1 Samuel who went often to the Temple to pray for a son and who promised to "lend" her son to the Lord to help Eli in the Temple. Come to the place where she brings her son to Eli and says:

> For this child I prayed; and the Lord hath given me my petition which I asked of him. Therefore also I have lent him to the Lord; as long as he liveth he shall be lent to the Lord. And he worshiped the Lord there.
>
> And Hannah prayed, and said, My heart rejoiceth in the Lord, mine horn is exalted in the Lord; my mouth is enlarged over mine enemies, because I rejoice in thy salvation. There is none holy like the Lord; for there is none beside thee, neither is there any rock like our God. (1 Samuel 1:27—2:2 KJV)

Not only is Hannah's specific prayer answered and her prayer of thanksgiving recorded for us as a help in our worship times, but her son Samuel "grew in favor both with the Lord and also with men." She also was given three other sons and two daughters. This was one of many women honored by God, as she worshiped and honored Him, trusting Him with her petitions, calling upon Him with love and faith in His power and might and with belief in His compassion.

In 2 Kings 20 Hezekiah pleads with God for a longer time to live. So many times in history people have asked for longer life although eternity is ahead and life here has been spoiled by the Fall and the abnormality that has resulted. God is patient and understanding, although He sees what is ahead as well as the devastation of lives and of His creation as they are *now*.

In those days Hezekiah became ill and was at the point of death. The prophet Isaiah son of Amoz went to him and said, "This is what the Lord says: Put your house in order, because you are going to die; you will not recover."

Hezekiah turned his face to the wall and prayed to the Lord, "Remember, O Lord, how I have walked before you faithfully and with wholehearted devotion and have done what is good in your eyes." And Hezekiah wept bitterly.

Before Isaiah had left the middle court, the word of the Lord came to him: "Go back and tell Hezekiah, the leader of my people, 'This is what the Lord, the God of your father David says: I have heard your prayer and seen your tears; I will heal you. On the third day from now you will go up to the temple of the Lord. I will add fifteen years to your life. And I will . . . defend this city for my sake and for the sake of my servant David.'"

Then Isaiah said, "Prepare a poultice of figs." They did so and applied it to the boil, and he recovered. (2 Kings 20:1-7 NIV)

Hannah had cried out to God in prayer. We are told she "wept sore;" she "poured out her soul before the Lord." She was deeply unhappy and intense in her longing for a baby. When she received the answer to her specific request, she was just as fervent in her thanksgiving to God, her Rock—and in her declaration of His holiness. She did not simply take the answer for granted without a deep appreciation and an expression of that appreciation.

Hezekiah had cried out with tears for fifteen more years. As the prophet Isaiah received an answer from the Lord and carried out the Lord's instructions, putting a poultice of figs on Hezekiah's boil, he told Hezekiah that he would have fifteen years added to his life and that God would defend the city for David's sake. This response showed to Isaiah, Hezekiah, and others of God's people through history that history is affected by human beings bringing specific requests to God. God has responded in space/time history in areas that have changed history. Hannah's son Samuel made a tremendous difference in history! And

Hezekiah's added fifteen years also affected history and the people living then.

In Isaiah 37 we have Hezekiah's prayer for victory over Sennacherib. This took place before he was told he would die, but it gives us some idea of how he honored and revered God:

> Hezekiah received the letter from the messengers and read it. Then he went up to the temple of the Lord and spread it out before the Lord. And Hezekiah prayed to the Lord: "O Lord Almighty, God of Israel, enthroned between the cherubim, you alone are God over all the kingdoms of the earth. You have made heaven and earth. Give ear, O Lord, and hear; open your eyes, O Lord, and see; listen to all the words Sennacherib has sent to insult the living God.
>
> "It is true, O Lord, that the Assyrian kings have laid waste all these peoples and their lands. They have thrown their gods into the fire and destroyed them, for they were not gods but only wood and stone, fashioned by human hands. Now, O Lord our God, deliver us from his hand, so that all kingdoms on earth may know that you alone, O Lord, are God." (Isaiah 37:14-20 NIV)

God did answer that prayer for victory and then later answered the plea for another fifteen years of life. Hezekiah's appreciation came in his prayer of thanksgiving in Isaiah 38. These verses could be our own prayer of thanksgiving, a resolution to live constantly closer to the Lord:

> "I cried like a swift or thrush,
>   I moaned like a mourning dove.
> I am troubled; O Lord, come to my aid!"
> But what can I say?
> He has spoken to me,
>   and he himself has done this.
> I will walk humbly all my years
> because of this anguish of my soul.
> Lord, by such things men live;
> and my spirit finds life in them too.
> You restored me to health and let me live.

Surely it was for my benefit
    that I suffered such anguish.
In your love you keep me
    from the pit of destruction;
    you have put all my sins
    behind your back.

(vv. 14-17 NIV)

How many people who have struggled through one or another kind of anguish, despair, distress, heartbreak, or grief have been brought through to a place of rest. Over and over again in the individual lives of God's people one after another has recognized what John Bunyan did as he pictured Pilgrim being given a delectable resting place where after answered prayer he looked back and recognized the protection that had been given and the benefit that had taken place not in spite of, but because of the painful and difficult times. We are with the multitude of the Lord's people when we recognize not only the sheer wonder of His strength having been given us in our weakness and of His grace having been really sufficient in our agonies, but also the value to us, in our own spiritual growth, of the lessons we could not have otherwise learned and digested.

Hezekiah states that what he has discovered in having gone through all the anguish will make him walk humbly. He is not simply excited and elated that he has had an answer to prayer, but with his thanks to the Lord, he vows to walk humbly! May we be as sensitive to the need to notice answers and thank God, but also to be more humble as a result. Quite the opposite from being proud because we have had an answer to prayer. At times we can pray with Hezekiah in this prayer, although centuries later we can identify with his anguish, with his thankfulness, and with his desire for honest humbleness.

There are many prayers one could study and learn from through the many years covered in the Old Testament. So often there is a cry of doubt and despair as in Job, Jeremiah, Ezekiel, and so on. Yet there is mercy and compassion shown to those who cry out to the Creator for help, for strength, for wisdom, for

direction and guidance, century after century, looking forward
with some measure of understanding to the promises of the future
as Job did when he declared:

> "Oh, that my words were recorded,
>   that they were written on a scroll,
> that they were inscribed
>   with an iron tool on lead,
> or engraved in rock forever!
> I know that my Redeemer lives,
> and that in the end he will stand upon the earth.
> And after my skin has been destroyed,
>   yet in my flesh I will see God;
> I myself will see him
>   with my own eyes—I, and not another.
> How my heart yearns within me!"
>
> (Job 19:23-27 NIV)

This is trust in the midst of despair. This has brought praise
to God in the midst of the battle. As we sing, or hear sung, "I
know that my Redeemer liveth" in the midst of Handel's *Messiah*,
we need to remember that Satan was trying to make Job curse
God and turn totally away from him. Prayer can express despair,
as when Jeremiah is in that horrible pit, and yet in the same
prayer, despair can be transformed into praise within a few
minutes:

> I remember my affliction and my wandering,
>   the bitterness and the gall.
> I well remember them,
>   and my soul is downcast within me.
> Yet this I call to mind
>   and therefore I have hope:
> Because of the Lord's great love we are not consumed,
> for his compassions never fail.
>   They are new every morning;
>   great is thy faithfulness.

I say to myself, "The Lord is my portion;
Therefore I will wait for him."

(Lamentations 3:19-24 NIV)

This really is a crystal-clear waterfall of poured out thankfulness and love to the Lord in the midst of the slimy, muddy horror of persecution, unfairness of men, torturous treatment,
rejection, cruelty. In Jeremiah's mind and memory he is going over
the truth of God's faithfulness in the past, and he pours out his
very real adoration and thankfulness to God. People in every
period of history have been enabled by God's grace to do this. The
next bit applies all through history to each one who has been or
is now in a place of distress and agony, longing for wings to fly
away.

The Lord is good to those whose hope is in him,
to the one who seeks him;
it is good to wait quietly for the salvation of the Lord.

(Lamentations 3:25 NIV)

The great cloud of witnesses all know the need of asking
help in waiting quietly and in waiting in a fog for the Lord to give
wisdom and strength for a decision or for the Lord's rescue out
of a place of danger. We are not alone in our experiences of critical need for rescue which only the Lord can give.

Micah in his review of all the distressing things that have
taken place speaks with assurance in honoring God:

But as for me, I watch in hope for the Lord,
I wait for God my Savior;
my God will hear me.
Do not gloat over me, my enemy!
Though I have fallen, I will rise.
Though I sit in darkness,
the Lord will be my light . . .
He will bring me out into the light;
I will see his righteousness.
Then my enemy will see it

and will be covered with shame,
she who said to me, "Where is the Lord your God?" . . .
The day for building your walls will come,
the day for extending your boundaries . . . .
Who is a God like you,
who pardons sin and forgives the transgression
of the remnant of his inheritance?
You do not stay angry forever
    but delight to show mercy.
You will again have compassion on us;
you will tread our sins underfoot
and hurl all our iniquities
    into the depths of the sea.
You will be true to Jacob,
    and show mercy to Abraham,
as you pledged on oath to our fathers
    in days long ago.

                (Micah 7:7, 8, 9b, 10a, 11, 18-20 NIV)

Then in Habakkuk 3:2 Habakkuk prays:

Lord, I have heard of your fame;
    I stand in awe of your deeds, O Lord.
Renew them in our day,
    in our time make them known;
    in wrath remember mercy.

                (NIV)

How we do echo that prayer of Habakkuk's as we fall on our knees or flat on our faces, walk along a dusty road alone, or sit on a rock in a field, walk on the side of a lake or the sea, or make our way up a mountain. *O Lord, please renew Your deeds of old, our very glorious Heavenly Father. In this tragic moment of history show people Your splendor.* Yet do we ask this as Daniel asked for safety in the lions' den and as the three men who approached the fiery furnace with "but if not" in our hearts as well as on our lips? Or do we have selfish reasons or think that our ideas are better than God's?

Habakkuk 3 continues with a review of the frightening power of God through history as Habakkuk experienced it and ends with a declaration of our need to ask God for grace to be true in our own prayer, even as it has been real in the prayer of saints through the ages.

> I heard and my heart pounded,
>   my lips quivered at the sound;
> decay crept into my bones,
>   and my legs trembled.
> Yet I will wait patiently for the day of calamity
>   to come on the nation invading us.
> Though the fig tree does not bud
>   and there are no grapes on the vines,
> though the olive crop fails
> and the fields produce no food,
> though there are no sheep in the pen
>   and no cattle in the stalls,
> yet I will rejoice in the Lord,
> I will be joyful in God my Savior.
> The Sovereign Lord is my strength;
> he makes my feet like the feet of a deer,
> he enables me to go on the heights.
>
> (Habakkuk 3:16-19 NIV)

This displays the kind of trust that can only be shown in the land of the living in a time when things are imperfect. We need to be able to say with a depth of true meaning, *O God, my God, nothing is impossible to You. Please hear my request and answer, but if the answer is no crops, no harvest in the fields, no good health, I will still trust You and will thank You for Your mercy and strength to go on in the midst of hardships, waiting for the future promises to unfold.*

As we come to the advent of the promised Messiah in the history given us in the New Testament, we see that His coming is an answer to prayer, as people had prayed for the Messiah. Mary in her trust and love of God had her troubled questions answered, and she bowed before God, willing for His will to be done in her.

When she comes to tell her cousin Elizabeth her amazing news, Elizabeth says: "Blessed is she who has believed that what the Lord has said to her will be accomplished." Mary's reply is a prayer of praise to the Lord and an acceptance of the truth of what has been told her. She has believed God without doubt.

And Mary said, My soul doth magnify the Lord,
And my spirit hath rejoiced in God my Savior.
For he hath regarded the low estate of his handmaiden;
    for, behold, from henceforth all generations shall call
    me blessed.
For he that is mighty hath done to me great things; and holy
    is his name.
And his mercy is on them that fear him from generation to
    generation.
He hath shown strength with his arm; he hath scattered the
    proud in the imagination of their hearts.
He hath put down the mighty from their seats, and exalted
    them of low degree.
He hath filled the hungry with good things; and the rich he
    hath sent empty away.
He hath helped his servant, Israel, in remembrance of
    his mercy;
As he spoke to our fathers, to Abraham, and to his
    seed forever.

(Luke 1:46-55 KJV)

Jesus, as He later went about His teaching, making clear who He was and healing the sick, "often withdrew to lonely places and prayed." Jesus, as Second Person of the Trinity, the Son of God, called upon His Father and spent time in prayer, often going to the hills or a place away from the press of crowds.

One of those days Jesus went out to a mountainside to pray, and spent the night praying to God. When morning came, he called his disciples to him and chose twelve of them, whom he also designated apostles. (Luke 6:12 NIV)

Right after the feeding of the five thousand:

Straightway Jesus constrained his disciples to get into a ship, and to go before him unto the other side, while he sent the multitudes away. And when he had sent the multitudes away, he went up into a mountain apart to pray: and when the evening was come, he was there alone. (Matthew 14:22, 23 KJV)

And it came to pass, as he was alone praying, his disciples were with him: and he asked them, saying, Whom say the people that I am? (Luke 9:18 KJV)

And it came to pass, that, as he was praying in a certain place, when he ceased, one of his disciples said unto him, Lord, teach us to pray, as John also taught his disciples. (Luke 11:1 KJV)

This is when Jesus gave them the prayer: "Our Father which art in heaven, hallowed be thy name. . . ." When the disciples asked Jesus for help in praying, it came as He was constantly and consistently in prayer. Jesus never did anything to simply entertain. When He healed someone, it was out of compassion for that person, as well as a demonstration or evidence of who He was. When He talked and carefully explained the truth to the woman at the well, He was treating her mind and understanding with respect, as well as telling her of her sin and her need of a Savior. When He prayed, Jesus was really praying to His Father in Heaven. God the Son was praying to God the Father through the power of the Holy Spirit. We do not know what Jesus prayed in those private times. We do know that it mattered . . . it mattered that the Son stay in communication with the Father, His Father in a unique way, the Father of the only begotten Son. But "Our Father which art in heaven . . ." has been given to each of us who comes truly believing, asking forgiveness for our sins, accepting Christ's death in our place, and becoming a child of God. Nothing is more moving than being able to say, "Our Father," and know that Jesus has accepted us into the family by teaching that the "our" is not presumptuous or too familiar with the Creator of the universe, the holy perfect God. However, this is not a prayer to be rattled off thoughtlessly by those who do not believe and who can not sincerely join in. It can then become flippant, disrespectful, even blasphemous.

When Jesus begins to tell the disciples He is going to leave them (John 16:17), that in a little while they will not be seeing Him, they are puzzled. In the rest of that chapter, Jesus explains to them and to us. This is in the context of His teaching more about prayer. From now on they and all since that time are to pray to the Father in Jesus' name.

> And in that day ye shall ask me nothing. Verily, verily, I say unto you, Whatsoever ye shall ask the Father in my name, he will give it you. Hitherto have ye asked nothing in my name: ask, and ye shall receive, that your joy may be full. (John 16:23, 24 KJV)

Then in chapter 17 we have Jesus' prayer for the apostles and for all believers. Do read it all as I will quote just a few verses here.

> These words spake Jesus, and lifted up his eyes to heaven, and said, Father, the hour is come; glorify thy Son, that thy Son may also glorify thee: As thou hast given him power over all flesh, that he should give eternal life to as many as thou hast given him. And this is life eternal, that they might know thee the only true God, and Jesus Christ, whom thou hast sent. I have glorified thee on the earth: I have finished the work which thou gavest me to do. And now, O Father, glorify thou me with thine own self with the glory which I had with thee before the world was. I have manifested thy name unto the men which thou gavest me out of the world: thine they were, and thou gavest them me; and they have kept thy word. . . .
> They are not of the world, even as I am not of the world. Sanctify them through thy truth: thy word is truth. As thou hast sent me into the world, even so have I also sent them into the world. And for their sakes I sanctify myself, that they also might be sanctified through the truth. Neither pray I for these

alone, but for them also which shall believe on me through their word; That they all may be one; as thou, Father, art in me, and I in thee, that they also may be one in us: that the world may believe that thou hast sent me. . . .

O righteous Father, the world hath not known thee: but I have known thee, and these have known that thou hast sent me. And I have declared unto them thy name, and will declare it: that the love wherewith thou hast loved me may be in them, and I in them. (vv. 1-6, 16-21, 25, 26 KJV)

This prayer of Jesus to His Father for those who are believers has been a fabulous encouragement through the centuries to all who are alone in deserts, mountains, or prisons, as well as to those who are in stress of one sort or another. Jesus our Shepherd has said He loves us. He prays for our sanctification. He also prays in verse 24 that we will see His glory. This prayer pours out the love of God for us and the faithfulness of the Trinity in opening the way to the glory ahead. In Hebrews 7 Christ is likened to Melchizedek, whom Abraham gave his tithe to, called "King of Peace." But unlike human priests, Jesus lives forever, always interceding. This is truly prayer without ceasing by the infinite One who is able to pray always, to pray continually, to pray without ceasing.

Now there have been many of those priests, since death prevented them from continuing in office; but because Jesus lives forever, he has a permanent priesthood. Therefore he is able to save completely those who come to God through him, because he always lives to intercede for them.

Such a high priest meets our need—one who is holy, blameless, pure, set apart from sinners, exalted above the heavens. Unlike the other high priests, he does not need to offer sacrifices day after day, first for his own sins, and then for the sins of the people. He sacrificed for their sins once for all when he offered himself. For the law appoints as high priests men who are weak; but the oath, which came after the law, appointed the Son, who has been made perfect forever. (Hebrews 7:23-28 NIV)

Continuity of prayer throughout history? The most thrilling continuity is Christ's always interceding for us. In our finiteness and weakness, in our limitedness and sinfulness, we are to have *His faithful prayer* as our example—but also as our comfort!

We have further assurance of continuity of help as we wait for future glory in the midst of sufferings, tribulations, shocks, and disappointments.

I consider that our present sufferings are not worth comparing with the glory that will be revealed in us. The creation waits in eager expectation for the sons of God to be revealed.

In the same way, the Spirit helps us in our weakness. We do not know what we ought to pray for, but the Spirit himself intercedes for us with groans that words cannot express. And he who searches our hearts knows the mind of the Spirit, because the Spirit intercedes for the saints in accordance with God's will. (Romans 8:18, 19, 26, 27 NIV)

How amazing is God's grace! How dazzling is his understanding of our need! His astonishing provision in the midst of the ongoing attacks of Satan and the ongoing troubles we have in this abnormal world since the Fall show us He truly understands our temptations. There are temptations to doubt, to complain, to fantasize as to how we might arrange history or someone's life or our own life if we had the power. As we contemplate the intercession of Christ, the intercession of the Holy Spirit for us without ceasing, it is like seeing a sudden stunning view of a sea or lake at sunset when the sky is gray. Suddenly there is a break in the clouds, and a streak of tangerine red-orange ripples the water before we look up to see where it comes from in the sky!

The holy Father, First Person of the Trinity, receiving intercession by Jesus Christ our Savior, the Second Person of the Trinity, and by the Holy Spirit who dwells in us, Third Person of the Trinity, in the midst of such weakness that we could not find strength, nor could we persist in keeping on—hears the intercession in our behalf!

We come to the Garden of Gethsemane and approach Christ's time of greatest agony in prayer. He had said to Peter and the two sons of Zebedee that He was going a little distance from them to pray. Then He said to them, "My soul is overwhelmed with sorrow to the point of death. Stay here and keep watch with me" (Matthew 26:38 KJV). Watch! Watch and pray! Isn't this exactly what we are told to be doing as we ask, "Thy Kingdom come, Thy will be done"? Watch and pray for the return of the Lord Jesus? Are we told not to sleep?

> Going a little farther, he fell with his face to the ground and prayed, "My Father, if it is possible, may this cup be taken from me. Yet not as I will, but as you will."
>
> Then he returned to his disciples and found them sleeping. "Could you men not keep watch with me for one hour?" he asked Peter. "Watch and pray so that you will not fall into temptation. The spirit is willing, but the body is weak."
>
> He went away a second time and prayed, "My Father, if it is not possible for this cup to be taken away unless I drink it, may your will be done."
>
> When he came back, he again found them sleeping, because their eyes were heavy. So he left them and went away once more and prayed the third time, saying the same thing. (Matthew 26:39-44 NIV)

Think about it again. Jesus was not praying falsely, simply as a script reading. Jesus was truly praying, pleading with His Father to remove that awful cup, the cup of death and torture, but more than anything, the cup of separation and aloneness, separation from the Trinity for the first and only time in all eternity. His prayer was a question that only He had the right to really ask. It was a question so many people ask: "Isn't there another way?" "There must be many ways to come to God." No, the answer was unmistakably clear. There is no other way given whereby sinful people can be saved. There is only one way. The Lamb must die, and the blood of the Lamb does cleanse us from sin.

Jesus understands what it is to have a prayer not answered, the fulfillment of a longing, a deep request. Had He not been given that most sorrowful answer, and had He NOT bowed before it and prayed to the Father, "Thy will be done," then not one of us could be saved; not one of us could come to God in prayer; not one of us could have the hope of eternal life in new bodies. The unanswered request of Jesus fulfilled His purpose in coming; the unanswered plea has given us life.

After Jesus' resurrection, He could show to the disciples what His resurrected body was like, to add to the excitement and glory of their hope and ours of future resurrection. But just before ascending to the Father, Jesus prayed with them for a last time as He lifted up his hands and blessed them.

As we go on in the book of the Acts of the Apostles, we find that there is no time when the continuity of prayer through the ages is cut off. Yes, there is the promised intercession of Jesus and of the Holy Spirit which has always continued, but also the believers were taught to continue praying as Jesus had taught them and also to intercede for others.

The early church met to praise God together, to break bread and have communion, to pray, and to include new believers who were being added as truth was made known and the eyes of their understanding were opened.

In Paul's letter to the Corinthians he recounts a time when he (or another) had an amazing experience of being caught up into Paradise where he heard things that could not be told. He speaks of this as something he would not glory in—he would not brag about it or continue giving an excited account about it—but rather he would tell about his weaknesses. Then he tells of his asking, pleading three times for a change in what he feels to be the last straw.

> To keep me from becoming conceited because of these surpassingly great revelations, there was given me a thorn in my flesh, a messenger of Satan, to torment me. Three times I pleaded with the Lord to take it away from me. But he said to me, "My grace is sufficient for you, for my power is made perfect in weakness." [The *King James Version* has: "my strength is made perfect in weakness."] Therefore I will boast all the more gladly about my weaknesses, so that Christ's power [God's strength] may rest on me. That is why, for Christ's sake, I delight in weaknesses, in insults, in hardships, in persecutions,

in difficulties. For when I am weak, then I am strong. (2 Corinthians 12:7-10 NIV)

Oh yes, Paul urges prayer, intercession for each other among the believers, and he expects answers and changes in history, but he truly understands the astonishing answer of the sufficient grace being given to enable us to continue in a very difficult circumstance which does not change. He magnificently understands the tremendous privilege that we have only in this life, only in suffering, only in disappointment of the reality of the strength of God, the power of Christ, being given us to accomplish what would be impossible in any other way. We could not do it ourselves no matter how miraculously our thorn or sickness was healed or our longing was fulfilled. Paul's trust of God is in the same stream of continuity as Micah's when Micah prayed and declared his trust:

> But as for me, I watch in hope for the Lord,
> I wait for God my Savior;
> my God will hear me.
> Do not gloat over me, my enemy!
> Though I have fallen, I will rise.
> Though I sit in darkness,
> the Lord will be my light.
>
> (Micah 7:7, 8 NIV)

We have all eternity to praise God in perfect bodies, in perfect surroundings, with beauty beyond our imagination now. We have only a very short time to make known to our Heavenly Father, our Savior and Shepherd, the Holy Spirit, our trust and love. Yes, we are to pray, knowing that nothing is too hard for Him, nothing is impossible for Him to do for us. But we join the martyrs through the centuries in tiny opportunities, or in major ones, to show the reality of our love for God.

As Paul prays for the Ephesians, we can pray for our family members, for our dearest friends, for those for whom the Lord gives us special responsibility, for people He brings to us to care for:

For this reason I kneel before the Father, from whom his whole family in heaven and on earth derives its name. I pray that out of his glorious riches he may strengthen you with power through his Spirit in your inner being, so that Christ may dwell in your hearts through faith. And I pray that you, being rooted and established in love, may have power, together with all the saints, to grasp how wide and long and high and deep is the love of Christ, and to know this love that surpasses knowledge—that you may be filled to the measure of all the fullness of God.

Now to him who is able to do immeasurably more than all we ask or imagine, according to his power that is at work within us, to him be glory in the church and in Christ Jesus throughout all generations, for ever and ever! Amen." (Ephesians 3:14-20 NIV)

Paul's prayer is a magnificent prayer for us to pray with the names of our beloved people, people we long to make these requests for in earnest. Of course we may come in our own wording, but as we kneel before the Father in secret whether in the woods or fields, in a room, a prison, or a park, or as we "kneel" within our minds in hidden prayer with people milling around us, this prayer of Paul's joins us with those who have prayed with this glorious context through the centuries.

Ephesians ends with the command to put on the armor of God in order to take a stand against the devil's schemes. The final portion of that admonition is:

And pray in the Spirit on all occasions with all kinds of prayer and requests. With this in mind, be alert and always keep on praying for all the saints. Pray also for me, that whenever I open my mouth, words may be given me so that I will fearlessly make known the mystery of the gospel, for which I am an ambassador in chains. Pray that I may declare it fearlessly, as I should. (Ephesians 6:18-20 NIV)

No matter how many times we read this, it should spur us on to DOING it more completely than we have before. The direct order is to pray always, suggesting that prayer can include a great variety of requests for one's own needs, indeed, but be for all saints as well. We are to be alert to the need to intercede for others. There were many different kinds of needs in that early church, from slaves in their work to very highly placed people. There would have been artists, soldiers, farmers, and weavers of cloth. As Paul asks for prayer for the right words, he is teaching us that prayer of intercession is needed, not only that those speaking or writing may be given strength to go on, but also that the content of the message given through them would be God's. He is not asking prayer for an easier time or that his chains might be cut off, but for help in making known what he needs to make known. Obviously we are being taught that prayer, interceding for each other, will bring results.

When we finally find out what took place in history because of a continuity of prayer we will discover whose faithfulness made astounding differences in individual lives or in the events of nations.

As Paul and Timothy write to the saints in Philippi, that epistle begins with prayer: "I thank my God every time I remember you." (Of whom can we say that? And do we spend time thanking God *directly* for some for whom we are really thankful?)

In all my prayers for all of you I always pray with joy because of your partnership in the gospel from the first day until now, being confident of this, that he who began a good work in you will carry it on to completion until the day of Christ Jesus. (Philippians 1:4-6 NIV)

Paul goes on to pray that their love may abound more and more in knowledge and depth of insight. However, he also speaks of the fact that people know that he is in chains for Christ and that other believers are encouraged because of that! Again, it is not that he must be released and have everything go well in order to have people be encouraged. Nevertheless, he asks that they pray on and expects that through their prayers he will be delivered, although he feels that the important thing is to pray that he will have *courage* so that whether by life or by death, Christ will be exalted.

Paul's prayer instruction to the Philippians should be carefully noted. Too often throughout history worry has characterized God's people. What word fits what happens to you, to me, when someone we love is in a dangerous place—an operating room, intensive care, playing some dangerous sport, in a fighter plane or a tank in a war, on a solo sail across uncharted seas, mountain trekking, fighting a forest fire, tending a very sick baby, in a landslide, flood, or avalanche? Is it fear, dread, terror, anxiety, tension, nervousness, suspense, distress? It is 3:00 A.M. and we toss in bed, worrying about lack of money to pay bills, fearing that a child of ours may not make it, anxious about possible unfairness of judges in a competition—whether violin or figure skating, whether art or skiing. We twist and turn and imagine results that stir our emotions, and sleep departs from us!

What to do?

> Rejoice in the Lord always. I will say it again: Rejoice! Let your gentleness be evident to all. The Lord is near. Do not be anxious about anything, but in everything, by prayer and petition, with thanksgiving, present your requests to God. And the peace of God, which transcends all understanding, will [keep] guard your hearts and your minds in Christ Jesus. (Philippians 4:4-7 NIV)

We are not told to "stop worrying." "Stop twisting and turning." "Everything will be fine." "Go to sleep." We are given very practical help. With thanksgiving, we are to pray. What are we thankful for? Not the thing we are worrying about. We are to review in our memories, as Jeremiah did in the slimy pit, the things God has done that are so marvelous. We are to recall in our minds what God has told of His diverse works in history. We are to think of Gideon, of Joshua, of David standing before Goliath, of Jesus causing the waves to calm. We are to verbalize our thankfulness that God is so great. We then need to go on with thankfulness for what God has done in our own past history and in the lives of people we have prayed for.

This takes time. It is not simply a sentence; it is to be a chapter of real review and recognition of the greatness and kindness of our Father and of the many things He has provided for us and His present availability. We offer thanksgiving that He has told us we may bring our requests. We are now in a changed place. That is, we are calmed to a place of making the requests for the immediate help we need within ourselves or in a situation many miles away—across mountains, lakes, rivers, seas. Our infinite God is able to respond, and we are to trust His response. But we are to take the time to pray in the manner we are given. After that the peace which is beyond our understanding fills us. In verse 9 Paul says:

> Whatever you have learned or received or heard from me, or seen in me—put it into practice. And the God of peace will be with you.

Turning to the Lord in prayer for help and interceding for those we are anxious for is not a casual or infrequent thing, not if we are going to put into practice what those in the continuity of Scriptural teaching have tried to follow.

In the beginning of Colossians, Paul prays a prayer that has been prayed through centuries for beloved children, beloved friends, families, and fellow believers. Through many, many years I personally have prayed this prayer as Paul prayed for those whose faith he had heard of in Colossae. It outlines what we need to pray—for growth in our own lives as well as in the lives of those whom we love. The need is NOT "dated"!

> For this cause we also, since the day we heard it, do not cease to pray for you, and to desire that ye might be filled with the knowledge of his will in all wisdom and spiritual understanding: That ye might walk worthy of the Lord unto all pleasing, being fruitful in every good work, and increasing in the knowledge of God; Strengthened with all might, according to his glorious power, unto all patience and longsuffering with joyfulness; Giving thanks unto the Father, which hath made us meet to be partakers of the inheritance of the saints in light;

who hath delivered us from the power of darkness, and hath translated us into the kingdom of his dear Son. (Colossians 1:9-13 KJV)

It is almost startling that the phrase, "I do not cease to pray," is so central. This continues the urging to keep on praying, to pray in the midst of all else throughout the days of life. Although we can be comforted and reassured that Jesus is interceding for us, we are meant to follow Paul's example and to always pray for fruitful lives, for ourselves and for the ones we love. This kind of continued faithfulness is meant to make a difference in many areas of history.

Epaphras, who is one of you . . . saluteth you, always laboring fervently for you in prayers, that ye may stand perfect and complete in all the will of God. (Colossians 4:12 KJV)

In this verse not only is the word *always* used, but so is *labor*. Prayer is *work!* Fervent prayer is not lackadaisical murmuring while thinking about something else, but a real work. As someone takes prayer as the main work for however much time in a day, it is labor, work, toil. In Hebrews 11:6 we gain further understanding of the same reality:

But without faith it is impossible to please him; for he that cometh to God must believe that he is, and that he is a rewarder of them that diligently seek him. (KJV)

We have considered before that the central need is to believe that God is, that God exists. But here the writer is saying that there must be faith and trust that God will respond, reply, answer those who sincerely, diligently call out to Him. In the rest of this chapter is a list of people who actually did do that in history through centuries. That list includes those for whom lions' mouths were shut, those for whom the fiery furnace did not burn, and those who suffered martyrdom and torture. God says He is not ashamed to be called their God.

Why?

But now they desire a better country, that is, an heavenly; wherefore, God is not ashamed to be called their God; for he hath prepared for them a city. (Hebrews 11:16 KJV)

As our Heavenly Father looks over all of space and time, over all of the ages of history, over all the centuries of people, over all the tribes and nations and kindreds and tongues, He alone knows the total sinfulness of their sin and its results. He alone knows what is ahead based on the heavy price paid for the atonement for sin. He also is the only One who knows what the indescribable glory ahead consists of. He is not ashamed to be called our God when the answer is, "My grace is sufficient for thee; My strength is made perfect in weakness," and we go on with no change in the circumstances that are so hard for us. He also is not ashamed to be called the God of our sister or brother, our son or our daughter, our friend or our fellow worker when the answer to that one's prayer is an exciting change in a difficulty or an amazing success that seemed an impossibility.

The criteria of answered prayer, as has been said before, are not a complete succession of things, events, improved human relationships, perfect scores in exams or competitions, but a balance of the two kinds of answers. It was so when the early Christians prayed for Stephen as he was being stoned, and he died. It was so when the early Christians prayed for Paul, and he lived through the stoning and also later was restored to them from prison.

God's love is not to be spoken of only in connection with things that have gone well, prayer that has brought someone through a fire alive, or has brought someone out of a cell. Paul tells of having learned to be content in all circumstances. He has learned to be abased—that is, to be persecuted, hungry, miserable, and poor—and to abound—that is to really experience a period of time in a measure of luxury. We are to be versatile, to be sensitive to what the Lord gives us in leading as we ask for His guidance. He places us in the circles of people, in the geographic areas of the world, in mountains or by the sea, in woods or in deserts, for a purpose—for the people we are meant to pray for because we come to know them, not just speak to them or hand them leaflets! We are to be ready to be abased or to abound in a variety of ways in different periods of our lives, in vastly different locations of the world, or in a seemingly never-changing rut. We cannot intercede fervently and very personally for people we do not know exist. God brings people to us in one way or another for us to have a responsibility for, in intercession, just as thoroughly as He brings some to us we are to give a cup of cold water to, or to help as a Good Samaritan in some critical need. We need to be aware of a thirsty person to draw water for and hand a glass to, to make a sandwich for and prepare on a plate, to be hospitable to, or to rescue from a fall. We can't do such things in our imaginations and feel comfortable about how kind we would be "if only . . ."! Just so in careful prayer for people, in serious intercession for others, prayer can be in secret, but we need to *know people*, personally or through others.

Wherever you are now, wherever I am now, there is someone whose need has been made known to us by telephone, by letter, by a knock on the door, by sitting beside someone on a bus or a plane, by hearing an ambulance go by. We also have people we know half the world away who suddenly come into our minds, though we are not sure what is going on. It is an important thing to pray for them immediately. If you or I are in a hospital waiting for an operation or waiting for someone else to be operated on, we might be the only one praying for some other person in the room, a stranger, whether nurse or patient! Of course, I am talking about silent prayer, in our minds, for people we may be close to in order to intercede—in a fish market or on the sidewalk!

Truth was meant to be relayed from generation to generation. God makes it clear in Deuteronomy 6 that parents are to tell their children to love the Lord their God with all their hearts and souls and all their strength. Questions are to be answered as children ask them that they may know the history of what God has done through the ages before. In 7:9 we are told that God is a faithful God, keeping His covenant of love to a thousand generations of those who love Him and keep His commands. But these thousand generations are meant to hear all about God's marvelous creation and the history of His great works from their fathers and mothers, uncles and aunts. Truth is meant to be relayed and *was* meant to be relayed through the centuries.

Just so, prayer was meant to be faithfully made for the next generation, and the next and the next.

Intercession was meant to be a relay.

Each new generation was meant to have faithful grandparents, great-grandparents, parents, uncles, aunts—all interceding for them. In the relay of passing truth to the next generation, God alone would be able to trace exactly who dropped the stick, so to speak, in the handing down of truth! In this relay of intercession, we are responsible to pray faithfully for the next generations, one by one, specific children of our own or children of others. We each are to be very careful to be a part of the continuity of prayer for the next generation. We should also thank God for those whose prayer affected us before we were ever born.

You, I, each one of us who is a child of the living God through faith in Christ our Savior is affected, is different, because of prayer. I believe we will discover in Heaven that much of what we have done, or what we have come to understand, is the result of prayer on the part of people or a person who faithfully prayed for us when we were still among the next generation.

Dropping the stick in these crucial relays has made a difference in history! This is not just a fanciful illustration; this relay is commanded in the whole teaching of prayer without ceasing, always praying for one another, interceding for the saints. The relay of truth, and the relay of intercession, is an imperative for your life and mine for present and future history!

One of my early memories as a very little girl in China was of walking along the paths of the China Inland Mission property in Shanghai. It was morning and the time when Dr. Hoste, the director of the mission (who followed Hudson Taylor), took his four hours daily of prayer for the mission, praying individually for every missionary in each province and for their children by name. I was a tiny four-year-old as I looked up to his height of about six feet. "Hello," I said, preparing to accompany him along those paths through shrubs and trees.

"Hello, my dear, you may walk with me, but you must not talk. I am praying, you see." He then continued to pray and walk. He prayed aloud and was very reverent in honoring God as well as earnest in naming people and their needs. I felt so pleased and excited when he prayed for Wenchow, my city, and all the missionaries there whom I knew, then for my mother and father, for Janet and Elsa—my sisters in Cheefoo School—and for Edith!

Oh, he prayed for me! I thought delightedly. *I guess I do matter.* I discovered when I got older that Dr. Hoste felt his most important work as director of the mission was to pray for each missionary and each child daily. He felt that intercessory responsibility was his first responsibility, coming before any kind of administrative work.

Each of us has SOME people for whom we are the intercessors, and each of us has some children for whom we need to pick up the stick in the relay of intercession.

Our finiteness and limitedness does not relieve us of the responsibility for some of those in this generation and the next in the relay of intercession. It is of utmost importance.

EIGHT

Continuity of Prayer Through Centuries

Part Two

You do remember that as Malachi wrote the closing portion of the Old Testament the Lord gave him a paragraph which has helped people of every generation. It is a fact that we need to remember as we read past history, as we live in the present period of time, and as we reread looking forward to the future, not only of our own lifetime, but the lifetime of all those who will be living when Jesus comes back again. God has said in Malachi 3:14-17 (in reply to people asking what they have said against God):

"You have said, 'It is futile to serve God. What did we gain by carrying out his requirements and going about like mourners before the Lord Almighty? But now we call the arrogant blessed. Certainly the evildoers prosper, and even those who challenge God escape.'"

Then those who feared the Lord talked with each other, and the Lord listened and heard. A scroll of remembrance was written in his presence concerning those who feared the Lord and honored his name.

"They will be mine," says the Lord Almighty, "in the day when I make up my treasured possession [my jewels]. I will spare them, just as in compassion a man spares his son who serves him. And you will again see the distinction between the righteous and the wicked, between those who serve God and those who do not." (NIV)

How reassuring as well as thrilling to think that all those centuries ago this stunning promise of the most holy God Almighty who keeps His promises pointed ahead to a time that we and they wait for! How exciting it should be, giving us real bubbles of joy inside, to know we really are joined with God's people, the ones He calls "My jewels" and My "treasured possession." The outcome of the centuries of people praying with trust in their Creator God, having deep faith in their Redeemer, from Abel on, from Job on, from Abraham on, from David on, from Peter on, from Hannah and Lydia on—the outcome is *sure*. God says the distinction will be seen between those who serve Him and those who do not.

A century ago a children's hymn was written that became a loving memory to many little children of believing parents as it was sung to them along with prayer at bedtime. Inspired by this verse in Malachi, two men, William O. Cushing (1823-1902) and George Fredrick Root (1820-1895), wrote the hymn.

When He cometh, when He cometh To make up His jewels,
All His jewels, precious jewels, His loved and His own.

(Chorus)

Like the stars of the morning, His bright crown adorning,
They shall shine in their beauty, Bright gems for His crown.
 Amen

Little children, little children Who love their Redeemer,
Are the jewels, precious jewels, His loved and His own.

As Malachi ends in the few short verses of chapter 4, the second verse tells all generations, "But for you who revere my name, the sun of righteousness will rise with healing in its wings." The last verse speaks of Elijah's coming to preach in the future: "He will turn the hearts of the fathers to their children, and the hearts of the children to their fathers."

Whether we are talking of a relay of truth or a relay of intercession, we are also talking of generation following generation.

We are talking of mothers and fathers, grandparents, aunts and uncles carefully teaching a basic understanding, a worldview based on the existence of the Creator. We are praying for, praying with the next generation, and we are teaching them to pray. Past, present, and future history is made up of people. Simplistic remark? Obvious? Perhaps, but we need to remind ourselves that although prayer is a very personal and private communication with God, pouring out our repentance and sorrow for sin, it is also to be a constant connection with God, an unbroken communication, a means of receiving assurance as to how to go on in this next hour in our work, and our means of receiving guidance. Prayer is also to be our means of receiving sufficient grace and strength to do what we are being guided to do. This reality is to be handed to the next generation, not to end when we die.

In Deuteronomy 4, right after God had told Moses He would not answer his prayer to go over Jordan but that Joshua would be the leader, God goes on to make clear that there are differences for those who cleave to the Lord.

What other nation is so great as to have their gods near them the way the Lord our God is near us whenever we pray to him? And what other nation is so great as to have such righteous decrees and laws as this body of laws I am setting before you today? Only be careful, and watch yourselves closely so that you do not forget the things your eyes have seen or let them slip from your heart as long as you live. Teach them to your children and to their children after them. (Deuteronomy 4:7-9 NIV)

The emphasis is on handing the knowledge of what has happened in history down to the children, on being certain that the next generation will have by word of mouth the flaming reality of what their parents' eyes have seen of the great works of the mighty God. How could they forget the Red Sea rolling back? Or the blazing mountain as Moses was up there with God? But we know they did let it slip from their hearts. This handing down of true facts is to insure love, worship, awe, and excitement for the wonders God had done and to encourage prayer that it might go on continually through the ages.

You remember when God told Joshua to select twelve men from among the twelve tribes and to have each one take up a stone from the middle of Jordan, where they had miraculously passed over that night, and to put it where they were going to stay for the night on the other shore? The purpose of that memorial was that God's answer would not be forgotten. It was for the children, the next generation. God strongly commanded the children to be continually reminded. There was to be no gap between generations. A new generation who would be far removed from living through agony of struggle, prayer for a solution, fasting and prayer for deliverance of one sort or another, was not to grow up and go on with a blindness as to the reality of what their parents had discovered concerning the trustworthiness of God and His continued availability.

> "In the future when your children ask you, 'What do these stones mean?' tell them that the flow of the Jordan was cut off before the ark of the covenant of the Lord. When it crossed the Jordan, the waters of the Jordan were cut off. These stones are to be a memorial to the people of Israel forever." (Joshua 4:6, 7 NIV)

Joshua speaks to the people after the stones had been set up, giving the message God had given him, very clearly:

> "In the future when your descendants ask their fathers, 'What do these stones mean?' tell them, 'Israel crossed the Jordan on dry ground.' For the Lord your God dried up the Jordan before you until you had crossed over. The Lord your God did to the Jordan just what he had done to the Red Sea when he dried it up before us until we had crossed over. He did this so that all the peoples of the earth might know that the hand of the Lord is powerful and so that you might always fear the Lord your God." (Joshua 4:21-24 NIV)

The blessing given in Psalm 128 is a family blessing for a person who "fears the Lord" and who "walks in his ways." This person works hard and will "eat the fruit of his labor." The wife will be "fruitful," which, it seems to me, indicates not only having children physically, but teaching those children, being an example to them so that they are full of the important knowledge of the Lord. The prayer for blessing at the end is that the Lord will bless the person all the days of his life and that he will see his children's children.

Now don't begin to grumble and feel left out because in this fallen world you personally don't have physical children. We are each meant to have spiritual children, people we have been spiritual parents for, children or young people we have adopted to pray for and care for, teach and love, taking the place of parents who have died or who have abandoned their children. Oh yes, some of us have both kinds of children, but each *one* of us has a responsibility for some specific children of the next generation, and maybe the next one after that! There is a special blessing that belongs to the ones who *are* faithful in prayer in this way. Peace be upon them all.

Jesus received little children and prayed for them.

Then little children were brought to Jesus for him to place his hands on them and pray for them. But the disciples rebuked those who brought them.

Jesus said, "Let the little children come to me, and do not hinder them, for the kingdom of heaven belongs to such as these." When he had placed his hands on them, he went on from there. (Matthew 19:13, 14 NIV)

As Jesus is our example in prayer, as well as in all His life, here He shows us how gentle we are to be in receiving children, not brushing them away as without importance. The importance of praying for and with the next generation, the value of human beings of a very young age, is sharply demonstrated here as Jesus gives an example to His disciples and to us.

We are commanded that a part of our growing Christian life is openness to others, that is, hospitality. Now hospitality is often thought of as serving a meal in one's house, or in a field, or in a tent, or in a row boat! We think of hospitality as giving some person in our own "circle" a warm welcome. As with everything we are to do, finiteness makes it impossible to invite the whole city, or town, or village into our space, but we are to include some.

Now as we think of intercession and consider the responsibility to intercede for a wider family of the next generation, it seems to me good to think of prayer as another form of hospitality. Prayer takes time and energy and is a matter of choice. As we each take a notebook, or a piece of cardboard, or a small sketch book and begin writing down the names of those for whom we want to intercede (this is just between ourselves and the Lord), we will soon discover how much choice is involved, and we will worship more deeply our infinite Intercessor, the Lord Jesus Christ who is not limited and does not have to choose which one to pray for today. Time does not suddenly slip away from Him.

That day as He took the little children on His lap and prayed for them, he did not have every child in the world on his lap, because at that time He was truly man, as well as truly God. He then could show us, as our example, how we are to give hospitality in prayer to the ones who come to us, into our minds or into our homes.

Who are children?

Who are the next generation?

One dictionary definition is that it is someone between infancy and youth! In other words it is a period of time in everyone's life! A generation is also a period of time; some speak of twenty years, others may take a different measure. At any rate, there are many children who need help because they have no loving parent to help them. Also there are many children who need prayer, and some need to be a part of our own prayer day by day.

However, as parents or adoptive parents, we call people our children for a lot longer than twenty years! It is a terrible thing to disown a child. It is shattering for child and parents. The parent-child relationship does not have a cut-off time. "From now on," someone says solemnly, "you are my son. I will be faithful in prayer for you and will provide whatever I can otherwise in the midst of my limitations!" That is a Christian's promise in adoption.

But there is another answer to the question, "Who are children?" found in Romans 8:16, 17.

> The Spirit himself testifies with our spirit that we are God's children. Now if we are children, then we are heirs—heirs of God and co-heirs with Christ, if indeed we share in his sufferings in order that we may also share in his glory. (NIV)

Then in Galatians Paul speaks of the believers as his children, the ones he led to the Lord. "My dear children, for whom I am again in the pains of childbirth until Christ is formed in you" (Galatians 4:19 NIV). These Galatians are people Paul is obviously praying for very earnestly, unsure whether they are really showing evidence of their Christian growth.

And in verse 28:

> Now we, brethren, as Isaac was, are the children of promise. (KJV)

The point here is that it is imperative to pray for the next generation. The next generation includes both meanings of the word *children*. In our prayer lists, we need to intercede for both kinds of children, children we have special responsibility for in our family life and the children of the Lord's family whom we believe have been born again.

Had all the people who should have been interceding for the next generation really been faithful, had true hospitality been given in intercession through the ages for the children coming along, there would have been an enormously different history, it would seem.

However, thank God there were always some who were faithful in intercession in every period of history. Had there not been, we would not be the ones involved in this relay. Had no one been faithful in spite of enormous persecution, torture, and temptation, the Word of God would not have been painstakingly written and passed on; people would not have known the truth to pass on. Had there not been faithful intercessors to pray for the next generation of believers, of children, neither you nor I would be looking forward to eternal life. Paul in the book of Romans is speaking of making the truth of the gospel known to Gentiles, but notice in chapter 10:1, 2:

> Brethren, my heart's desire and prayer to God for Israel is, that they might be saved. For I bear them record that they have a zeal for God, but not according to knowledge. (KJV)

This striking combination of Paul's preaching to the Gentiles, yet yearning for his own people, the Jews, to be saved, shows that in his longing for them he puts prayer for their salvation as primary. Oh yes, he does go on his missionary journey; he makes known, with words spoken in audible voice, the truth at Mars Hill; he faces dangers and persecutions by preaching under terrible circumstances, but he does it with prayer. Generations of believers have followed Paul and Peter, Timothy and his mother and grandmother; generations have been prayed for, as well as having been taught to pray, one by one, for the next generation.

Thy Kingdom come, we pray.

> Then the angel showed me the river of the water of life, as clear as crystal, flowing from the throne of God and of the Lamb down the middle of the street of the city. On each side of the river stood the tree of life, bearing twelve crops of fruit, yielding its fruit every month. And the leaves of the tree are for the healing of the nations. No longer will there be any curse. The throne of God and of the Lamb will be in the city, and his servants will serve him. They will see his face, and his name will be on their foreheads. There will be no more night. They will not need the light of a lamp or the light of the sun, for the Lord God will give them light. And they will reign forever and ever.
>
> The angel said to me, "These words are trustworthy and true. The Lord, the God of the spirits of the prophets, sent his angel to show his servants the things that must soon take place." (Revelation 22:1-6 NIV)

Ever since Jesus taught His disciples the Lord's prayer, there has been a succession of generations, faithfully praying for *this* marvelous Kingdom to come, praying for the second coming of the Lord Jesus Christ. As the throne of God and of the Lamb are so gloriously described at the beginning of this last chapter of Revelation, the end of the chapter is first an invitation to the people we are praying for, the ones we long to have become "children" in this Kingdom. That invitation comes in verse 17:

The Spirit and the bride say, "Come!" And let him who hears say, "Come!" Whoever is thirsty, let him come; and whoever wishes, let him take the free gift of the water of life.

Then follows a very strong command with a penalty added to it to not take away any of the words from this book of prophecy.

The very last words of Revelation are a prayer, a prayer that continues the Lord's Prayer, "Thy kingdom come." John, who is closing this piece of work he has accomplished under difficulty on the Isle of Patmos, makes certain that all readers will know that what he has written is not coming from his own imagination, but is truth, given to him to write: "He who testifies to these things says, 'Yes, I am coming soon.'" The final prayer then is: "Amen. Come, Lord Jesus. The grace of the Lord Jesus be with God's people. Amen."

What magnificent continuity! How gloriously God encourages us and gives us incentive to keep on despite all hindrances, to keep on with the relay of intercession, the prayer without ceasing, the carrying out of our part in the succession of his children who have been told to watch and pray.

We know from the book of Acts that just before His ascension, Jesus gave a commission, a command that was not temporary, but was to be relayed from generation to generation. They had asked when he was going to restore the Kingdom, and the answer was that no one is to know. "But you will receive power when the Holy Spirit comes on you; and you will be my witnesses in Jerusalem, and in all Judea and Samaria, and to the ends of the earth" (Acts 1:8 NIV). At the end of the book of Mark the same moment is reported as the disciples are told to preach the good news to all creation.

No individual has been perfect, and no generation has been perfect, but if this were a book about the spread of the gospel, the spread of the good news, it would have to begin with a thorough study of Paul's missionary journeys. We would have to study the preparation of Peter to go to Cornelius and the astonishment that Gentiles were also to be included as God's children if they believed and accepted the work of Christ's atonement for them. The message indeed was to be taken to all creation.

In that same tenth chapter of Romans where Paul speaks of his prayer for Israel, his desire for their salvation in verses 12 and 13, Paul goes on to say that the same Lord is Lord of all and richly blesses all who call on Him. Calling on the Lord is prayer. However, it is made clear that people need to know who the true God is in order to pray in this very basic way of asking for salvation.

> How, then, can they call on the one they have not believed in? And how can they believe in the one of whom they have not heard? And how can they hear without someone preaching to them? And how can they preach unless they are sent? As it is written, "How beautiful are the feet of those who bring good news!" (Romans 10:14, 15 NIV)

(The last bit comes from Isaiah 52:7.)

Intercessory prayer is threaded through all of this. The relay of truth as to who God is, how to come to Him, and how to call upon Him in prayer for salvation is also threaded through these passages which tie in quotes from Isaiah, Deuteronomy, Joel, 1 Kings, and so on with what Paul is preaching and writing to the Romans. How long did Paul have to teach, preach, write, and pray for the people to whom he was giving truth and for whom he was burdened? For how many years were the prayers of faithful Christians responsible for snatching Paul from danger in shipwreck, keeping him from death in stonings, preserving him in the midst of tortures and afflictions of all kinds? How long did Paul live anyway?

He was born about A.D. 1; he stopped killing Christians and persecuting them when he was converted at the Damascus road meeting with the Lord when he was about thirty-three years old. So it was in the next half of his life that all he accomplished in preaching and prayer took place. Paul's time of learning to be content, whether being abased or whether abounding, whether being persecuted and tortured or whether being treated well and meeting many leading people, was only about thirty-three years altogether! Paul's time on earth to "pray always," to "pray continually," to "pray on every remembrance of you" for all those for whom he faithfully promised to pray, and did pray for, was just this same number of years. He needed to pray with worship and adoration of the Lord, to pour out his confession of sin and to ask mercy, to pray for the thorn to be removed, to cry out for the Lord's strength to carry on what he was doing in his own weakness, to ask for the Lord's strength over and over again. He needed to write, to travel, to teach, and to continue interceding!

What a titanic amount to accomplish in thirty-three years, on top of some eating, sleeping, enjoying the beauty of land and sea, discussing deep things with the Roman philosophers, and gently answering questions of simple people.

As we glance through history and absorb what we read, (and truly a glance is all we can have even if we read prolifically because there is so much history behind us and we are such limited, finite people during our own short "moment") this glance is enough to inform us how important the relay of truth and the relay of intercession have been. You see, the glances we have, no matter what authors we read or what depth of study we have gone to under professors, is enough to give us some recognition of how sinful human beings, even when doing great exploits for the Lord in the power of the Holy Spirit, are never perfect, and therefore are never perfectly balanced in their understanding. Such disagreements that occurred in the early days of the spread of Christianity and through all history will not continue after we are changed. Although we "see through a glass darkly" now, when we are changed and when we see Him face to face, we will have a very different measure of understanding! " . . . Now I know in part; then I shall know fully, even as I am fully known" (1 Corinthians 13:12 NIV).

> Behold, I show you a mystery: We shall not all sleep, but we shall all be changed, in a moment, in the twinkling of an eye, at the last trump; for the trumpet shall sound, and the dead shall be raised incorruptible, and we shall be changed. (1 Corinthians 15:51, 52 KJV)

> How great is the love the Father has lavished on us, that we should be called children of God! And that is what we are! The reason the world does not know us is that it did not know him. Dear friends, now we are children of God, and what we will be has not yet been made known. But we know that when he appears, we shall be like him, for we shall see him as he is. Everyone who has this hope in him purifies himself, just as he is pure. (1 John 3:1-3 NIV)

What magnificent continuity God has given us throughout Scripture, making clear in different portions at different times in history where *we* fit in! Yes, indeed, "children" are little children, and they are loved and received by Jesus, but we too are children, children of the Father, whom we may call "our Father" *with* Christ because of Christ's death in our place. We too are His "jewels," His "precious possessions," and we await His coming. As we await or watch for that coming and pray as He has commanded us, our prayer is to be for growth in holiness. We are to pray that we may be constantly more purified by the hope that is in us, that is, the hope for His return. This is where if fits in for us to think about what a short time Paul had to live his exhausting life of prayer and a great diversity of things along with suffering.

As we contemplate the need to use our time for intercession well—for our children, adopted or otherwise, for the lost children, and as we consider the need to be where the Lord would have us be, it is necessary to remember that no one else can be the Holy Spirit to us. We need not try to copy someone else's life. We can learn something from each other and be prayed for by each other, but we need to trust the Lord to open a door for us if we are to walk through a new door, or we need to stay right where we are with our hand in His.

Another reading of Isaiah 50:10, 11 is needed here as a constant reminder to wait and pray when we are unsure.

> Who among you fears the Lord
> and obeys the word of his servant?
> Let him who walks in the dark, who has no light,
> trust in the name of the Lord and rely on his God.
>
> (NIV)

This warning does not change with the period of history. God is able to answer our prayer for guidance and to make the next stepping stone clear, to make the water recede so that it appears! If the waters are swirling around us and the fog is dense, the leading is to wait. We are not out of touch. We are not isolated from communication with the Lord; we must trust Him at that time, and we must rely on Him. The word *rely* also means "look to," and our way of looking to the Lord is to pray.

Verse 7 in that chapter of Isaiah has said:

> Because the Sovereign Lord helps me,
> I will not be disgraced.
> Therefore have I set my face like flint,
> and I know I will not be put to shame.

What a firm determination is set forth. How courageous were the people through history who did exactly this—Paul, John, Peter, Augustine, Irenaeus and on through generations. Ragland the pioneer in taking the gospel to India in 1845 was the first young man going from England. His years were few, but he planted a seed, not only in that land and in many people in that area, but also in the minds of others who would then begin to pray about what they should do. Hudson Taylor as a very young man "set his face like flint" and went forth to China. Oh yes, through centuries of the relay of truth and the relay of intercession, through centuries of prayer for the sovereign Lord's help hour by hour, people have trusted the Lord in the face of ridicule and persecution as they relied upon God and looked to Him in prayer with trust.

The eleventh verse provides a contrast, ending with a negative promise.

> But now, all you who light fires
>   and provide yourselves with flaming torches,
> go, walk in the light of your fires
>   and of the torches you have set ablaze.
> This is what you shall receive from my hand:
>   You will lie down in torment.

The *King James Version* speaks of lighting sparks. All through the centuries people have needed to pray earnestly for increased trust of the Lord, for patience and strong determination to wait for Him and for sensitivity as to the real danger of lighting their own sparks. Today, this day when I am writing this and the day when you are reading it, you and I need to pray: *Lord, have mercy on me. I need Your help in recognizing where I am in danger of lighting my own sparks and of rushing ahead to walk in the light of my sparks instead of waiting for Your help.*

If we alone or we as a family or we as a group of people in some sort of leadership are on such a tightrope, in danger of slipping off on the side of lighting our own torch, this is the time for a day of fasting and prayer, for a block of time in the night to pray. This warning is not to be taken lightly today. It is a warning of very real danger, not just picturesque poetry to be enjoyed.

A double danger for all believers through the ages has been the choice time after time of the wrong time and place for the next step. What is the double danger? First, our own inclination to light our own sparks; second, the fact that we have an enemy throwing temptations at us, temptations to turn aside, or hindrances that rise up like a huge rock on a downhill ski run, a rock hidden around a bend! How have people through the centuries avoided crashing headlong into the obstacles, or turning aside when waiting seemed too slow?

The answer is prayer—prayer on the part of the person himself or herself and intercession for that one by others.

Let us go back and remind ourselves again of Paul and Timothy's letter to the Philippians. Paul feels the intense responsibility for continuing faithfully in prayer for them, and he counts just as fervently on their prayers making a difference in his life and Timothy's life hour by hour. What takes place in their ministry is attributed to people whose names we do not know, but God does know them. What has happened in the spread of the gospel, the good news, the truth, has come about because of the faithfulness in prayer of countless people whose names are written in the Book of Life in Heaven, but who are not given credit in any honor roll on earth. There will be a day, I believe, during the believers' judgment when they will receive their reward!

I thank my God every time I remember you. In all my prayers for all of you, I always pray with joy because of your partnership in the gospel from the first day until now, being confident of this, that he who began a good work in you will carry it on to completion until the day of Christ Jesus . . .

And this is my prayer: that your love may abound more and more in knowledge and depth of insight, so that you may be able to discern what is best and may be pure and blameless until the day of Christ, filled with the fruit of righteousness that comes through Jesus Christ—to the glory and praise of God. (Philippians 1:3-6, 9-11 NIV)

Earnest intercessory prayer indeed, with a primary desire for true growth in righteousness which would be demonstrated by fruit. We know from Galatians 5:22 that the fruit of the Spirit, which is a result of walking in the Spirit, is made up of things that are not tabulated in statistics nor hung on a wall with trophies, but are what we are to pray for, *for* ourselves and for each other, and are to count (in modern designation) as REALITY! "But the fruit of the Spirit is love, joy, peace, longsuffering, gentleness, goodness, faith, meekness, temperance . . ."

We can't be longsuffering unless someone is annoying us or frustrating us in some way. The opportunities to be longsuffering are many! When those moments arrive, one after another, our prayer for the fruits of the Spirit can be, *Lord, please help me to bite my tongue, to be silent, to really be longsuffering now.*

After Paul tells of his being in chains because he has been speaking the Word of God and says that some other brothers are therefore encouraged to speak more courageously, he goes on to urge the Philippians to continue praying for him. Philippians 1:19-22A gives us an idea of what he asks them to pray for in the midst of his troubles:

> Yes, and I will continue to rejoice, for I know that through your prayers and the help given by the Spirit of Jesus Christ, what has happened to me will turn out for my deliverance. I eagerly expect and hope that I will in no way be ashamed, but will have sufficient courage so that now as always Christ will be exalted in my body, whether by life or by death. For to me, to live is Christ and to die is gain. If I am to go on living in the body, this will mean fruitful labor for me. (NIV)

Paul goes on to say he does not know which he would choose, but he does declare he is convinced that the believers need him to continue with them at this time. He urges them not to be frightened by those who oppose them, but to remember that they are going through the same struggle he has been having.

Remember that these epistles, letters, communications, encouragements, and teachings to the churches in Corinth, Thessalonica, and Ephesus were written to give understanding and knowledge to people who had become believers and were now called Christians. The Bible, God's Word, is always written for an astoundingly real continuity of generations. The epistles were for the adults who believed in Paul's time and also for their children and grandchildren alive then. However, you and I are a part of the flow of generations who are meant to pay attention to what is being given. As we read and pray for understanding, worship together, pray together, and pray alone in secret, we are meant to have a growing balance, not just in understanding in our minds or hearts, but also in our doing, i.e., our practical living, our attitudes, our creativity, our human relationships, and our diligence in work.

We can't simply go to a Bible class and feel the lesson has been good and then go on about the day or the week without having some change. It might not be a noticeable change to anyone, not that day; it might not be an earth-shaking change bringing about an immediate flood of results, but we are to approach very thoughtfully and recognize where we have been failing to do the things meant to be a part of our sanctification. You see, we ARE in the process of being sanctified after we have been justified through accepting Christ as Savior. All Christians throughout history who have been true Christians, and God alone knows who they are, have been living day by day in the process of sanctification. It is only when we step into Heaven that we will be glorified! 1 Thessalonians 4:11, 12 clearly states the importance of doing well the work we are doing:

> Make it your ambition to lead a quiet life, to mind your own business and to work with your hands, just as we told you, so that your daily life may win the respect of outsiders and so that you will not be dependent on anybody. (NIV)

Yes, Paul and Silas, Timothy and Peter are making the truth of the gospel known. Yes, they are urging people not to be ignorant about the reality of Jesus coming back someday, at which time the dead will rise, and we will hear the voice of the archangel and the trumpet call of God. We are to BE encouraged and to encourage other people with this glorious hope.

But we are to go on working with our hands, bringing forth creative things, caring about doing *well* what we are to do in fields, forests, in the sea, in the air, at looms, with wood, with our pens or paintbrushes, or in preparing food. We are to do work that will win respect.

Oh yes, as 1 Thessalonians ends, the command to "pray always" is not to be canceled out by working carefully and diligently. The request, "Brothers, pray for us," is not to be disregarded because of being *too* loaded down with work!

As centuries of real people—weak, sinful, with varying battles against temptation—strived for spiritual growth and righteousness, for great reality in praying continually, there was no real break in the relay of truth and the relay of intercession and of work.

We have looked extensively at Philippians 4:4-7 where we and they are given clear instruction as to how to deal with anxiety, worry, and fear, let us say, at 2:00 and 3:00 A.M. We are to get out of bed and on our knees to pray with thanksgiving, or perhaps remain there in bed and bow in our hearts and minds and pray. Here at this point, I want to back up a few lines to marvel and thrill over those to whom Paul and Timothy were talking originally, although it is also for us!

I plead with Euodia and I plead with Syntyche to agree with each other in the Lord. Yes, and I ask you, loyal yokefellow, help these women who have contended at my side in the cause of the gospel, along with Clement and the rest of my fellow workers whose names are in the book of life. (Philippians 4:2, 3 NIV)

Notice that some of Paul's fellow workers in making known the truth of the gospel were women. However, as we step into the next period of history, it is exciting to realize that we have names of some who lived after Paul. The spiritual children Paul led to Jesus will be living after Paul died. These are the ones he is instructing to "pray continually," not just to pray up to his death! The Bible gives us names of some who *continued* to live and pray. The death of Paul took place in about A.D. 65.

This is not a book of church history, nor can it record prayers of people all through the ages! But in helping us to feel the reality of you and I being a part of this stream of the continuity of prayer through history, it seems a helpful thing to look at some of those prayers, not just for curiosity, but to help us to pray. We have much to learn. We should humbly continue to ask, *Lord, teach us to pray.*

This same Clement who was a fellow worker with Paul and whose name is in the Book of Life is also being given the instruction as to what to do when anxious or worried. This same Clement lived to the year A.D. 100. He is called Clement of Rome.

The following is one of his prayers preserved for us in the *Ante-Nicene Fathers,* volume 2 (Eerdmans, Grand Rapids, MI, page 295). As you read this, do pray in Clement's words, slowly and thoughtfully, *Grant to us who obey Thy precepts, that we may perfect the likeness of the image.*

Remember that Jesus said, "Be ye perfect as my Father in heaven is perfect." He died that through His atonement we might someday be perfect. He gave us perfection as our standard, and too often our shrug of a shoulder simply removes us from any remorse for sin or any recognition of the need to repent, to ask forgiveness, or to examine ourselves honestly.

Clement's prayer, his hymn to Christ the Savior, and his praise to God the Creator are taken directly from the book I have referred to above. All that remains, therefore, now, in such a celebration of the Word as this, is that we address to the Word our prayer.

PRAYER TO THE PEDAGOGUS

Be gracious, O Instructor, to us Thy children, Father, Charioteer of Israel, Son and Father, both in One, O Lord. Grant to us who obey Thy precepts, that we may perfect the likeness of the image, and with all our power know Him who is the good God and not a harsh judge. And do Thou Thyself cause that all of us who have our conversation in Thy peace, who have been translated into Thy commonwealth, having sailed tranquilly over the billows of sin, may be wafted in calm by Thy Holy Spirit, by the ineffable wisdom, by night and day to the perfect day; and giving thanks may praise, and praising thank the Alone Father and Son, Son and Father, the Son, Instructor and Teacher, with the Holy Spirit, all in One, in whom is all, for whom all is One, for whom is eternity, whose members we all are, whose glory the aeons are; for the All-good, All-lovely, All-wise, All-just One. To whom be glory both now and forever. Amen.

And since the Instructor, by translating us into His Church, has united us to Himself, the teaching and all-surveying Word, it were right that, having got to this point, we should offer to the Lord the reward of due thanksgiving—praise suitable to His fair instruction.

As we think of Malachi speaking of the time when the Lord will gather up His jewels and our study of the various meanings of "children" it is such a clear flow of continuity to find Clement praying with request for the Lord's graciousness "to us Thy children." The spread of truth, or the relay of truth, continually was accompanied by the relay of intercession, prayer for one another. The "simple children," you will notice, are a part of Clement's hymn of praise below.

A HYMN TO CHRIST THE SAVIOR

I.

Bridle of colts untamed,
    Over our wills presiding;
Wing of unwandering birds,
    Our flight securely guiding.
Rudder of youth unbending,
    firm against adverse shock;
Shepherd, with wisdom tending
    Lambs of the royal flock:
Thy simple children bring
In one, that they may sing
In solemn lays
Their hymns of praise
With guileless lips to Christ their King.

What a beautifully expressed description of what Christ the Savior *is* for us and *does* for us. Think of the martyrs of that time singing about Christ their "rudder," guiding the "unbending" youth who are kept firm against adverse shock. Courage was shown forth in those days in the face of many adverse shocks, courage similar to that of Daniel as he approached the lions' den. In Clement's day, however, the lions were not standing with their mouths closed! Early Christians were thrown to the lions in Rome, and they did not deny the Lord who died for them, in order to save their own lives.

Fran always had a print of an old etching titled in French, *Diane ou Jesus-Christ?* on the wall in his office, or on the back of a closet door in our Chalet les Mélèzes bedroom (as the bed was his desk in the daytime). He said it was to remind him of what the martyrs of the early church considered necessary in being truly faithful to the Lord. On the back of this framed picture is an explanation in French. A young woman is being urged to put a grain of incense in front of a statue of the goddess Diana. Her fiancé is urging her to put down "just one grain" so that she will be set free, but she shakes her head. She will not deny Christ and worship Diana. She knows the alternative to freedom is being thrown to the lions.

You may not need this picture to remind you to pray for courage in the times we face today, but it is important to be reminded that we need to pray for mercy and for help. We need to pray for the Lord's strength in our weakness to resist temptation, to resist the devil even if that temptation is not so serious as throwing incense in front of a false god, denying our Savior.

We may face martyrdom. Many in today's world do, but also there are many small "deaths" that are hard for us to be willing to face. The idea of becoming a kernel of wheat and falling into the ground and dying may be figurative, but it often is a very hard kind of sacrifice, which is not easily recognized as fitting into what Jesus is asking each of us who is one of His people to do.

Jesus replied, "The hour has come for the Son of Man to be glorified. I tell you the truth, unless a kernel of wheat falls to the ground and dies, it remains only a single seed. But if it dies, it produces many seeds. The man who loves his life will lose it, while the man who hates his life in this world will keep it for

eternal life. Whoever serves me must follow me; and where I
am, my servant also will be. My Father will honor the one who
serves me." (John 12:23-26 NIV)

Yes, the early Christians prayed for strength and God's sufficient grace to stand firm at any cost, to not deny the Lord who
died for them. They also interceded for each other for protection
from their enemies. But if the dreaded time of separation was to
come, they prayed for strength to be given in the weakness of the
moment of torture and death.

Our own need is the same, even if we are not at the moment
facing lions. The very hard struggle we personally may be having—to really be honest in serving the Lord without placing other
things or other requirements as conditions of doing His revealed
will—can be seen by the Lord as a refusal to "fall to the ground
and die" to *that* particular condition for doing His will or following His leading.

We don't need to wear hair shirts or put dried peas in our
shoes to practice suffering difficulties purposely; there are many
opportunities to put aside the thing we would prefer doing or to
turn from some special plan we had in order to quietly usher in
the "interruption" and to serve someone God has sent to us or
put in our path so that we may be the Good Samaritan in some
practical way. Others of us may need to go to the place of God's
choice for us when we would rather stay and can give the Lord a
lot of reasons why we think it better to stay.

As we grow day by day, it is important to seriously consider
in our own times of prayer just how we are fulfilling that which
Jesus has described in John 12 as following Him, as well as praying for strength to keep on and be real and not false.

Stephen, in his great speech to the Sanhedrin in Acts 7, had
tremendous power and courage to speak forcefully and honestly
in the midst of dangerous opposition. At the end of his giving the
complete and powerful history starting with Abraham, his audience took up stones to stone him. I've spoken of this before, but
at this point it is important to us to note two areas of prayer under
seemingly impossible circumstances.

While they were stoning him, Stephen prayed, "Lord Jesus, receive my spirit." Then he fell on his knees and cried out, "Lord, do not hold this sin against them." When he had said this, he fell asleep. And Saul was there, giving approval to his death. (Acts 7:59–8:1 NIV)

Stephen prayed for himself as he was being struck with the awful blows of the stones, and he prayed for the people stoning him. His prayer to be immediately taken to the Lord was answered. Saul, who helped organize the stoning, was among those Stephen prayed for. Saul's conversion was the answer to Stephen's last prayer. Stephen literally fell to the ground and died that day in his following Jesus up to his last compassionate prayer, and the multiplication of that kernel of wheat in Paul's ministry is still continuing in present generations. What an answer to Stephen's prayer under costly conditions!

There is such a stream of martyrs through all the generations of believers that we could not in this book begin to trace their prayers. It is clear that they were men and women of solid faith and sincere prayer and that we need to read more about them, not forgetting that there are also men and women of our own century who were (and will be) faithful martyrs, loving and trusting Jesus Christ, praying for themselves and interceding for others up to the last moment. Results of their prayers are continuing, whether among the Auca Indians or among many in China, India, Africa and other parts of the world

It is helpful in worship to bow, alone or with the church, and declare to the Lord our certainty of what is true, what we believe. Irenaeus, who lived in A.D. 130-200, knew Polycarp who had known the Apostle John. Among Irenaeus's writings during that time is "Against Heresies" (from *The Lion Concise Book of Christian Thought* by Tony Lane), which showed the central points of his understanding of the Christian faith. This would be a basis of his prayer life and of course helped many people. You will recognize much of this was later to be found in the Apostles' Creed. We can thrill in the continuity of this summary of his understanding, and of ours today.

The church, though scattered throughout the whole world to the ends of the earth, has received from the apostles and their disciples this faith: in one God, the Father Almighty, maker of heaven and earth and the sea and all things in them; and in one Christ Jesus, the Son of God, who was made flesh for our salvation; and in the Holy Spirit who through the prophets proclaimed God's saving dealings with man and the virgin birth, passion, resurrection from the dead and bodily ascension into heaven of our beloved Lord Jesus Christ and his second coming from heaven in the glory of the Father to sum up all things and to raise up human flesh so that . . . he should execute judgment upon all men.

Irenaeus not only lived a life of prayer, he studied and wrote, taking a stand on the Scriptures against the Gnostics. However, some Christians felt the necessity to live a life of prayer so completely that they went out into the Egyptian desert to live alone as hermits, striving to pray without ceasing. In later years this concentration on a life of prayer became communities of monks and nuns.

It was Basil the Great (A.D. 330-379) who began his monastic life by starting a community, which he favored more than the solitary ascetic life. He pointed out that many of the commands of Christ could only be carried out when living with others. One alone cannot serve others and prefer others before himself or herself. To really intercede for another person, we need to know something of that person's needs. We cannot have close friendships with a multiplied number of people, but God has given us a capacity to have compassion on, to be sensitive to the difficulties of, and to keep in touch with the struggles of a multiplied number of people and to really intercede for them.

Basil the Great taught that monks should help each other rather than competing in holiness, and he started seven periods of prayer at regular hours of the day. He also began a plan for his monks to care for the poor and the sick. He considered it dishonoring to Christ if such people were neglected. Therefore, he started a hospice for strangers, a hospital, special care for lepers, a school, and a program for social help. As we see from the dates, he only lived to be forty-nine.

It is truly valuable for us, I speak to myself in this, to remember that we cannot assess with any objective certainty what is the most important day of our lives, what is the most important thing we will ever do, who is the person the Lord would have us talk to or pray for who will in turn make the greatest difference in history for Jesus Christ and the Word of God. Our most important task can easily be the successive times we spend in prayer through the days, weeks, months, and years. Are Basil's forty-nine years or John and Betty Stam's brief years in China (they were martyred in 1933) of less importance than those of someone who lived to be one hundred? Is a life of praying in the desert more effective than a life of praying in a wheelchair? Is the preaching to a thousand people more important than sitting by the side of a well, talking to a Samaritan woman? Jesus did both. He is the example of each one who has been a Christian through the ages. In our finiteness there is one way of "multiplying" our time—prayer.

The following prayer of Basil's is taken from *A Pocket Prayerbook for Orthodox Christians* (Antiochian Orthodox Christian Archdiocese, Englewood, NJ, 1956). As we read this fourth-century prayer, we can continue to pray in his words; our need for *preparation* to make other requests is just the same today. We can come with a psalm or at times with this prayer.

In a time when confusion reigns in all the world—political, moral, and ethical confusion, as well as confusion about what is true and false—it is a comfort to be able to pray in continuity through the centuries for our "eyes of understanding" to be enlightened, and then for the eyes of understanding of those for whom we pray to be enlightened.

A PRAYER OF ST. BASIL THE GREAT

We bless thee, O God most high and Lord of mercies, who ever workest great and mysterious deeds for us, glorious, wonderful, and numberless; who providest us with sleep as a rest from our infirmities and as a repose for our bodies tired by labor. We thank thee that thou hast not destroyed us in our transgressions, but in thy love toward mankind thou has raised us up, as we lay in despair, that we may glorify thy Majesty. We entreat thine infinite goodness, enlighten the eyes of our understanding and raise up our minds from the heavy sleep of indolence; open our mouths and fill them with thy praise, that we may unceasingly sing and confess thee, who art God glorified in all and by all, the eternal Father, the Only-Begotten Son, and the all-holy and good and life-giving Spirit: now and ever, and unto ages and ages. Amen.

In Francis Schaeffer's Bible he had written the following poem at the front. Some biographers say it was not really St. Patrick who wrote this poem, known as "The Breastplate," but it indicates a longing to fulfill a growing reality of sanctification in the midst of times of failing.

Christ be with me
Christ within me
Christ above me
Christ below me
Christ before me
Christ behind me
Christ on my right
Christ on my left
Christ all about me
To guard and direct me
That each meeting
Each work undertaken
May be by, with, and in Him
*   done to his glory.*

St. Patrick (389-461)

So often the struggles of young men and women for a reality of righteousness, a growing closeness to the Lord, and victory over the deluges of temptation are put aside because of busyness in work, and that work may be so-called full-time Christian work.

There can be a hardness of conscience, a coldness and insensitivity to sin, growing so gradually that it is not noticed.

John Bunyan wrote *Pilgrim's Progress* in the Bedford jail where he had been locked up for preaching the Bible, the gospel. Bunyan's struggles and his vivid description of the Christian life with all its pitfalls is must reading for anyone who would understand the need of prayer for help in keeping from "falling into a slough of despond." We need to be more aware of the need to pray for ourselves and then for others in the area of thoughts, words, and deeds.

Thomas à Kempis (1379-1471) wrote *The Imitation of Christ* (Grosset & Dunlap, New York, n.d.), which has been translated and read by people in as large a number of countries and language groups as *Pilgrim's Progress*. Here is his prayer for the power of God to continue working in his life.

A PRAYER FOR ENLIGHTENMENT OF THE MIND

O good Jesus, enlighten me with the brightness of Thine inward light, and remove from the sanctuary of my heart all manner of darkness. Restrain my wayward thoughts, and destroy the temptations that so vehemently attack me. Fight mightily for me, and drive out the perilous desires of the flesh that assail me like evil beasts; that peace may be restored by Thy virtue and power, and that abundant praise may resound to Thee in Thy holy court, the court of a pure conscience. Command Thou the winds and tempests; say unto the sea: Be still, and to the north wind: Blow not; and there shall be a great calm.

Send out Thy light and Thy truth that they may shine upon the earth; for unless Thou enlighten me, I am as earth that is empty and void. Pour forth Thy grace from above; bathe my heart in Thy heavenly dew; send fresh streams of devotion to water the face of the earth, that it may bring forth good and perfect fruit. Uplift my mind, weighed down with a heavy burden of sin, and raise my whole desire to heavenly things; that having once tasted the sweetness of supernal joy, my mind may turn away from the contemplation of earthly things.

Snatch me away, and deliver me from all transitory conso-

lation of creatures; for no created thing can fully comfort me,
or appease my desire. Join me to Thee with an inseparable bond
of love; for Thou alone dost satisfy the soul that loveth Thee.
Without Thee, all things are worthless.

The following three prayers are taken from *The Book of
Common Prayer and Administration of the Sacraments:
According to the Use of the Church of England (1662)*.

*Blessed Lord,
Who hast caused all holy Scriptures
    to be written for our learning;
grant that we may in such wise hear them,
    read, mark, learn, and inwardly digest them;
that, by patience, and comfort
    of thy holy Word,
we may embrace, and ever hold fast
    the blessed hope of everlasting life,
which thou hast given us in our Savior Jesus Christ.*

———

*Almighty God,
by whose grace alone we are accepted and called to
        your service:
strengthen us by your Holy Spirit and make us worthy of
        our calling;
through Jesus Christ our Lord.*

———

*Almighty Father,
whose Son Jesus Christ has taught us
that what we do for the least of our brethren
    we do also for him;
give us the will to be the servant of others
    as he was the servant of all,
who gave up his life and died for us,
but is alive and reigns with you and the Holy Spirit,
one God, now and for ever.*

Here is a favorite prayer of mine by the English poet George
Herbert (1593-1632):

OUR PRAYER

Thou hast given so much to me,
give one thing more
A grateful heart.
Not thankful when it pleaseth me,
As if thy blessings had spare days
But such a heart
whose pulse may be thy praise.

It is true that there is danger in praying in the words of the prayer book, of a set liturgy, a danger of having one's mind wander, of simply saying words, of doing what is described in Ezekiel 33:32:

And, lo, thou art unto them as a very lovely song of one that hath a pleasant voice, and can play well on an instrument; for they hear thy words, but they do them not. (KJV)

But there is danger of that *same kind* of lack of worship, of being bodily in the place of prayer but with the mind and heart far away, even when the words are original. Yes, there is a danger of being false when piously repeating, "make us worthy of our calling," with no feeling of repentance for being unworthy. A terrible danger of lying exists for each of us when we plead in prayer for the will to be servant of others, as Christ was the servant of all. We need to stand in the place of the Sadducee asking for mercy as a sinner in our danger of perjury when we are openly in a place of worship or even praying alone.

Is this danger only present when praying in the words of the Psalms, Isaiah, Jesus, Paul, John, Clement, St. Basil, John Wesley, Luther, Amy Carmichael, or repeating the Apostles' Creed, or the Nicene Creed, or praying in the words of the liturgy in the prayer book?

I would strongly say no. There is danger constantly of our slipping into what I call nonattention and having our minds wander off into other areas, especially if we have active creative minds full of ideas. Yes, there are people who don't really believe and

who are simply going through the motions of worship physically
with voices and hands doing the "right thing." But even those
who earnestly long to pray, whether privately or with other
believers, need to ask, *Help me, Lord, speak truth to You as I
come cleansed by the blood of Christ in the Holy Spirit's power.
May I not be in any way less real in my worship and fervency than
the words being said.* This is needed when we use our own words
as much as in a liturgy.

As I read and pray about the men and women throughout
the centuries, covering only a minimal number of books compared with what exists, I wish I could be sitting with you who are
reading this, discussing the sheer wonder of the relay of both truth
and intercessory prayer. We could perhaps cover more in an afternoon of talking than I can in writing! It is an awesome thing to
me as I discover in a fresh way the influence and life-changing
effect one life has on another, one man's writing has on another,
one man's courage and loyalty to God and His Word has on
another—often without the person realizing who is being influenced or who is watching him or her, who is being inspired, or
who is being discouraged and turned aside.

Another important individual in the relay of truth was
Martin Luther. According to *Great Leaders of the Christian
Church* by Robert Godfrey (page 189):

> Luther had a scholarly education preparing him to go on into
> law studies in the university, but he had wanted to become a
> monk, as he felt the monastic life was the highest form of reli-
> gious devotion. He joined the monastery of the Augustinian
> hermits in Erfurt where he devoted himself to study, prayer,
> and the use of the sacraments, with long periods of fasting and
> prayer and confession. His studies of the Scriptures were thor-
> ough as he learned Greek and Hebrew to recapture the sources.
> . . . Luther was ordained a priest in 1507 and taught at Erfurt
> and Wittenberg Universities, receiving his doctoral degree in
> 1512. In receiving his degree, Luther took the traditional vow
> to teach and defend the Scriptures faithfully. He never viewed
> himself as a rebel, but rather as a theologian fulfilling the vow
> impressed upon him by the medieval church.

This book on prayer is not a church history, but we need to have some feel of the depth of reality of various people praying who cried out to God for help in understanding justification and sanctification. How could one be sure of having enough righteousness to please the perfectly holy God? Luther's struggle and prayer to God the Father for help was answered with what he believed to be a *great* answer, that is, *understanding*. To have one's eyes of understanding opened is one of the greatest possible answers to prayer. He was reading Romans 1:17. How could knowing about the righteousness of God be good news? And he suddenly saw it—the righteousness of Christ fulfills God's demands for perfect righteousness and is imputed to the ones who come in faith, believing in Christ's atoning death in our place. This indeed is good news. We can sing, praying as we sing, putting this praise of Luther's, this declaration to our great God directly, as our own determination to serve HIM. It *is* a solemn prayer indeed and has strengthened those who have prayed it either with loud voices or tearful voices in many countries and languages, when they have prayed it with intent to keep these promises to put the mighty Triune God and His Word before all else in loyalty and devotion, even to martyrdom.

A mighty fortress is our God, A Bulwark never failing;
Our helper He, amid the flood Of mortal ills prevailing.
For still our ancient foe Doth seek to work us woe;
His craft and power are great, And, armed with cruel hate,
On earth is not his equal.

Did we in our own strength confide, Our striving would
*   be losing,*
Were not the right Man on our side, The Man of God's
*   own choosing.*
Dost ask who that may be? Christ Jesus, it is He;
Lord Sabaoth His name, From age to age the same,
And He must win the battle.

And though this world, with devils filled, Should threaten
*   to undo us,*

We will not fear, for God hath willed His truth to triumph
     through us.
The prince of darkness grim—We tremble not for him;
His rage we can endure, For lo! his doom is sure,
One little word shall fell him.

That word above all earthly powers—No thanks to them—
     abideth;
The Spirit and the gifts are ours Through Him who with
     us sideth.
Let goods and kindred go, This mortal life also;
The body they may kill: God's truth abideth still,
His Kingdom is forever.

                            Martin Luther (1483-1546)

Less than two hundred years later, Charles Wesley wrote a hymn that we should sing as a very deeply moving liturgical prayer. Never should we sing this without truly speaking it with our heart, actually *praying*, really communicating to God. We should sing it in a worship service, or we should sing it all alone as we begin our prayer time by the kitchen sink, or in the woods, on a porch, on a balcony. Or we should sing it in our minds on a subway train! It is a preparation for prayer indeed. It is a beginning as we come with thanksgiving to make our requests. It helps us to join with myriad believers adoring and loving God.

And can it be, that I should gain An interest in the
     Savior's blood?
Died He for me, who caused His pain? For me, who Him to
     death pursued?
Amazing love! how can it be That Thou, my God, shouldst
     die for me?

'Tis mystery all! Th' Immortal dies! Who can explore His
     strange design?
In vain the first-born seraph tries To sound the depths of
     love Divine!
'Tis mercy all! let earth adore, Let angel minds inquire
     no more.

He left His Father's throne above, So free, so infinite
    His grace;
Emptied Himself of all but love, And bled for Adam's
    helpless race;
'Tis mercy all, immense and free; For, O my God, it found
    out me.

Long my imprisoned spirit lay Fast bound in sin and
    nature's night;
Thine eye diffused a quick'ning ray, I woke, the dungeon
    flamed with light;
My chains fell off, my heart was free; I rose, went forth, and
    followed Thee.

No condemnation now I dread; Jesus, and all in Him,
    is mine!
Alive in Him, my living Head, And clothed in
    righteousness Divine,
Bold I approach th' eternal throne, And claim the crown,
    through Christ my own.

Charles Wesley (1707-1788)

George Muller, born in Prussia in 1805, has been to many an example of an intercessor, faithful and childlike in his trust of the God to whom he prayed for the supply of all the needs of his work in Bristol for orphans. However, he did not begin his life that way. As a boy and as a young man, he lied and stole and spent money wildly, taking money his father's clients had paid and telling his father they had not paid. The night his mother lay dying, George, fourteen years old, was reeling through the streets of the town drunk. The story is a long one including a time in prison and various fraudulent schemes, although his father sent him to Nordhausen where he studied hard in the classics and later became a divinity student, but continued to be a hypocrite. His conversion came when he was in Halle, and a student invited him to a small Bible class in a professor's home. At the end of the study people knelt in prayer, the first time Muller saw anyone kneel to pray. In his church everyone stood in prayer. Somehow that simple act of kneeling before God penetrated George Muller's mind and heart, and when back in his room, he bowed in repentance before God alone, asked forgiveness, and believed. This was a real conversion, as he truly became a new creature in Christ Jesus, and his life changed.

For two months George Muller lived in an orphanage, which also lodged poor theological students. It was built by A.H. Francke, a professor of divinity at Halle who had died one hundred years before in 1727. This man had founded this orphanage in dependence on God to provide the funds needed. It was this tangible proof to young Muller which so impressed him that the living God hears and answers prayer and gave him the courage and determination as well as the example to found in later years his orphanages in Bristol, determining to pray specifically for the needs to be cared for by God's hearing and answering prayer in His own way.

The continuity of lives based on prayer and work based on prayer being relayed is startling when one begins to trace the connections through the centuries. George Muller said when he started his homes for orphans that he wanted to prove to widows that they could trust their Heavenly Father to answer prayer for their needs in their old age, as they would watch the way God sent potatoes, apples, wood for fires, and so on just in the nick of time when needed at the orphanage, rather than just talking about what God could do.

It was in 1836, after a series of events Muller accepted as God's leading to step out by faith and start the first orphanage, that a gift of ten shillings was given in answer to prayer, and a woman offered to work to care for the children! Small beginnings, and in the course of years there was never a time when there was a comfortable cushion. There was plenty of opportunity to trust in God alone and to remember that He continued to be the God of Gideon and of Elisha!

Hudson Taylor was seventeen years old in 1849. He had been brought up in a Christian home, but had not just acquiesced to what he had been taught, but had a deep struggle alone in becoming a Christian. His sister Amelia had been a help to him, but as she went off to college, and he lived with a cousin who was not interested at all in the Bible or prayer, Hudson felt he was not growing. One Sunday morning, December 2, 1848, he stayed at home, sick with a cold. His thoughts turned to Amelia, and he wrote her a letter that records what happened that day. A few sentences taken from that letter give us a glimpse of the spiritual depth of this teenager:

> Pray for me, dear Amelia. . . . I am so unworthy of God's blessings. . . . I so often give way to temptation. I am frothy and giddy, and sometimes yield to my teasing disposition. . . . I have read a very interesting paper on the beauty of holiness in the *Wesleyan Magazine* for November. What a happy state it must be!

> *Oh, for a heart to praise my God, A heart from sin set free,*
> *A heart that always feels Thy blood So freely shed for me!*
> *A heart in every thought renewed, And full of love divine;*
> *Perfect, and right, and pure, and good, A copy, Lord,*
> > *of Thine!*

In this long letter he quotes much Scripture and shows a state of longing similar to Augustine's. Fervently he prayed that God would show him what the hindrance was. In the midst of such earnest prayer one day alone on his knees, he promised God that he would go anywhere, do anything, suffer whatever would be needed if only God would deliver him from his backsliding and keep him from falling.

> Never will I forget the feeling that came over me then. Words can never describe it. I felt I was in the presence of God, entering into a covenant with the Almighty. I felt as though I wished to withdraw my promise, but could not. Something seemed to say, "Your prayer is answered; your conditions are accepted." And from that time on the conviction never left me that I was called to China.

"From that hour," his mother wrote, "his mind was made up. His pursuits and studies were all engaged in with reference to this object, and whatever difficulties presented themselves, his purpose never wavered."

When he was seventeen and a half, Hudson obtained a copy of the Gospel of Luke in Mandarin and went to a Methodist pastor in his town to ask if he could borrow a copy of Medhurst's *China.*

When asked why he wanted to read it, the boy replied, "God has called me to spend my life in missionary service in that land."

"And how do you propose to go there?"

"Probably I will have to go as the twelve and seventy did in Judea, go without purse or script, relying on Him who is sending me, to supply my need."

"Ah my boy," replied the minister, "as you grow older you will be wiser than that. Such an idea would do very well in the days when Christ Himself was on the earth, but not now."

Hudson was not turned aside. He felt he must begin right where he was to live a life without the usual comforts, in order to prepare himself for China, so he slept on the floor and ate very meager food, apples and brown bread and tea, mainly. He also began to visit the poor and do what he could practically for the sick, feeling it was imperative not to neglect the present opportunities to help people in physical and spiritual need, simply because he was expecting to go to China. He also began to pray and get others to pray for China, to give and encourage others to give in preparation for going.

The story of this teenager's amazing single-mindedness and his courageous determination to search out every way to go to China, as well his faithful prayer for each detail of the steps to be taken, is told in Dr. and Mrs. Howard Taylor's two-volume work *Hudson Taylor and the China Inland Mission* (London: China Inland Mission, 1918, over 1000 pages). The above quoted material was taken from this work. Hudson Taylor's story has also been written by others.

Again, let me say that I am not attempting to write a complete history, nor even a partial history of centuries of time. But as Hudson Taylor was influenced by Wesley and by George Muller's work as well as by his own deep struggle against sin and weaknesses, and as he set forth to relay truth into every province of inland China and to live as the Chinese and not as a foreigner, either in dress or in location, some knowledge of this strategic portion of the relay of truth and of intercession MUST be known about. The similarity of struggle to live righteously and to follow Christ's example is not one of an explainable thread of connection except through the reality of the Trinity—the Father, Son, and Holy Spirit—responding to earnest, sincere prayer by hearts truly seeking forgiveness and salvation, mercy and help to DO what God would have done.

Was anyone ever perfect in this stream of continuity? No. Not one. No one except God the Father, God the Son, and God the Holy Spirit is perfect in this life. Our hope is in the resurrection and the "forever" time when there will be no more tears, no more sorrow, no more struggling against sin, no more walking in a dark or fog, for "we shall be like Him, for we shall see him as He is." How marvelously comforting are His promises and His revelation of some of what is ahead of us.

The day came in London (after young Hudson Taylor had spent a term in a coastal town in China under the Church Missionary Society, during which he had shocked the missionaries by growing his hair long so that he could have his own pigtail and pass unnoticed by country Chinese) when Hudson went to the Bank of England and stood before a window, taking a deep breath. He had prayed and prayed for inland China where no one was even thinking of going.

"Lord," he prayed, "I believe You are guiding me to do this."
Then he spoke to the cashier. "I want to open a bank account," he said, putting down all his money, which amounted to ten English pounds (about $50 in those days).

"Under what name shall I enter it?" asked the cashier.

He hesitated, not having thought of a name; then firmly it came out for the first time. "Under the name of the CHINA INLAND MISSION."

He had resolved that it would be a missionary work to "relay the truth of the gospel to China," but the basic resolve was also to have it be a work of intercession, intercession for the Lord to put it into the minds and hearts of young people to go out to do the work, wherever in the world they might be now, and intercession that the supply of funds for boat fares, for housing, for language study, for all the needs that would multiply in days ahead would come in in time in answer to prayer. It was also to be intercession for the Chinese people who would be hearing the message, that their "eyes of understanding would be opened," and their "ears of understanding" also.

China Inland Mission prayer meetings began to be weekly times of very devoted and faithful prayer. First in England, then in Sweden, Switzerland, Norway, Germany, Austria, Czechoslovakia, Poland, Russia, Canada, Australia, New Zealand, U.S.A., and other countries. But all this was far ahead, and it took place gradually.

TIME in history is important. How long did mainland China stay "open"? Hudson Taylor rightly heard the Lord's call, and the harvest is still being gathered, but China is closed at present! As I have told before, I was born in China. I would not exist had not my father heard of Hudson Taylor's mission in Pittsburgh where he was teaching Greek and Latin at a boys' school, and had not my mother, studying in Toronto Bible College, been moved to apply to the China Inland Mission a year before that. Mother and Father met in Wenchow, China, and were married in Shanghai. Who interceded most effectively for me? Only God knows, but I am sure the prayers of my Chinese Amah, the Chinese pastor, and other Christian Chinese in Wenchow led to the Lord by my parents and others, were being answered for me. The new Chinese convert's prayer is just as powerful as the missionary's prayer.

The relay of truth and the relay of intercessory prayer is never a "we and they" situation . . . never! Wherever in the world the truth is spread and people understand and believe, the first-generation Christians coming out of whatever nation, kindred, tribe, or tongue, language group are so often the most sincere, tender in conscience, serious about following Jesus in the way He taught, just as were the "first-generation Christians" like Paul and Clement in the early days of Christianity. Not always, but all too often children of Christians forget how truly overwhelming Christ's death for us really is, because they have not heard with the awe and fresh understanding of someone hearing for the first time. They have let themselves "turn off" familiar words and think about something else!

However, Amy Carmichael was not a first-generation Christian. She was born in County Down, North Ireland, of a family who had been at least for several generations God-fearing people with several ministers among them. Eldest of seven children, Amy was brought up in a happy family, with memories of the wind sighing down the nursery chimney, her father's voice reading the Bible at family worship, the view from the house of the gray sea. As her father read, "Let the sea roar; let the floods clap their hands," it all blended together in her memory with the sea and days of playing in the lovely garden. She always counted her earliest memory of prayer as the time when at the age of three she prayed most earnestly that her brown eyes would be changed by God to blue and then climbed up on a chair in the early morning to look disappointedly into the mirror and find the same brown eyes! At that early time she was taught and kept it as a part of her prayer life's warp and woof that answers to pray are "no" and "wait," as well as "yes." This story she often repeated to her beloved Indian children many years later!

Amy Carmichael was born in 1867—a vivid, poetic, beauty-appreciating, intense person, whose prayer as a young woman was like others we've looked at in this continuity of prayer, a prayer for reality in an honest and unselfish way, "Lord, let the glow of Thy great love through my whole being shine." She knew

Hudson Taylor and had applied to the China Inland Mission, but was turned down for "health reasons" by the mission doctor!

How astounding it is to find a record of a choice like this by a mission doctor and to realize what a titanic difference it has made in history! Had she gone to China, the life of thousands of children in India would have been different. Her brown eyes and dark hair, which helped her to move among the market places in her Indian sari and sandaled feet (having stained her skin brown to be less noticed), were God's provision. The Lord's answer was in the "no" for China, as well as in the "no" to her request for "blue eyes like the skies." She was needed in India at just that time of history, and her brown eyes were the best equipment.

You need to read the story of Amy Carmichael. Her story and her books have been a part of my own life. During the very first year of L'Abri, the two Stammer Sisters, Joan and Pauline, one a missionary with Amy Carmichael and the other in a mission work in Beirut, joined with us on that first day of fasting and prayer on July 30, 1955. Their decision to stay in Beau Site, a pension then next to Chalet les Mélèzes, was made without any knowledge on their part as to how we had come there, and we had had no idea who "the two little ladies" vacationing there were.

In 1893 Amy Carmichael set sail for Japan and worked some years there, but felt deeply that she wanted to be more a part of the people and not live a separate life of "we and they." That had a lot to do with her prayer for direction and her ending up in India. It was March 6, 1901, that her work for the temple children began. So many Western people who think Hinduism is "beautiful" have no understanding of the system that was very strong then and is coming back. Baby girls were sold to the temple to be raised as temple virgins, actually prostitutes, with sexual practices being a part of the temple worship. Amy was overwhelmed with love for these baby girls and prayed long and passionately for the possibility of snatching some of them out of this life, of rescuing them and bringing them up with an education, beauty, love, and knowledge of God.

She resolved that it would be a work of prayer. She would

not apply to churches in England for support, but would pray that God would touch the hearts of those who truly love children and give them a desire to send what was needed—money, oranges, help to build buildings, clothing, sheets, medical supplies, and so on. She prayed for one Indian woman to begin this work with her, and God gave her a very special person who worked by her side through the years.

The work was physically very hard and extremely dangerous. Hindu relatives tried to kidnap the children as time went on. The first two babies died, and Amy almost gave up then. But as she prayed for protection and the Lord's victory over myriad attacks, she often spoke of the reality of the Lord's placing "a wall of fire" around the compound to keep off the demonic influences as well as human attacks. Prayer was central in this work—prayer for strength and for guidance, as well as for so much else.

Sometimes she questioned her guidance, especially as requests came to her from all over south India to come and help what seemed to be "fields white to harvest." *What am I doing,* she queried, *changing diapers, nursing fretful sick children through the nights, being a nursemaid to Indian babies.* It was then that she read the words from John 13 about the Lord of glory who "took a towel and girded Himself" to wash his disciples' feet. Never again did she question whether her gifts were being wasted. She was sure the Master never wastes his servants' time. This was his work for her, she was sure. It was after that that the babies began to come in amazing ways.

Her work, called Dohnavur Fellowship, left no time for writing. The physical work of caring for growing numbers of baby girls, and later boys too, teaching and caring for them, took all the time. It was in 1931 that her accident took place. She had a terrible fall into a cesspool while walking over a plank that had been laid over it as entrance to an outdoor toilet. The plank broke. Not only did she suffer a broken hip, but all sorts of infection. A succession of painful results (with cancer in later years) kept her bedridden for twenty years unable to direct her work except from her room. It was then she began writing. Her books were born out of affliction and prayer, in a very literal way.

She also suffered painful attacks from Christians who wrote her letters telling her that she could get up and walk and be rid of her pain if only she had enough faith! I think most of God's treasured servants who have suffered and who have been given His sufficient grace to go on have had to endure such attacks, just as Job did.

The books she wrote during those years in bed, from 1931 to 1951, have been an immeasurable help to uncounted numbers of people. She was able to write as one suffering to those suffering, with understanding the Lord was giving her in answer to prayer. And her books encouraged many to pray believing that there is nothing impossible to the living God, Creator of all things, whether to give sufficient grace and strength in our weakness to go on or to provide a surprise supply for a need. She enjoyed the trees surrounding her room; she delighted in the arrival of new babies rescued; she prayed for each worker, each baby, for the spiritual needs and choices of each one. Those were fruitful years with a harvest we will be aware of in Heaven, but she did not have physical healing in her lifetime. She is among the cloud of witnesses watching us run the race! It is a competition. We are to run well the race set before us! We need to pray one of her beautiful prayers with her as we press on!

God of the gallant trees,
  Give to us fortitude;
Give as thou givest to these
  Valorous hardihood.
We are the trees of thy planting, O God,
  We are the trees of thy wood.

Now let the life-sap run
  Clean through our every vein.
Perfect what thou hast begun,
  God of the sun and rain,
Thou who dost measure the weight of the wind,
  Fit us for stress and for strain.

NINE
If God Is Sovereign, Why Pray?

This question has been asked many times—by all ages of people in many parts of the world. It is not a question about the importance of bowing before the most holy God with prayer of repentance, with prayer asking forgiveness and mercy, with prayer of adoration and worship. Communicating thanksgiving to God and bringing appreciation to Him in the variety of ways we have talked about is not what the troubling question refers to, or so it seems to me.

What nags at people when they are all alone and have a troubling problem, a sudden shock that came out of a "blue sky," is: If God is sovereign how can I ask anything and have it make any difference in history? Doesn't sovereign mean that everything is cut and dried? Doesn't it mean that there is no way of having anything change because of prayer? How can you intercede for another person, ask for a rebel to be given understanding, if everything that happens was going to happen anyway? What is the difference between fatalism and the Bible's teaching?

A lot of difference! God did not create puppets. God did not create people to be like programmed computers. God did not create people as slightly higher animals. We need to continue thinking about creation in order to increase our awe of our unexcelled, mighty, unparalleled, majestic, magnificent Triune God. His creation is far beyond our understanding. Who was there when He created light or the seas or the distant stars? We are never going to be able to reach a mathematical formula that will enable us to say, "Oh yes, that is it; that is how God's thoughts or ideas or plans work." The creation of the whole universe is fantastic, but the creation of human beings is beyond all else, in that God made human beings in His own image. Animals operate by instinct. Human beings have to make choices constantly in all their creative works, both in verbalizing and in designing things they make from available resources.

I'd like to quote a few lines from Mortimer J. Adler's book *Intellect: Mind Over Matter.* Mortimer J. Adler is professor at the University of North Carolina at Chapel Hill, Chairman of the Board of Editors of the Encyclopedia Britannica, Director of the Institute for Philosophical Research, and Honorary Trustee of the Aspen Institute for Humanistic Studies. It seems to me that some of the keen observations Professor Adler makes are important to consider as we prepare to answer our deep question about prayer. I will quote some lines from chapter 3:

> With regard to most of the similarities just mentioned, human beings and other animals differ in degree. But there are two exceptions and these two go to the heart of the matter. They give us a clue to the mind's uniqueness, which consists in its having intellectual powers not possessed by other animals.
>
> While thought is present in both man and the higher animals, animal thought is perceptual thought; only human thought is conceptual. While motivating appetites or desires are present in both men and other animals, only man has an intellectual appetite, a will that is able to make free choices.
>
> Other animals live entirely in the present. Only human individuals are time-binders, connecting the perceived present with the remembered past and the imaginable future. Only man is a historical animal with a historical tradition and a historical development.
>
> It is not enough to say that man is the only manufacturing animal. The kind of thought that is involved in designing and building a machine betokens the presence of an intellect in a way that the use of hand tools does not.

Professor Adler goes on to speak of the difference between the songbirds' music, made for enjoyment, and human artistry, which is not instinctive. I quote again:

To say that human artistry is creative, not instinctive, is to say that it consists of acts voluntarily done, involving both thought and choice on the part of the individual artist.

The difference is one of kind and it can be explained only by the uniqueness of the human mind because of its intellectual powers—conceptual thought and free choice.

Only human beings live with the awareness of death, and with certain knowledge that they are going to die. Only human beings use their minds to become artists, scientists, historians, philosophers, priests, teachers, lawyers, physicians, engineers, accountants, inventors, traders, bankers, and statesmen. Only among human beings is there a distinction among those who behave ethically and those who are knaves, scoundrels, villains and criminals.

Only among human beings is there any distinction between those who have mental health and those who suffer mental disease or have mental disabilities of one sort or another. Only in the sphere of human life are there such institutions as schools, libraries, hospitals, churches, temples, factories, theaters, museums, prisons, cemeteries and so on.

The thing that excites me about all this is the recognition that stands out in this man's analysis that human beings are a distinctly different kind of being, made with minds that can have ideas and make choices, in verbalizing as well as in being creative in making things. It seems to me that Adler sets forth his logic brilliantly, based on what is observable in God's creation. Observing astutely, Adler points out the sharp difference that intellect, minds with ideas and choice, and the diversity of creativity makes between human beings and all else.

Even as we are meant to be aware of God's existence because of the heavens declaring the glory of God and the firmament showing His handiwork, it seems to me inexcusable to fail to recognize the marvel of God's creation of human beings with ideas, choice, and creativity as pointing to his glorious *power* of creation. It is a staggering thought that God could and did create the human mind and intellect with all its incredibly diverse potentialities and that He has said we are created in His image. The artistic understanding and accomplishments of some human beings, the scientific and mathematical achievements of others, the physical abilities of others, and so on and on cause us to marvel at this wonderful creation of God—man and woman with generation following generation.

But being made in God's image does not mean being made equal to God.

Lucifer, the highest of the angels, rebelled against God and commenced a coup in Heaven. What he was determined to do was to make himself *equal* to God.

> You said in your heart,
>   "I will ascend to heaven;
> I will raise my throne
>   above the stars of God;
> I will sit enthroned on the mount of assembly,
>   on the utmost heights of the sacred mountain.
> I will ascend above the tops of the clouds;
>   I will make myself like the Most High."
> But you are brought down to the grave,
>   to the depths of the pit.
> Those who see you stare at you,
>   they ponder your fate:
> "Is this the man who shook the earth
>   and made the kingdoms tremble,
> the man who made the world a desert,
>   who overthrew its cities
>   and would not let his captives go home?"
>
>   (Isaiah 14:13-17
>   NIV)

This was the temptation Lucifer offered, coming in the form of a serpent and first putting doubts into the minds of Eve and Adam that it was of any use to obey God's one commandment to them. Then he dangled an even greater temptation before Eve. What was the temptation? It was to be like God, to know what God knows, to gain wisdom by refusing to trust that God spoke the truth. Eve ate the forbidden fruit and gave it to Adam to eat in order to gain more than had been given them. God had said death would be the result. They used, first Eve, then Adam, their power of *choice* to choose death! Oh yes, they did not believe what God had said, that the result would be death, and they chose to act on their belief that God's verbalized word was not true. God is perfect in His holiness and justice, as well as in His mercy, compassion, and grace. In God's mercy He unfolded a solution, a way whereby there could be forgiveness of sin, a way of coming to Him through the Lamb.

God did not wipe out the human race.

God did not strike Adam and Eve dead.

God did not destroy the possibility of family, which was His creation.

God did not destroy intelligence and creativity.

God did not wipe out choice.

Love and communication are only possible with choice.

Only human beings can pray.

As we have seen in the rest of this book, communication, love, and trust are essential in real prayer, but so is choice. We have the wonderful invitation that must be responded to; we may choose to pray. When we recognize our sin, we may choose to bow before the Lord and repent; we may choose to ask for His mercy; we may choose to declare our love for Him; we may choose to pour out our thanksgiving for all He has done; we may choose to accept what we read in His Word, "For God so loved the world that he gave his only begotten Son, that whosoever believeth in him should not perish, but have everlasting life." We may choose to accept this as true and to accept Christ's death for us. Choice is involved in this because God astoundingly created human beings with real choice.

But prayer is also asking, making needs known, as we come moment by moment. Of course the basic need is wisdom, His guiding us as to the next step and giving us sufficient grace to go on, His strength in our weakness—but we are meant to ask for it. Prayer is meant to have results in history. All through the Bible we are given examples of prayer being answered in a way that changed history (as well as all through the centuries we have skimmed through in our search), and then also we have so many true examples in our own lives.

One of my favorite examples of prayer for something specific in the Bible is in Genesis 24. Abraham is sending his servant to his relatives to find the right wife for his son Isaac. You may remember that the servant went to the town of Nahor and had his camels kneel down near the well outside the town later in the afternoon just when the women would be going to the well to get water. Then he prayed:

"O Lord, God of my master Abraham, give me success today, and show kindness to my master Abraham. See, I am standing beside this spring, and the daughters of the townspeople are coming out to draw water. May it be that when I say to a girl, 'Please let down your jar that I may have a drink,' and she says, 'Drink, and I'll water your camels too'—let her be the one you have chosen for your servant Isaac. By this I will know that you have shown kindness to my master." (vv. 12-14 NIV)

This is a prayer with a detailed request for guidance. The servant wants to be sure as to which girl will be right for Abraham's special son Isaac. He needs to be very sure. He wants an answer that will comfort Abraham as well as an assurance as to which woman is right for Isaac. Now his asking for guidance in such specific ways reminds me of Gideon asking for the fleece to be wet and for another sign the next night, for the fleece to be dry and the ground to be wet. God showed patience in these times and in so many other instances of sincere seeking for the Lord's help in knowing what to do.

Before the servant had finished praying, Rebekah came out with a jar on her shoulder. We are told she was very beautiful and a virgin. The detail of her beauty is a touch that shows us that this bit of "left-over beauty" of form and face was added to by her thoughtfulness for the servant's thirst and for the thirst of the camels. Rebekah's beauty also lay in her sensitivity to a stranger's need and her willingness to serve someone else. Her choices demonstrated her character.

The servant presented her with a gold nose ring and two gold bracelets, after having watched carefully to see if she seemed genuine and discovering whose daughter she was (a relative of Abraham). She invited him to stay in her father's house for the night and said there was plenty of straw and fodder for his camels also.

The reason it is good to remember this story in the midst of thinking of specific prayers and the Lord's answers is that it should be a help in our own lives. The servant's reaction was to bow down and worship the Lord saying, "Praise be to the Lord the God of my master Abraham. . . . As for me, the Lord had led me on the journey to the house of my master's relatives." The servant is thankful for his own answer to prayer for leading.

We can't take space to relate the whole wonderful story here, but that answer to prayer involved Abraham, Isaac, the servant, Rebekah, and all the history that followed! Each person is an individual, with an individual significance in history, and stands alone before the Lord in prayer even when someone else's life seems to be central in the results of the request.

God made very clear the choice of life or death to Adam and Eve in the garden. And the choice set forth through Moses speaking in Deuteronomy 30 is just as clear:

> See, I set before you today life and prosperity, death and destruction. For I command you today to love the Lord your God, to walk in his ways, and to keep his commands, decrees and laws; then you will live and increase, and the Lord your God will bless you in the land you are entering to possess.
>
> But if your heart turns away and you are not obedient, and if you are drawn away to bow down to other gods and worship them, I declare to you this day that you will certainly be destroyed. You will not live long in the land you are crossing Jordan to enter and possess. This day I call heaven and earth as witnesses against you that I have set before you life and death, blessings and curses. Now choose life, so that you and your children may live and that you may love the Lord your God, listen to his voice, and hold fast to him. For the Lord is your life, and he will give you many years in the land he swore

to give to your fathers, Abraham, Isaac and Jacob. (vv. 15-20 NIV)

Later as Joshua leads the people, he speaks with strong emphasis on the results, depending on what choice the people would make.

"Now fear the Lord and serve him with all faithfulness. Throw away the gods your forefathers worshiped beyond the River and in Egypt, and serve the Lord. But if serving the Lord seems undesirable to you, then choose for yourselves this day whom you will serve, whether the gods your forefathers served beyond the River, or the gods of the Amorites, in whose land you are living. But as for me and my household, we will serve the Lord." (Joshua 24:14, 15 NIV)

An invitation to make a choice is extended all through the ages by God's prophets; an invitation to make a decision is given all through Scripture. It is God who created human beings with minds that can consider the truth of what is being made clear and can understand the alternative results set forth. Life or death are pretty clear alternatives.

"Come, all you who are thirsty,
     come to the waters;
and you who have no money,
     come, buy and eat!
come, buy wine and milk
     without money and without cost.
Why spend money on what is not bread,
     and your labor on what does not satisfy?
Listen, listen to me, and eat what is good,
     and your soul will delight in the richest of fare.
Give ear and come to me;
     hear me, that your soul may live. . . ."
Seek the Lord while he may be found;
     call on him while he is near.
Let the wicked forsake his way
     and the evil man his thoughts.

Let him turn to the Lord, and he will have mercy on him,
> and to our God, for he will freely pardon.

"For my thoughts are not your thoughts,
> neither are your ways my ways," declares the Lord.

"As the heavens are higher than the earth,
> so are my ways higher than your ways
> and my thoughts than your thoughts.

As the rain and the snow
> come down from heaven,

and do not return to it
> without watering the earth and making it bud
> > and flourish,
> so that it yields seed for the sower and bread for the eater,

so is my word that goes out from my mouth:
> It will not return to me empty,

but will accomplish what I desire
> and achieve the purpose for which I sent it.

You will go out in joy
> and be led forth in peace;

the mountains and hills
> will burst into song before you,

and all the trees of the field
> will clap their hands.

Instead of the thornbush will grow the pine tree,
> and instead of briers the myrtle will grow.

This will be for the Lord's renown,
> for an everlasting sign,
> which will not be destroyed."

(Isaiah 55:1-3a, 6-13 NIV)

This which is being given by God through the prophet Isaiah precedes by over seven hundred years what Jesus says in the Gospel of John, yet it is the same invitation pointing to "bread" and "water" that will satisfy forever! It was after the feeding of the five thousand that Jesus answered those who were seeking him and said:

"I tell you the truth, you are looking for me, not because you saw miraculous signs but because you ate the loaves and had your fill. Do not work for food that spoils, but for food that endures to eternal life, which the Son of Man will give you. On him God the Father has placed his seal of approval."

Then they asked him, "What must we do to do the works God requires?"

Jesus answered, "The work of God is this: to believe in the one he has sent."

So they asked him, "What miraculous sign then will you give that we may see it and believe you? What will you do? Our forefathers ate the manna in the desert; as it is written: 'He gave them bread from heaven to eat.'"

Jesus said unto them, "I tell you the truth, it is not Moses who has given you the bread from heaven, but it is my Father who gives you the true bread from heaven. For the bread of God is he who comes down from heaven and gives life to the world."

"Sir," they said, "from now on give us this bread."

Then Jesus declared, "I am the bread of life. He who comes to me will never go hungry, and he who believes in me will never be thirsty. But as I told you, you have seen me and still you do not believe. All that the Father gives me will come to me, and whoever comes to me I will never drive away. For I have come down from heaven not to do my will but to do the will of him who sent me. And this is the will of him who sent me, that I shall lose none of all that he has given me, but raise them up at the last day." (John 6:26-39 NIV)

Just three chapters before in John 3 Jesus said:

"For God so loved the world that he gave his one and only Son, that whoever believes in him shall not perish but have eternal life. For God did not send his Son into the world to condemn the world, but to save the world through him. Whoever believes in him is not condemned, but whoever does not believe stands condemned already because he has not believed in the name of God's one and only Son." (vv. 16-18 NIV)

In Ezekiel 33 the responsibility of warning people, of blow-

ing a trumpet to tell of danger, is put forth as extremely important. Verses 10 and 11 strongly urge people to choose correctly:

> Therefore, O thou son of man, speak unto the house of Israel;
> Thus ye speak, saying, If our transgressions and our sins be
> upon us, and we pine away in them, how should we then live?
> Say unto them, As I live, saith the Lord God, I have no plea-
> sure in the death of the wicked; but that the wicked turn from
> his way and live: turn ye, turn ye from your evil ways; for why
> will ye die, O house of Israel? (KJV)

It is very striking to compare this with Jesus' warning
against blind guides and His denunciation of the hypocritical
Pharisees in Matthew 23. Matthew 23:37 sets forth His compassion and sorrow because of a negative choice:

> "O Jerusalem, Jerusalem, you who kill the prophets and stone
> those sent to you, how often I have longed to gather your chil-
> dren together, as a hen gathers her chicks under her wings, but
> you were not willing." (NIV)

Along with the many invitations to choose the Lord, to
choose life, to choose to turn away from lies and false gods, are
these glimpses of the sorrow the false choices, the bad choices,
have brought to God the Father and God the Son. This is shown
in Mark 3:5: "He [Jesus] looked around at them in anger and,
deeply distressed at their stubborn hearts, said to the man,
"'Stretch out your hand'" (NIV). The Holy Spirit also is grieved
by our bad choices. "And do not grieve the Holy Spirit of God,
with whom you were sealed for the day of redemption"
(Ephesians 4:30 NIV).

These are choices being put forth to the believers. Think for
a while as you read this chapter. We need to choose to be kind and
compassionate, not to let the sun go down on our anger, to do
something useful with our hands and work. All these things are
urged as choices to be worked on day by day.

It continues to be overwhelming that our Creator is so
great that He could create people, human beings, men and

women and children so uniquely different from all else, to operate in every area of life—from major earth-shaking decisions to
the tiny choices without being programmed! What a brilliant,
yet frightening creation that has caused the Creator so much
suffering.

"But," you say, "Ephesians starts by talking about predestination, so it all seems to cancel out the power of choice."

Praise be to the God and Father of our Lord Jesus Christ, who
has blessed us in the heavenly realms with every spiritual blessing in Christ. For he chose us in him before the creation of the
world to be holy and blameless in his sight. In love he predestined us to be adopted as his sons through Jesus Christ, in
accordance with his pleasure and will—to the praise of his glorious grace, which he has freely given us in the One he loves.
In him we have redemption through his blood, the forgiveness
of sins, in accordance with the riches of God's grace that he lavished on us with all wisdom and understanding. And he made
known to us the mystery of his will according to his good pleasure, which he purposed in Christ, to be put into effect when
the times will have reached their fulfillment—to bring all things
in heaven and on earth together under one head, even Christ.
In him we were also chosen, having been predestined
according to the plan of him who works out everything in conformity with the purpose of his will, in order that we, who were
the first to hope in Christ, might be for the praise of his glory.
And you also were included in Christ when you heard the word
of truth, the gospel of your salvation. Having believed, you
were marked in him with a seal, the promised Holy Spirit, who
is a deposit guaranteeing our inheritance until the redemption
of those who are God's possession—to the praise of his glory.
(Ephesians 1:3-14 NIV)

That does say that God has power to choose before the
foundation of the world. Does it cancel out all the strong invitations, all the clear freedom given to human beings, urging people
to make a choice? Does it cancel out Revelation 22:17: "And the
Spirit and the bride say, Come. And let him that heareth say,

Come. And let him that is athirst come. And whosoever will, let him take of the water of life freely"? It seems to me that the warning given at the end of the last book of the Bible, Revelation, applies very seriously to this question. We are not to take away anything from the Word of God; we are not to add anything to it.

In theological discussions through the ages in a variety of theological colleges, in all-night discussions by young students preparing for the ministry, or in long sessions on the part of older men and women, human beings who insist on finding a solution which they can argue "fits" display a kind of arrogance. It is the arrogance that also appeared among angels. It is the arrogance that was the sin of Lucifer. It is the insistence on being equal with God.

The fallacy, it seems to me, which is a terrible fallacy, is to fail to recognize that there remains a mystery that God has not explained to us, which He does not need to explain. We are finite; God is infinite. We are limited; God is unlimited. We have been made in the image of God to have minds that can understand many things, but we have not been created equal to God. We cannot know all that God knows nor understand all that God understands. When we are told that we now see through a glass darkly, that is precisely describing our limitations. We are meant to go into all the world to make known the gospel. We are meant to intercede. We are not meant to sit down and say, "It is no use, because if God has already chosen, then my prayer is worthless."

Why pray?

Paul in Timothy gives a command that is not to be turned from:

I urge, then, first of all, that requests, prayers, intercession and thanksgiving be made for everyone—for kings and all those in authority, that we may live peaceful and quiet lives in all godliness and holiness. This is good, and pleases God our Savior, who wants all men to be saved and to come to a knowledge of the truth. For there is one God and one mediator between God and men, the man Christ Jesus, who gave himself as a ransom for all men—the testimony given in its proper time. And for this purpose I was appointed a herald and an apostle—I am telling the truth, I am not lying—and a teacher of the true faith to the Gentiles.

I want men everywhere to lift up holy hands in prayer, without anger or disputing. (1 Timothy 2:1-8 NIV)

We are meant to have faith, to trust God in the "fog" or the "dark," to stop insisting on being able to understand "how it works." The greatness of God and the overwhelming suffering of God for the terrible choices of human beings should be sufficient to cause us, you and me, to worship Him more all the time—in amazement for His power and majesty and the reality of His thoughts being so far, far above our thoughts! Rather than arguing over the "impossibility," we should spend those hours worshiping God and trying to carry out His direction to us to pray continually.

Years ago on a day of prayer in Swiss L'Abri, I was up in the thicket of trees at the top of the field above Chalet les Mélèzes. I was lying on my back with my feet up against a tall, straight tree trunk, my Bible in my hands, and a prayer list with some extra requests on it for that day. I had several hours, so there was time to read and pray, read and pray. In the midst of asking for honesty before the Lord in bringing a particular request, I began to go back and forth in my own attempt to be truly willing for the Lord's will and yet at the same moment believe with faith in His promises, such as the ones in John's Gospel concerning *asking*. I struggled with the apparent canceling out. "Do I truly trust God's will about this?" "Am I in this same minute really asking with faith believing that nothing is impossible to Him, asking in the manner He has said to ask?"

Was this new to me? Of course not. Since childhood it had bothered me that people prayed "if it be Thy will, if it be Thy will" so constantly that it seemed to me there wasn't a moment to even think about how fantastic it was that we were allowed to make requests. Oh no, it wasn't new to me, that struggle. But this time I was trying to pray properly all in the same moment of time and with a double fervency of making a request and wanting God's will with equal emotion.

I closed my Bible, opened my eyes (which don't have to be closed, but they were), and wept for a few minutes. I was really frustrated. Truly upset. Suddenly I looked up that tree trunk. My eyes went slowly up until I was enjoying the green leaves, seemingly touching the clear blue of the cloudless sky. A rare day! My eyes shifted to the left and noticed that those leaves were mingled with the leaves of another tree. Then my eyes traveled down that second tree trunk, and it was as straight as the first one. *Parallel lines—meeting in the sky,* I thought to myself. *This is a great illustration of God's sovereignty and man's free will, or of God's having no chance behind Him* (my husband's way of saying it) *and man's reality of choice.* The treetops, by optical illusion, seemed to really touch the sky, to meet each other in the heavens. *What is the matter with theologians,* I thought to myself, *is the insistence of making those parallel lines only meet in God's mind. They can't leave alone what God has kept as a mystery, or behind the dark glass.*

I began to remember theological discussions in Scotland, in Holland, in other places through history, and I thought to myself with an unnoticed pride entering in, *Oh well, that isn't my problem. I've left all that as parallel lines which don't meet down here. I've realized that God is far, far above us.*

Then suddenly, as if lightning had struck me, I realized something. "Why, Edith Rachel Merritt Seville Schaeffer," I said aloud to myself, "that is exactly what you have been trying to do in your prayer today. You have tried to force those parallel lines to meet in your prayer. You have been tearing yourself apart attempting to understand something you are not given to understand—as a human being. You are not emotionally equipped to be sure you are honest in asking for God's will and asking with faith for your request, all in the same split second of time."

Then I did something you may think childish, but it helped me that day and has been a help since. I picked up my Bible again, and, leaving my feet propped up on that tree, I prayed to the Lord this way, *O Lord, I can't be sure of my praying properly so I am*

*going to separate my time of praying in this way. I am going to
concentrate on asking for Your will as I have my feet on this tree.*

In my imagination I wrote the word *trust* on the top of the
tree. Then I wrote the words *God's will* beneath that. After that,
I began to pray for honesty and sincerity in wanting His will. At
that point I opened my Bible to passages in Isaiah, in the Psalms,
in Job, and so on—passages that became a crescendo of speaking
of the greatness of our magnificent Creator God. I read, and I
acknowledged my sin and my ignorance, compared to His perfect
holiness and perfect knowledge and wisdom.

This took a period of time. Reading, asking for honesty, and
coming to feel a great and growing trust. "Who else," I asked
myself, "who else could I trust completely to know what is right
for me or for any of the people for whom I am praying?"

I prayed then concerning that which troubled me, asking
that I might be sincere in wanting His will, asking for it to be
unfolded, and then asking for His strength to DO His will when
it would be unfolded. (We constantly need to pray for strength
and help in doing His will, and also for strength and help in the
results of answered prayer!)

Taking my prayer list, I carefully went through this for each
request on it. *Please cause_____to be honest and sincere in
wanting your will. Please show him or her the next step. Please
show what Your will is concerning L'Abri at this time.* And so on
throughout the long list, reading only, in between prayer, the passages magnifying the Lord, not reading the promises concerning
our requests.

Then I literally slid myself across the ground, the dry grass,
and leaves until I could put my feet up on that second tree. I was
disciplining myself and my emotions to deal in one period of time
only with what I could handle as a human being with a finite
mind. I was preparing to act on that which God has given us, to
follow what He has said we are to do, without trying to solve the
mystery He has hidden from us.

Now I looked up to the branches of that second tree, and in
my imagination I placed the word *faith* up there and under it,
faith in God's promises. I then opened by Bible to Philippians 4:6

and (in my imagination) wrote it on the tree trunk! "Do not be anxious about anything, but in everything, by prayer, and petition, with thanksgiving, present your requests to God" (NIV). At that point I began to thank God for many, many things, first in his Word, both Old and New Testaments, in the history of the ages, and in my own life and the lives of my family and others. Then I began to read other portions of the Word that give promises connected with asking. In the context of this reading, separated emotionally from the first tree, I relaxed and concentrated in asking specific requests connected with my own need, the needs of each family member, and needs of the wider circle of friends, people who had come to L'Abri, and so on.

The result of making requests is outlined in Philippians 4:6. In the next period of time, I found it to be true that the peace of God, which transcends all understanding, guarded my heart and mind in Christ Jesus.

A prayer time like this is not a once-for-all time. That is to say, as we go on in life, we need to return over and over again to praying "on two trees," so to speak. We need to divide our emotions in a manner that releases us to concentrate on pleading for God's will, for His guidance and direction to be given for the next step in our lives, our work, our geographic location, and for whomever we have taken responsibility to pray for in that way. We need to continue to ask for His strength and help in properly trusting Him.

Then, we need to shift over "to the other tree," figuratively speaking, and concentrate on coming with requests, believing with ever-deepening faith that God has *told* us to ask, and we are meant to *act* on those promises, not to push them aside as having been canceled! God is so GREAT that He has created the reality of choice in prayer to make a difference in history!

TEN
Creativity and Prayer

Creativity communicates. God the Creator has communicated through His creation.

The heavens declare the glory of God;
    the skies proclaim the work of his hands.
Day after day they pour forth speech;
    night after night they display knowledge.
There is no speech or language
    where their voice is not heard.
Their voice goes out into all the earth,
    their words to the ends of the world.

                                    (Psalm 19:1-4 NIV)

For since the creation of the world God's invisible qualities—his eternal power and divine nature—have been clearly seen, being understood from what has been made, so that men are without excuse. (Romans 1:20 NIV)

"I have never seen God's love. I have never experienced God's love," said the young man flatly to Prisca Sandri as she walked and talked to this student looking for answers at Swiss L'Abri.

"Never seen God's love! Look around you; look at His fantastic creation." They were walking in early spring Alpine fields full of the bursting forth of purple violets, yellow cowslips, and other May flowers. Just then a startled deer ran across an opening and disappeared into the woods again; a bird called out from a tree, to be answered by another close by. Prisca was thinking of Romans 1:20 as she pointed out the beauty of the snow-covered peaks against the incredibly blue sky, the sparkle of the Rhone

River twisting its way down the valley, the butterfly just drying its wings, preparing to fly. "You are without excuse, really. The truth is you have never stopped to really examine these glorious wildflowers and think about the creation of sheer beauty. Your need is to recognize what you see of God's love in what He has made and to thank Him with true appreciation."

Paul is speaking in that strong sentence in Romans to those who have turned away from God and have worshiped false gods. They have turned away from His clearly seen creation and are without excuse. People are meant to understand something of God—the Artist, the Creator of beauty to be enjoyed—meant to understand that He has communicated and does communicate through His creation, as well as through His Word.

We have this understanding in a thanksgiving prayer from Clement who labored with Paul among those named in Philippians 4:3:

GOD THE CREATOR

*You have shown by what you have made and done
how the world has been planned from eternity.
The earth is your creation, Lord,
yours that are true to every generation
just when you judge,
your strength and splendor a marvel.
Such competence yours in creating,
such skill in setting firm the things you make,
your goodness apparent in this world we see.
You are loyal to those who trust you,
merciful, compassionate.*

To me, it is very exciting to find Clement speaking of the communication of creation, "You have shown by what you have made." Perhaps you have never walked in early spring in Swiss Alpine fields; perhaps you have never watched Australian horses gallop across the vast plains of tall grass; perhaps you have never walked in the woods of Finland and delighted in the soft green carpet of moss even in the winter, as the trees form a ceiling and walls; perhaps you don't know the beauty of bluebells painting the countryside with a magic brush full of blue; perhaps you haven't walked under magnolia trees of the South or cherry blossoms in Washington. . . look around you. Are you on a farm plowing? Are you in a city with a lake or a park? Do you have a tiny garden or a large one with sprouts of tulips or vegetables piercing up from the earth? Can you see the sky when the stars come out? Have you a place where you can watch the sunset sky with a new moon appearing in the midst of fading apricot which had just been blazing? A hostage, a prisoner in a cell, or a patient in a hospital bed must see only in memory.

But, whatever shuts out the splendor of God's creation, it is there speaking of His existence and His love. If ever you have had opportunity to dive down, even thirty feet, below the surface of the sea in a place where the fish swim by, grouped in families in a gorgeous variety of colors and shapes, of stripes and bands of contrasting color, you have had the breathtaking experience of discovering another world hidden from eyes that never look below that surface. If ever you have had your first glimpse of a giraffe looking through your car window, or several galloping freely not too far from you, you have realized suddenly that the diversity of God's ideas in creation carry out in astounding ways His provision for our enjoyment. In variety of color, texture, fragrances, shapes, and sizes of everything from the tropical fruits, flowers, birds, and tress of Jamaica to the totally different ones of Alaska, God has shown His goodness and love in providing things for people's enjoyment, as well as for their food, clothing, and raw materials for their own creativity.

In 1 Timothy 6:17 you will notice the specific statement that God has really created many, many things, beyond our possibility of ever listing all, especially for his people to enjoy.

Command those who are rich in this present world not to be arrogant nor to put their hope in wealth, which is so uncertain, but to put their hope in God, who richly provides us with everything for our enjoyment. (NIV)

Take time to consider how many kinds of marble exist or colors of quartz—the pink quartz from the Namibia desert, the green slabs of flagstone found in Zermatt used for the roofs of chalets or flagstone terraces but designed and put in the mountains by the Creator. Think of the rushing tumbling mountain streams that turn into ice sculpture through chill winds, with no human hands. Remember the waterlilies in a quiet pond and consider the purple lilacs in a hedge as thoughts of the same Artist! Picture a field of wild daisies with the beauty of children enjoying the unlimited picking of flowers, or an adult reading a book or resting, surrounded by the unstinted arrangements of the divine Decorator! Become a birdwatcher for a period of time, long enough to realize in some measure how enchantingly satisfying it is to watch cardinals and hear their delightful mating calls and to try to identify whatever birds are in your area. Go out in a canoe, a rowboat, a sailboat on some stream, lake, or sea and watch gulls swoop or cranes stand on one leg or swans flap their wings and glide to a graceful landing. It depends on where you can find water and a raft or boat, but the provision God the Creator has made surrounds water, floats on it, as well as under it, for us to richly enjoy.

This Creator who communicates the sheer wonder of His attention to detail speaks of His delight in beauty in so very many ways that to try to list them would be like trying to count snowflakes or stars! And this communication of His magnificent creation can be "heard," in all the world, whether people are looking at the things on this planet earth—the mountain peaks and rolling hills, the deserts and seas—or at the skies, the sun, moon, planets, and stars. Read again and absorb Psalm 19:1-4: "The heavens declare the glory of God." Whether the before-sunrise light in the skies or the cloud formations that painters love to paint, whether the northern lights or a falling star, the glory of God is being declared or announced, and the skies are proclaiming the work of His hands. We are told that we need no language translation for the speech being made by this gloriously obvious work of the Creator who had these endless ideas and brought them forth. We are told that the voice telling of His glory in all that He has made goes out everywhere. Everyone can see and hear this communication.

In any language the statement is there to be discovered: "The One who made this cares about beauty; sheer beauty is important to Him." Yes, it is also obvious when one examines the balance of oxygen, water, and essential nutrients that exist on this planet that the earth was made to be inhabited! Just as it says in Isaiah, God's creation is habitable. But far more than that, His creation is enjoyable and full of fresh surprises and discoveries. The diversity of colors, fragrances, textures, shapes, and flavors in such profusion declares God's unlimitedness. The vast extent and preciseness of the cosmos communicates the marvel of His infiniteness. Human beings have not deciphered the extent of God's glory through the ages of scientific research, as both the complexity and simplicity of His creation continue to "speak" as people study and do research.

God has communicated in His written Word, the Bible, and it remains fresh and gives deeper understanding as we read and reread, but as He has told us that His creation communicates His glory to us, His revelation also never comes to an end. We are to search for more understanding and appreciation of who our Redeemer is, who our Eternal God is, as we walk through woods with a friend or with children, as we ski over fresh powder snow or along a lake on cross-country tracks, as we hike up hills or mountains, or as we walk along a sandy beach or sit on a rock and examine a beautiful insect or a wildflower.

Just as in an art museum we are to enjoy the work of an artist and be glad that Rembrandt painted as he did or that Mary Cassatt's paintings of mothers and children delight us as they do, we are also to search for understanding of the artist. Just so, God's creation is to be enjoyed, but we are to be sensitive to the reality of what we are finding out about Him, the way we are getting to know *Him*.

We are a part of God's creation. Human beings have been made in the image of the Creator. God made beauty to be enjoyed, and He made man and woman with eyes to see, ears to hear that beauty. He gave taste buds to distinguish myriad flavors, the sense of smell to enjoy fragrances and to distinguish odors, hands to make a countless variety of things and endless materials with which to make small houses and enormous buildings, fabrics, sculpture, paintings, jewelry, or musical instruments. Making the earth to be inhabited included making it with an overwhelming variety of materials for the countless ideas, imaginations, and inventions that human beings would have.

The making of human beings with a capacity for creativity was not an accident, but a glorious creation which could bring a two-way communication, a response to what God has given so generously and lovingly to be enjoyed. The heart of man, the heart of woman, the hearts of children, had people not been blinded by selfishness and sin, would overflow with thankfulness in every form that fertile imaginations could express it! Worship and adoration of the magnificent Creator would have been spontaneous, had it not been so horribly spoiled.

Let me quote from my book *Forever Music* (pages 106, 107):

> Francis Bacon, who lived from 1561 to 1626, was a lawyer, essayist, and Lord Chancellor of England. He could be called the major figure of the scientific revolution, and he took the Bible seriously, including the historic Fall and the revolt of woman and man in history in a geographic location. He said in *Novum Organum* (1620):
>
> "For man by the Fall, fell at once from his state of innocence and from his kingship over creation. Both of these misfortunes however, can, even in this life, be in some part repaired; the former by religion and faith, the latter by the arts and sciences.
>
> For the curse did not make creation entirely and forever rebellious, but in virtue of that edict, 'In the sweat of thy brow shalt thou eat bread,' it is now by various labors (assuredly not by disputations or idle magical ceremonies) at length in some measure subdued into supplying bread for man; that is, to the uses of human life.
>
> Natural philosophy is given to religion as a most faithful handmaiden, the latter manifesting His will, the former His power."

I was so thrilled with what Francis Bacon expressed in his writing more than 360 years ago. What an understanding, I thought, of the abnormal world following the Fall, which introduced death and destruction. Yet what an understanding of the "left-over beauty" of God's creation. When Francis Bacon said, "For the curse did not make creation entirely and forever rebellious," he referred to what I call left-over beauty.

I have been describing the beauty that people have been able to see—the beauty that speaks, declares, makes known the glory of God! It is true that human beings see enough of the beauty of God's diverse creation to be without excuse as to realizing that there is a Creator, the Creator God who brought forth into history that which was hidden in His mind. Although we are also told that His creation was spoiled so that we do not know what perfection is, yet there is left-over beauty that is not as spoiled, which is sufficiently wonderful to give us a glimpse of what God is like as the Creator. The avalanches have not wiped out all the Alps; the beauty of those mountains is sufficient to give us the desire to worship the Creator. The earthquakes and hurricanes have not destroyed every part of the world, blotting out what was there before. We continue after centuries to have trees, flowers, bushes, rivers, lakes, seas, birds, great varieties of animals, and so on. The left-over beauty in nature is sufficient for people to thrill over a walk in the snow at sunset.

Yes, the Fall brought about devastation, and nothing has been perfect since, but God did not blot out everything He had made and turn it into gray slime! There is sufficient left over after the Fall to give people no excuse to say, "I see no signs of the Creator." There is sufficient of the marvel of His creation to give us cause, we who are His children through the work of the Lamb, to worship Him and to long to do so in ways which will let Him know of our trust and love. There is sufficient of the marvel of His creation to also cause those who are not yet His children to seek Him with all their hearts, to be sincere in wanting to find Him.

God's creation communicates.

We are to respond to His creation with specific thanksgiving for specific things we appreciate, hour by hour. However, we are a very special part of His creation. Read once again these familiar words from Genesis:

> Then God said, "Let us make man in our image, in our likeness, and let them rule over the fish of the sea and the birds of the air, over the livestock, over all the earth, and over all the creatures that move along the ground."
>
> So God created man in his own image, in the image of God he created him; male and female he created them.
>
> God blessed them and said to them, "Be fruitful and increase in number; fill the earth and subdue it. Rule over the fish of the sea and the birds of the air and over every living creature that moves on the ground."
>
> Then God said, " I give you every seed-bearing plant on the face of the whole earth and every tree that has fruit with seed in it. They will be yours for food. And to all the beasts of the earth and all the birds of the air and all the creatures that move on the ground—everything that has the breath of life in it—I give every green plant for food." And it was so. (Genesis 1:26-30 NIV)

Human beings are created in the image of God, the Creator. Man and woman were created fantastically with the capability to verbalize, to communicate in spoken and written language, to understand and to respond to ideas. Of course man and woman were finite and limited before the Fall, before they had sinned, but they had been created in the image of the great Creator with a capacity to be creative, to have myriad ideas as to the possibilities of being creative with the abundant variety of things surrounding them. Their eyes could enjoy the lush garden; their hands could feel the diversity of texture, from rough bark to smooth leaves. They could taste such a difference in flavors and distinguish the fragrance of flowers, and they could feel the cool breezes and the difference between air and water.

But the central wonder of people being made in the image of God is the basic possibility of creativity, of what could be done with ideas, imagination, and raw materials—a good curiosity to explore and discover and to work with the hands to make things. The human brain is astounding. Multitudinous ideas flow through it in just moments of time. The ideas may be creative—planning paintings or sculptures, designing a dress or an apron or a house, arranging the plants (mentally) in a vegetable garden, choosing colors for a car or a bicycle, arranging haystacks in rows, making an apple pudding for supper, composing a song or a symphony—or they may be negative ideas with unpleasant projects being planned because of living in the abnormal history after the Fall.

I'd like to quote from Mortimer Adler's *Intellect: Mind Over Matter* (pages 17, 38):

> You and I and everyone else are directly acquainted with the acts of our own minds. We know the difference between thinking and remembering, between remembering and imagining, between imagining and perceiving, between perceiving and desiring, between desiring and feeling or emotion. . . .
>
> Only human beings use their minds to become artists, scientists, historians, philosophers, priests, teachers, lawyers, physicians, engineers, accountants, inventors, traders, bankers, and statesmen.

The reality of human beings being made in the image of God is vivid. How can that be when God is perfect, good, holy, righteous, merciful, just, all-powerful, unlimited, infinite?

Human beings are creatures created by the Creator. Human beings are finite, limited and are meant to always worship God, not to be worshiped by anyone. To have been made in the image of God is to have been made fantastically different from animals, birds, fish, and all the rest of creation, to have been made with minds that can *think* abstract thoughts as well as learn how to do carpentry, but most of all to have ideas! We have been made to have creative ideas, ideas of how to invent something, whether the wheel or a computer, a wind instrument or a telephone, a sailboat or a cathedral, a pair of skis or an airplane, a printing press or a television.

Minds are the marvelous design of God, enabling human

beings to be capable of creative acts. Hidden in our minds are ideas which will never be known unless we express these ideas in writing or speaking in some language, or by creating something that can be seen and will communicate what was hidden. It is fantastic that one can imagine tastes in one's mind, not just in memory, but in creating a new dish. Good cooks are especially talented in this. Mozart could hear his compositions in his mind before he wrote the notes down and performed the music so that other people could hear it. Beethoven was deaf when he wrote the *Emperor* Concerto. He could hear it in his mind even though sadly he never heard it with his ears, and we can hear years later what was in his mind that day so long ago! The creation of that music had to take place first in Beethoven's mind.

A seemingly endless variety of human creativity communicates what was in the mind of the Creator to other people. Sheep are cared for properly and then at the proper time shorn of their wool. The wool is carded, spun into long skeins of thread, ready for knitting or weaving. Wool is dyed with red from beets or yellow from onion skins. In whose mind was the sheep? The mind of the Creator God. In whose mind came the ideas of cutting the wool, carding it, spinning it, weaving blankets and coats, knitting sweaters and scarves? In the minds of human beings, creatures created in the image of the Creator. Human beings think of endless possibilities for using what the Creator God created or made as raw materials, available for great varieties of imaginations, creative ideas, and skillful hands to make into marvelously beautiful or tremendously practical things to make life on the earth interesting and enjoyable.

The Fall brought death—little deaths of thorns, thirst, and virus spoiling efficiency and energy—as well as hindering pain and the separation of soul and body. Death removes one by one human beings who would prefer to go on living and creating! The Fall also brought about a change in God's creation of nature— potato bugs, tree diseases, blights, and crop-destroying hailstorms. As far as human beings go, the rebellion brought about continuing sin, with Cain's murder of Abel as the first war and the beginning of unending attacks of person against person, group against group, nation against nation. We are told that among them all, that is, among all who have ever lived, "there is none righteous, no not one; there is no one that doeth good." We know that *perfection* among human beings does not exist, so that added to physical illness and accidents to the body, there is moral illness, imperfection, and sin. It stands to reason, then, that human minds are not what they would have been had not the Fall taken place. Creativity would have reached greater heights than it has ever reached, had there not been the hindrance of the Fall.

Just as the Fall failed to wipe out all the beauty of God's creation in nature, so also it did not destroy all the capacities of the human mind, the skill of human hands, or the achievements of human athletes, artists, musicians, instrument makers, and makers of myriad unique things. There is left-over beauty in human beings, which gives a glimpse of what God created in the first place.

The uniqueness of the human mind with all its capacities of thinking, having ideas, choosing, and communicating with creative acts as well as with language, points to the greatness and magnificence of the Creator God. With what awe we should approach such a Creator God who could make such beings. The fascination of shucking an ear of corn on the back porch while the twilight and first stars appear, accompanied by the evening songs of the birds, causing a thrill of deep thankfulness to the Creator of it all, should be similar to the recognition of that same magnificent Creator who created such amazing human beings with eyes, ears, hearts, hands, with minds that could compose music such as Handel's *Messiah*, Bach's Toccata and Fugue, Beethoven's Concerto no. 2, Scott Joplin's jazz piano compositions, and of course many many more! What an incredible blend of the creations of people's minds were made possible by God the Creator. The compositions of music brought forth by composers through centuries could not be heard without the genius that found the perfect wood for violins, cellos, pianos, harps, and so on, nor without the brilliant ideas that brought forth the metal and the perfection of balance of the wind instruments. Nor could our ears have heard what was in the minds of the composers and

instrument makers without the performers with a genius or natural talent added to by diligence and discipline.

Now how is it that human beings, who had rebelled against
God, who had made false gods to worship, who had denied the
existence of the God of Scriptures and attributed His creation to
chance, could compose, make instruments, and perform in solos,
trios, quartets, and orchestras, bringing forth such glorious
music?

Some great composers, instrument makers, artists who are
performers, as well as artists who are sculptors, painters, architects, city planners, scientists, landscape gardeners—in other
words some of the most outstanding creative people through the
centuries have been believers in the God of creation; some have
been Christians. But others have not. What is your explanation
for the fact, because it is a fact, that some very wonderful things
have come forth from both streams of people?

My own answer would be that there is left-over beauty in
God's creation of human beings in both their physical and mental capabilities and accomplishments. The Fall did not wipe out
all the beauty of nature. The heavens are still declaring His glory.
Just so the Fall did not wipe out all the amazing wonder of His
creation of human beings—their minds, their physical achievements, and their physical health and beauty. As we watch the
Olympics and see a teen-aged Finnish boy do the ski jumps in an
unbelievably special way, or the Norwegian cross-country skiers
lead everyone else, or the downhill ski racers come flying down,
and the figure skaters twirl and glide as gracefully as the most
graceful sweep of the birds, most of us know we could not do
that. How come? We, that is to say I, do not have the particular
talent needed for that level of tennis or diving or speed swimming,
whatever it might be. That bit of left-over beauty is not in us,
though some other kind might be our special talent.

The point is that the marvel of God's creation of complex
human brains or the complex agility of human bodies is still able
to be seen in *some* human beings, just as the beauty of the sunrise is still able to be seen. We can't know what perfect human
beings would be like, but we do have glimpses of some of the

diverse aptitudes or talents that may have been in all of us, or at least would have been far more widespread, had not the Fall taken place. We observe enough of the left-over beauty in human beings, in spring in Dutch tulip gardens, Swiss Alpine flower fields, New York's and Philadelphia's and Boston's flower shows to be able to understand something of our loving Father God's mind, of what He wants to communicate to us.

Let me say before going on that one can appreciate music, can worship the God of creation with great fervor (silently) in the midst of a symphony concert being given by musicians, many, or even most of whom are not believers. We may know that in this particular orchestra several of the violinists plus the violists and the cellist are Christians. We may know the conductor is a very deep believer, but we do not sit and try to appreciate only the believers! We simply thank God for the blend of great talent, for the blend of great instruments, for the marvelous composition, which may be our favorite Schubert or Rachmaninoff piece, and enjoy what God has given us richly to enjoy and thank Him in silent prayer for His creation of the fertile, versatile creativity of the human mind. We do not need to limit our enjoyment to Christian music or to Christian musicians because we are enjoying the results of God's creation, the portion of it that we are still able to see before He restores everything. What is really important is giving our children and family a growing understanding of the difference between mediocre music and great music, between mediocre art and great art, between mediocre books and great literature, between mediocre education and that which produces truly educated people who know how to go on throughout life reading, studying, and discovering more about a variety of things, with a thirst for knowledge and for new areas of creativity.

God's creation communicates something of His splendor and skill and love. Our creativity in a variety of areas communicates something of what we are capable of doing, but also it is a communication beyond that. We can communicate love for another person by the imagination and time, work and carefulness with which we make something for that person. Talking face to face or in letters, telegrams, or phone calls can communicate with another person. However, we also communicate with our dear friends, family members, or someone we want to help through our creative skills. We plant a garden of vegetables, flowers, bushes, flowering tress, or make a bench in that garden to give enjoyment to others, make an atmosphere that communicates care. We can play an instrument privately for one friend or a few friends, or paint a water color or an oil painting. We can cook a surprise meal with an imaginative table setting to cheer someone who is down, to help our children in the middle of exam study, to prepare a sunny spot on a fog-filled day when the freezing rain seems to penetrate everyone's emotions. Candles lit, a fire in a fireplace, or an oil lamp lit can say something to the person or people for whom we are doing that.

We were given minds with which to think, to have ideas, to form sentences, and communicate to others what is going on in our minds. But we were also given other ways to communicate, the things in our minds being brought forth into the seen world where others can see, hear, taste, smell, or feel what was taking place in the creative ideas and pictures in the mind—hidden until they took shape.

Some people find it difficult to find words to say what they want to communicate to people; they find it easier to say it with a clarinet like Benny Goodman. A ballet dancer who came to Swiss L'Abri at one time felt she simply could not communicate in words what she wanted to express even to her husband. She really felt her only freedom of expression was in her dancing. Some pianists feel that way about their piano playing. They feel awkward in trying to communicate their ideas in words, but find their expression flows easily when they play a composition or improvise on the piano. People differ of course, but everyone has some form of creativity with which to say something that comes across as real, not artificial fluff.

Now in prayer we first of all need to respond to and thank God for all He has given us in his Word, the Bible. Then we need to be very careful to respond to His communication in creation, by noticing and expressing our appreciation for specific things day by day. However, we have a freedom in addition to our verbalized prayer. Our prayer at times can be in the form of expressing ourselves to God in a creative way, a way that is natural to us and a part of who we are.

One of my granddaughters used to take her flute out into the woods, away from the ears of any audience, and express herself to the Lord in music as a part of the day of prayer. Many musicians, who are full of music and find expression flows from inside through their instrument, have times of playing, alone or with one or two others, to be times of articulating deep things that are very real, telling more than any words could. For such sensitive musicians, playing their instrument for the Lord's hearing is prayer. Such prayer does not need translation for other people; it can be very private prayer which God will understand. It is God who made it possible to communicate in such ways.

Others express themselves in sketching, painting, weaving, or other art forms. When alone and in prayer, those who want to say something very deep to the Lord, not as an art work to exhibit, but directly to Him (maybe in a small sketch book just for prayer) can pray in this form. For example, when I have felt inundated by waves of difficulties, I have at times sketched a tiny rowboat with waves coming in, picturing to the Lord my need of His being in the boat with me. This is not a picture for other people, but truly is an intense form of prayer.

Thanking the Lord for beautiful wood and praying for that wood to be appreciated could make carving wood, making things of beauty, actually a time of prayer if it is done for the Lord who created the wood. For a man or woman who loves birds and wood and the Lord who made them, carving birds could be a time of prayer rather than a commercial project.

It seems to me that the art works God commanded to be made for the Temple would have been made by some of those Israelites as an act of worship and praise. They were accustomed to singing to Him and praising Him with instruments, instruments also made beautifully.

Sing joyfully to the Lord, you righteous;
    it is fitting for the upright to praise him.

Praise the Lord with the harp;
    make music to him on the ten-stringed lyre.
Sing to him a new song;
    play skillfully, and shout for joy.
For the word of the Lord is right and true;
    he is faithful in all he does.
The Lord loves righteousness and justice;
    the earth is full of his unfailing love.
By the word of the Lord were the heavens made,
    their starry host by the breath of his mouth.
He gathers the waters of the sea as into a heap;
    he puts the deep into storehouses.
Let all the earth fear the Lord;
    let all the people of the world revere him.
For he spoke, and it came to be;
    he commanded, and it stood firm.

                                        (Psalm 33:1-9 NIV)

People who are unable to hear sign to each other with their hands and of course pray with their hands too. However, they also have other forms of creativity which could be used to give another dimension to their communication with God. People who have lost their sight have a different kind of hindrance. They cannot see the stained-glass windows, paintings, and the instruments they hear. Verbalization may come easily, but so might ideas to what their sensitive fingers could make with materials they can feel. Such creations could bring forth a message, a communication to the people to whom they want to express something, but these creations could also be prayers. I recently watched a blind man working on a piece of sculpture with a delicate touch. Painting a painting would be difficult without sight, but the feel of clay in the fingers, the feel of marble or wood stimulates the creative brain not just in forming something, but in the area of what the person wants to say, to ask, to be thankful for, or to declare with honest love and worship. This can be very real prayer, not an artificial experiment.

Slavery is a horrible thing, as human beings are sold to other human beings, but in the middle of hard work and often deep affliction, music came forth with creative genius from black men and women who composed and sang while working. Many times it was natural prayer. "Nobody knows the trouble I've seen; Nobody knows but Jesus." This spiritual is a calling out in music that speaks to the Lord with trust and at the same time comforts the ones working and singing together. Gospel music and all the Negro spirituals, as well as the blues, were born to communicate something that needed expression. For those who loved the Lord and contributed to the birth of this American music, the singing and playing of instruments was indeed a communication to God of their need for help, as well as their praise of Him, His creation, and His mercy.

Through the ages the Psalms have been sung as praise, and prayer, and worship, with or without any instrumental accompaniment. They can be sung by any one of us alone as a part of our own private prayer time.

> Have mercy on me, O God, have mercy on me,
>   for in you my soul takes refuge.
> I will take refuge in the shadow of your wings
>   until the disaster has passed. . . .
> My heart is steadfast, O God,
>   my heart is steadfast;
> I will sing and make music.
> Awake, my soul!
>   Awake, harp and lyre!
>   I will awaken the dawn.
> I will praise you, O Lord, among the nations;
>   I will sing of you among the peoples.
> For great is your love, reaching to the heavens;
>   Your faithfulness reaches to the skies.
> Be exalted, O God, above the heavens;
>   let your glory be over all the earth.
>
>   (Psalm 57:1, 7-11 NIV)

But the Psalms also give words to our prayer in the midst of depression and struggle, in the midst of agony of one sort or another.

Save me, O God,
   for the waters have come up to my neck.
I sink in the miry depths,
   where there is no foothold.
I have come into the deep waters;
   the floods engulf me.
I am worn out calling for help;
   my throat is parched.
My eyes fail, looking for my God. . . .
You know my folly, O God;
   my guilt is not hidden from you.
May those who hope in you
   not be disgraced because of me,
O Lord, the Lord Almighty.

                      (Psalm 69:1-3, 5, 6a NIV)

All of this Psalm is a cry for help, a plea to be lifted out of the mud. Yet later there is a declaration, an expectation of answers:

I will praise God's name in song
   and glorify him with thanksgiving.
                   (v. 30)

Prayer alone can be an expression of agony, not just pictured in words, but in sketching, painting, with dark mournful music, by dancing a feeling of despair. But the hope, expectation of an answer, and thankfulness for the trustworthiness of God must follow at some time, when contemplation of God's past great works brings thankfulness. It is so important in all of our prayer, as well as in our communication with human beings, to ask God to help us be solid wood, not a thin veneer covering an inferior wood inside, not a thin coating of silver covering lead. *Please help me*, we need to ask. *Please help me to be real, to say things or express things in music or in my gardening, painting, building, or communication that is true to what I am honestly and sincerely communicating of repentance, of asking for mercy, of bringing praise*

or thanksgiving, or making as a tribute to You, Heavenly Father,
for the enjoyment Your creation has given to me.

Some very creative communication to the Lord, worked on
perhaps for years—as by some of the artists who carved doors,
designed and made stained-glass windows, painted murals,
painted multitudinous paintings, hand-copied portions of
Scripture with annotated letters, each one a long labor of love—
has gone on throughout all the centuries. How can we know
which artist actually painted, or carved, or sculpted, or built a
building with a desire to do it as a communication to the Lord of
creation? We can't know, and we don't need to know. The Lord
knows, and what we need to do is to search for our own talents
and attempt to enrich our own prayer by some creative communication of our own, in addition to our verbalized outpouring of
prayer, our praying in the words of the Psalms or in great hymns,
or in poetry of our own spontaneous composition, or in the
words of the saints who have gone before us.

I was deeply moved last summer, when in Czechoslovakia,
to meet and talk with some very special artists. It was exciting to
see and hear about what had been going on during years of being
shut in, that is, shut in physically within the borders of the country and shut in by attempts to keep out any other worldviews
except that of atheistic communism. We who were there speaking in a seminar found out that in some very subtle ways artists—
musicians who play a variety of instruments, painters, sculptors,
writers, poets, and songwriters—had been producing a diversity
of communications (not without danger). These were communications to God the Creator, as well as communications which
would open cracks in the walls that kept out any word about
Him. In other words some creative work had been done that
made clear that there was "another answer to life," another
worldview worth examining or searching for.

Rodica from Romania, wife of a sculptor (who could not get
away to come to the seminar), was very eager to draw me a
diagram of what she and her husband had accomplished. A truly
remarkable creative communication, which I would say was a
prayer to the Lord, as well as that which could open up questions

and a search for Him. We were sitting outside in a gravel court-yard along with her friend Ileana, a medical doctor, wife of Marius who for a long time played the first bass in the Timisoara Symphony Orchestra. We leaned over the round table, slid our glasses of lemonade out of the way, and watched while Rodica drew the diagram in my day book, so that I would not lose it. Pieces of paper have a way of slipping away, not to be found again!

Living in a drab block of flats, with a similar building next door, Rodica and Liviu discussed the thin piece of land between the two buildings. It was full of trash and unsanitary as well as ugly. This long thin strip was too narrow to do anything with, but when they tried to get permission to clean it up and plant grass, they were refused. After weeks of persistence in prayer, asking the Lord to open up the way to do something with this strip of earth and persistence in asking over and over again for permission, suddenly one day the permission was given. They had to promise to fence it in and put a gate across it to keep out everyone. It was not to be a public park.

With very hard work, these two university art students cleaned up the trash and took away much broken glass, tin cans, broken bricks and so on, and planted grass. That was only the beginning. Near the building an intricate fountain was made, with a wooden bucket to pull up water. A path circled this well-fountain arrangement, and then a straight, long path went to the gate. It was interrupted, however, by two curved paths that looked easy but led to dead ends. To keep straight ahead, a person would have to bend down very low to go under a very low opening in a tall wooden structure (a square column) that had an uprooted tree on top, the roots exposed to the air, the branches down! A person could only go up the bush-bordered path, flanked by grass, and on to the water by bending down under that low opening and crawling through, with that uprooted tree above causing a deep curiosity.

There were flowers planted around the well, and the whole place had beauty, as well as being puzzling! There was a doorbell to ring in that gate so that if Rodica or Liviu were home, one or the other would go and inquire who was there. Many curious visitors came to walk through the paths, to discover that only the straight path led to the right place and that one had to humble oneself and bend down to go through to arrive at that beautiful flowered place with water. An incredibly clear picture could be presented because of the imaginative ideas, the skill, and hard work that had gone into preparing a very vivid communication. The Bible was prohibited, but the communication was there. The dead tree, the humbling place of bowing, the amazing transformation of a dump yard into a place of beauty, water at the end of the straight path, curved paths that led to dead ends!

We can be interceding for people who are lost in the dark with our faithful prayer for them, and at the same time grow closer to the Heavenly Father to whom we are praying. But we can also pray to our Father with an act of creativity, using the land he has given us as he has told us to use it, growing vegetables and flowers and bringing forth beauty from a place that has been neglected. Beyond that we can, if our ideas unfold and if our skill in landscaping is unusual, declare or say something even more specific in a place where such a message would be shut out if we attempted to put up a soap box and shout or print Scripture verses and glue them on walls or tack them on trees.

I saw another example of creative communication in Gothenburg, Sweden, in the summer of 1991. Blake Mosher, Franz Mohr, and I were there right after the L'Abri conference in Mollë. Dr. Johan Holmdahl had arranged a Sunday evening meeting for people interested in music, and Franz and I were to speak on the topic "Forever Music." The next morning as Franz went off with his Swedish piano tuner friend who had studied with him in the Steinway headquarters in New York, Dr. Johan said he would take Blake and me to see a very special church before we had to go on to a folk art school for my afternoon speaking engagement.

You probably know that Gothenburg is a seaport on the Swedish coast. I discovered that one could take a freighter to Hong Kong from there. Of course it takes a month, but the cost is less than flying. As we walked up the steep incline to the church, my active imagination was carrying me out to sea on this voyage, thinking of watching gulls and the wake behind the ship—with the feeling that it was turning into wishful thinking. The steepness of that hill reminded me a lot of "the mound" in Edinburgh, Scotland. The church tower on top can be seen from the sea.

We walked into the church and were very impressed by the beauty of carefully carved wood and the light coming through stained-glass windows. We were saddened to hear from Johan that the truth of the Bible is not at present preached from that pulpit. As the three of us decided to sit down at the front of that wonderful building to pray for the future to open up a possibility of a Biblical message to ring from the walls and beams in some way, we looked up to the ceiling for a moment and caught a marvelous sight.

There, hanging on chains from a beam like a wonderful chandelier, was a beautifully made model, a large one, of a sailing ship with full sails. "Ohhh," I exclaimed, "how very beautiful! I never saw anything more beautifully made. Tell me about it." Johan explained that for many, many years Swedish churches have had these works of art, the creative work of artistic people who produce a model ship that fits in with the beauty of the wooden pews and pulpit and other wood in the church, to be hung where people will be sure to see it.

What is the significance of the boat? It is exactly the topic of this chapter, creativity and prayer mingled in a special way. Sweden has been a nation of seafaring people. Through the ages many Swedish women have spent weeks alone, concerned about their husbands, fathers, and sons off at sea on fishing boats or freighters. The ships hanging in churches remind people to pray for those at sea, for their safe return, for their needs, whatever those needs might be. The boats also draw people together in prayer—praying for other people's sons, fathers, husbands, or daughters at sea for one reason or another—and bind people together in times of mourning and "weeping for those who weep" when a ship is lost at sea.

Of course as we prayed there, the three of us together, we did pray for people on the sea, but also we prayed for those spiritually "at sea" who have no anchor at all, who are adrift with no compass because of listening to "false prophets" or because of having a truncated guidebook, a map with parts clipped out, having no way of reaching the proper destination.

Creativity does give us amazingly fresh ways of communicating our thanksgiving to God and fresh ways of interceding for those we would like to see kept safe.

It is important to say again right here that music, art, drama, architecture, landscape gardening, weaving fabrics, making ceramics, sketching, making instruments, reforesting land, researching in science or medicine, engineering, or making films need not have a "message" tacked on to make the day's work what it should be before God. Whatever we do, we are to do well—in any area from sports to education, from banking to packaging orange juice, from flying a plane to being captain of a boat. We are to do the normal work we are in the midst of doing as well as we can. That is a part of our glorifying the Lord.

But as we continue to attempt to pray continually, to pray without ceasing, to live a life of prayer, we can have an increasing sensitivity as to how we could be truly praying in some of the *other* ways we express ourselves—not for other eyes to see, not for the praise of men, but directly to glorify, worship, and praise the Lord for His creation of our minds, our hands, our potentialities. Yes, it is important to be humble. But it is also very important to recognize that it is because God created human beings in His image with great potential that we have had in history Bach, Michelangelo, Horowitz, and so forth, on and on, and that we can pray, *I want to use this talent for You, O God, because of Your fantastic creation of human beings. Therefore, as I weed this garden and transplant these strawberries, as I paint this painting or play this violin, as I bake this bread and make this jam from the plums I grew, it is truly a prayer because, God, You gave me the possibility of communicating with my creativity, to You, as well as to other human beings.*

People differ, places differ, possibilities differ, problems differ, pressures differ, stresses and strains differ, needs differ, hungers differ, sensitivities differ. No person is identical to anyone else, and no one faces the same combination of circumstances in the same place at the same time. The atmosphere that surrounds a person affects one person more than another, true. But the atmosphere can be changed in some instances, in one way or another. I'm thinking about attempting to find one or another place for prayer, a place that will be helpful and not a hindrance.

We talked about people living in crowded conditions in Hong Kong and other places. Of course Bombay and Calcutta are just as crowded and present many difficulties as to not only places, but atmosphere in which to pray. Imagination and creativity are needed to find a spot or to prepare a place that is helpful and conducive to thinking about God the Creator of all things, a place that enables us to communicate our thanksgiving, anxieties, and requests to our Father in Heaven to whom we come through the Lord Jesus Christ in the power of the Holy Spirit.

It is important that each one of us find a way to remove ourselves from hindering surroundings. Sounds, sights, smells *can* be a hindrance to our thoughts and concentration. That is true in a college dorm, a noisy apartment building, a street where a parade is passing, as well as in earshot of noisy worship of idols of various sorts. A Christian family I know lives in an apartment in a house in Katmandu, Nepal. The house had been dedicated to the snake god, and next door is a temple to the snake god.

This is not a book of the history of the church, nor the history of missionary work, nor a thorough description of *any* geographic spot in the world. But before speaking about the first Christian Arts Festival in Katmandu, we need to realize that Hindu music, Hindu art, and Hindu statues depict the various Hindu gods and communicate Hindu philosophy. Surrounding a distant village, five days' walk into the mountains, are plenty of rocks, trees, mountain streams, and fields to walk in, and fresh air to breathe—places where a day's picnic with children could take place or private time of prayer. But the atmosphere is not all one of freedom from hindrances even up there. Nearby is a cave in the rocks, a temple without light or windows, used to worship Satan. Without going into any detail, for this is not a list of "curious places," I want to stress that there are real hindrances in many parts of the world to communication with Jehovah, the God of the Bible, to whom people must come through the Messiah. Those hindrances are increasing in the West. Not only are Eastern temples springing up in Western countries, but there is a "corner" of a church in New York that now has a shrine to an Eastern god.

So don't gather your jacket around your shoulders and raise your eyebrows with a bit of detachment! We need to search for more understanding as to what can hinder an atmosphere and preparation for prayer. We also need discernment as to how to use our creativity to "pray" and glorify our most holy God. There cannot be a mixture of the true and false in such worship, as we thought deeply about in the first chapter.

Just recently when new freedom to worship God, to teach about God and the Bible, to teach Christianity came to what was the Soviet Union, a new freedom came to Nepal too. The government allowed people to be Christians and to go to church if they were already Christians.

Recently in the midst of this freedom, a small number of Nepalese Christians prepared an arts festival to exchange ideas and to encourage each other in the creative arts. This was not to transplant Western culture nor Western ideas of art and music, but to recognize and discuss how to produce creative works which would not communicate Hindu philosophy nor point to the Hindu gods. They wanted to create works that would be distinctly their original painting, weaving, sculpting, drama, music, and other sorts of creative art.

There were forty or so people who came with eager expectancy, some from long distances down narrow trails. Yes, communication in many languages is thrilling to know about as we hear of people becoming believers from many tribes and nations and kindreds and pouring out their prayers to the Lord. However, it is also important to make known the truth that creative works can be a form of communication to the Creator who tells us His creation declares His glory to us. When people are surrounded, flooded, with the atmosphere of creativity that denies the holiness of the one and only Creator God, then time and teaching and example are necessary to bring discernment. People need to understand what the wrong message is, the message coming from that which creates a contrary, hindering atmosphere.

Once more I must inject the fact that Christians who are composers, writers, painters, sculptors, musicians, actors, dancers, filmmakers, engineers, architects, doctors, lawyers, military persons, nurses, or whatever do *not* need to make their creative work into evangelistic works or messages. That is not what is being said here. People need discernment, along with increasing sensitivity, understanding, and knowledge, to recognize the communication of an enemy of God's Word and what produces an atmosphere or climate opposed to prayer and glorifying God. That is not to say we cannot pray in the middle of an alien atmosphere or a den of thieves if we find ourselves in such places. We can be separated into God's presence and ask for His protection and help, His mercy and strength wherever we are.

I am talking about something quite different. We are not to use our creativity to produce anything that leads to *the worship of a false god*. And for confused people who have had no previous background of teaching, we need to make the difference crystal clear, opening new doors to beauty and enjoyment of all that God gives us so richly, without worshiping idols or false gods.

Music has been a part of God's creation—the songs of the birds, the rolling drumbeat of thunder, the sound of waves coming in with rhythmic regularity, the variation of rain from a gentle spring rain on new green leaves to the beating of freezing rain blown by wild winds, the waterfall's resounding splash as it enters the river's rapidly flowing waters. Genesis tells of Jabal, the father of those who lived in tents, and he had a brother named Jubel, father of all who play the harp and flute. We realize that very early in the history given us in the Bible, musical instruments were designed by people with ideas in their minds, were made by skillful and successful hands, and were played. God created human beings to have minds with such an infinite variety of creative ideas, and among them have been those who produce music. People really need music. It is part of being human. Now it is not only important to encourage the differing peoples in various parts of the world to compose and sing and play their own music, being sensitive to what it is saying, but it is essential for peoples from different cultures to have some way of having what they are "hungry for" in the way of music.

Thinking of Nepal for a moment, there are a few westerners there—a doctor who is a fine pianist, a mother who has a trained voice and plays the recorder well, and some others who have arranged some concerts for other westerners hungry for Bach and Vivaldi and so on. Music is like water to a thirsty person on a desert. Frazier, a pioneer missionary to the Himalaya Mountains some years ago, worked and prayed, fasted and prayed, sat by smoky fires in small huts, slept on the ground, and did not complain as he literally gave his life to learn the language and make known to the dear Lisu tribespeople the truth of the gospel. However, he had left a career as a concert pianist to do what he was sure he had been called to do. One time he stayed briefly in China for a few days where there was a piano. He didn't want to eat or sleep, but just to play Chopin, Beethoven, Bach, and Vivaldi for hours, feeding on the music with his fingers as well as his ears. He took back with him to the mountains sheets of classical music although he had no instrument to play, but sitting on the back of a mule climbing steep paths, he "played" in his mind the great music he had been so thirsty for. He played it as prayer, thanking God for his mind, for the reality of music, for the designers of such things as pianos—truly a crescendo of just what I am trying to unfold in this chapter, the awesome possibilities of communicating to God with our diverse forms of creativity, even as we are enjoying His communication of His love and His glory to us in His creation.

Nothing could be more beautiful for a mountain climber than some of those views in the Himalaya Mountains, and God could hear the music being brilliantly played in the mind of this wonderful artist as easily as if he had been sitting at a Steinway on the stage of London's Albert Hall. That creativity bringing forth worshipful prayer in the mind is heard just as verbalized prayer is. It is always astonishing to me that we can communicate to God without any other ears or eyes being aware of it.

Praise is communication.

Praise is prayer.

Psalms 149 and 150 need to be in this chapter to help us see something clearly in case our "windows are fogged."

Praise the Lord. Sing to the Lord a new song,
  his praise in the assembly of the saints.
Let Israel rejoice in their Maker;
  let the people of Zion be glad in their King.
Let them praise his name with dancing
  and make music to him with tambourine and harp.
For the Lord takes delight in his people;
  he crowns the humble with salvation;
Let the saints rejoice in this honor
  and sing for joy on their beds.

(Psalm 149:1-5 NIV)

Praise the Lord. Praise God in his sanctuary;
  praise him in his mighty heavens.
Praise him for his acts of power;
  praise him for his surpassing greatness.
Praise him with the sounding of the trumpet,
  praise him with the harp and lyre,
Praise him with tambourine and dancing,
  praise him with the strings and flute,
Praise him with the clash of cymbals,
  praise him with resounding cymbals.
Let everything that has breath praise the Lord.
Praise the Lord.

(Psalm 150 NIV)

Paul's letter to the Ephesians continues this command to us all.

Speak to one another with psalms, hymns and spiritual songs. Sing and make music in your heart to the Lord, always giving thanks to God the Father for everything, in the name of our Lord Jesus Christ. (Ephesians 5:19, 20 NIV)

It is a deeply moving thing to be able to join in with those who have so long been in Heaven, knowing that our hearts can communicate with the same creative poetry to both "praise the Lord" and "speak to one another" with hymns. Our own original and private prayer is open to us at any time, but we also have a richness open to us in the thrill of joining in with those whom we will one day see as well as with others with whom we sing now.

In the eighth century John of Damascus wrote a hymn, but it was not translated until 1853 (by John Mason Neale). That is a period of more than ten centuries! Yet we can sing this hymn with great depth of worship and prayer, alone or with others.

Come, ye faithful, raise the strain Of triumphant gladness;
God hath brought His Israel Into joy from sadness.
Loosed from Pharaoh's bitter yoke Jacob's sons
*   and daughters,*
Led them with unmoistened foot Through the Red
*   Sea waters.*

'Tis the spring of souls today, Christ hath burst His prison,
And from three days' sleep in death As a sun hath risen.
All the winter of our sins, Long and dark, is flying
From His light, to whom we give Laud and praise undying.

Now the queen of seasons, bright With the day of splendor,
With the royal feast of feasts, Comes its joy to render;
Comes to glad Jerusalem, Who with true affection
Welcomes in unwearied strains Jesus' resurrection.

"Hallelujah!" now we cry To our King Immortal,
Who, triumphant, burst the bars Of the tomb's dark portal;
"Hallelujah!" with the Son, God the Father praising;
"Hallelujah!" yet again To the Spirit raising. Amen.

Venantius H. C. Fortunatus lived from 530 to 609. Perhaps John of Damascus sang the following Easter hymn written by Venantius a hundred years before. We thrill as we can sing these same words in celebrating the truth of the resurrection of Christ our Savior and Lord, and we should be excited at the continuity of creative prayer as we join in, looking forward to the certainty of the resurrection in eternity ahead of us. The translator of this hymn was John Ellerton, and the music was arranged by John B. Dykes in 1868 from the music of Franz Joseph Haydn. What does it matter? It matters a lot to be able to *feel* as well as understand the unchanging content of what is being sung and to contemplate the exciting ideas that came into the minds of these men in their bursts of creativity—a hymn that became communication and prayer to God, as well as a gift to other people through the ages, enabling all to join in with the same prayer.

"Welcome, happy morning!" age to age shall say;
"Hell today is vanquished, heaven is won today!"
Lo! the Dead is living, God forevermore!
God, their true Creator, all His works adore!

Chorus: "Welcome, happy morning!" age to age shall say.
    (Amen.)

Earth with joy confesses, clothing her for spring,
All good gifts return with her returning King:
Bloom in every meadow, leaves on every bough,
Speak His sorrows ended, hail His triumph now.

Months in due succession, days of lengthening light,
Hours and passing moments praise Thee in their flight;
Brightness of the morning, sky, and fields and sea,
Vanquisher of darkness, bring their praise to Thee.

Come then, true and faithful, now fulfill Thy word,
'Tis Thine own third morning, rise O buried Lord!
Show Thy face in brightness, bid the nations see;
Bring again our daylight; day returns with Thee.

Amen is the appropriate ending to prayer. As we join in praying with people in the sixth century, with overwhelming gratefulness for God's mercy and amazing grace that caused Jesus to "tread the path of darkness, saving strength to show," we acknowledge that to be able to answer our prayer for strength in our weakness, He had to walk through a dark path indeed.

Where are we, you and I, others of God's people around the earth, when we sing in our minds or with our voices this creative communication that came from that man of God born in 530? Perhaps one of us is sitting on the grass or standing under a tree by the grave of a loved one, thinking of the second coming, having prayed, "Thy Kingdom come." We go on now with that last verse, requesting as we pray, "Raise to life again . . . Bring again our daylight." Perhaps we are in a hospital bed or sitting on the ground in Africa praying for eyes of understanding to be opened to the hope which Christ died to give. Perhaps we are in a dangerous city slum in Washington or San Francisco or simply sitting on a bench alone at sunrise on Easter morning, thankful for the reality of the Lord's presence and for His ear open to hear our recognition of His love. Yes, of course we have times of joining our voices with other believers, but I'm thinking of the added dimension of praying *with* the hymn writers as a help to our own longing to meditate day and night on the Lord and to pray always, joining in with their creative expression during their time on earth.

There have been so many hymns through the centuries. This is not an attempt to make a study of them. Jane Stuart Smith and Betty Carlson have written and are writing books with good hymn studies. However, to talk about creativity and prayer communicating to God would be far too incomplete. Bach's manuscripts often had "praise to God" or "for the glory of God" written in the margins beside the notes. His writing of music, not just his church music, was truly creative prayer, that is to say, his creativity communicating appreciation, love, and worship to the Creator.

The following hymn, ascribed to Bernard of Clairvaux (1091-1158), was translated into German by Paul Gerhardt in 1656 and into English by James W. Alexander in 1830. What a tapestry of real people who loved the Lord and prayed in their own time, as "threads" of lives touched each other over the centuries. Hans Leo Hassler wrote the chorale in 1601, but it was harmonized by Johann Sebastian Bach in 1729. As Bach died in Leipzig in 1730, he must have arranged this just a year before he died.

> O sacred Head, now wounded, With grief and shame
>   weighed down,
> Now scornfully surrounded With thorns, Thine only crown;
> O sacred Head, what glory, What bliss till now was Thine!
> Yet, though despised and gory, I joy to call Thee mine.

As we sing and pray these words that have expressed so passionately appreciation to Jesus Christ in His suffering, we need to realize that the words and deep prayerful thoughts go back even more centuries to Isaiah, for we read:

> Surely he hath borne our griefs, and carried our sorrows; yet we did esteem him stricken, smitten of God, and afflicted. But he was wounded for our transgressions, he was bruised for our iniquities. . . . (Isaiah 53:4, 5a KJV)

Now we go on with the hymn:

> What Thou, my Lord, hast suffered Was all for sinners' gain:
> Mine, mine was the transgression, But Thine the deadly pain.
> Lo, here I fall, my Savior! 'Tis I deserve Thy place;
> Look on me with Thy favor, Vouchsafe to me Thy grace.

> What language shall I borrow To thank Thee, dearest Friend:
> For this Thy dying sorrow, Thy pity without end?
> O make me Thine forever; And should I fainting be,
> Lord, let me never, never Outlive my love to Thee.

> Be near me when I'm dying, O show Thy cross to me;
> And for my succor flying, Come, Lord, to set me free.
> These eyes, new faith receiving, From Jesus shall not move;
> For he who dies believing, Dies safely through Thy love.
>   Amen.

What language shall I *borrow* to thank our beloved Savior for His pity without end? Our hearts respond to this question